AF379543

a clinician, this book is deeply affecting. It fosters healing and resilience and brings a huge level of recognition to the importance of self-awareness and its role in healing. The author intersects the multiple and layering dimensions of self-discovery and highlights one's unique and vulnerable journey to faith. This book is beautifully crafted and flawlessly describes the complex and unsettling nature of trauma and its ability to subconsciously implant itself throughout and within our lives.

The author's description of physical dissociation is relatable beyond linguistics, and for those who can resonate with the author's story, you feel this read. Outside of the context, this is poetry; deeply sad, lost, found, and aware.

I strongly recommend this book to any collegiate program or athletic team looking to optimize the entire well-being of their college athletes. It provides a significant contribution to the holistic understanding of an individual's health and highlights how the mental, emotional, physical, social, and spiritual factors of our lives interact and impact our well-being."

—DR. CAITLIN SWALLOW, PhD, LMFT

"Kelsey's story reads like the sound of glass shattering against the wall. It's hard to imagine the impact of so many dehumanizing experiences. Broken pieces everywhere. See grace gather them up, binding her wounds through unexpected encounters with a love so great, no darkness could hide it."

—BROCK STAMPS,
Campus Pastor at LifeFamily Dripping Springs

"This book is the bravest, most courageous thing I have ever read! The beautiful thing is that Kelsey was able to voice so many things that I have thought and felt myself over the years. I believe reading about her journey healed a deep part of me that I did not know needed healing, especially so many years later, and I am so grateful.

Folly is the truth about how hard it is to break free from the pulls of the world, whether it be the sins we have committed or the lure of wealth and other people's 'love' and 'desire' for us. Kelsey's remarkable story captures our incessant need to both pursue worldly love and acceptance and our own internal struggle to find what we all somehow know is the truth of who we are, down deep! The book clearly points out how distraught we can become when we let the world identify WHO we are ... be it our vocation, our wealth, our status, our supposed contributions/actions or any other world-given names or titles we choose to adopt as our false identity. The truth that Kelsey points to is that God created us as ENOUGH, and because of that, we can do all things through Christ!"

—JOAN DANIELS
Founder, Dream Catalyst Life & Business Coaching

"*Folly* is an impactful story that will inspire those who are looking for purpose or who may be struggling with the direction of their lives. The book also reinforces support for those working to become closer to God and desiring validation, peacefulness, and fulfillment.

The inspirational theme of the book emphasizes that despite the pain caused by the harmful actions of self-serving individuals, the faith of others can help one accept God's grace and achieve a renewed, free, and abundant life."

—JOHN E. GAMBLE, Ph.D.
Professor of Management, former Business School Dean, and co-author of multiple editions of *Crafting & Executing Strategy*, a leading strategic management text.

"Unlike Kelsey, some of us have been fortunate enough to have had support systems from our childhood that have kept us from straying too far, if at all, from the path God chose for us. While it is upon each person to have the courage to embrace Jesus, just as Kelsey did, it is also upon us to accept those less fortunate. Instead of judging them, we should offer the acceptance they seek, which could alter the course of their lives. We thank God for using us to play a small part in the grand scheme of Kelsey's life, helping guide her toward Him.

In *Folly*, Kelsey is taking it a step further. We applaud her for having the courage to embrace Jesus and to tell her story, which we pray will serve as a beacon for the countless thousands who are trying to find their way to a better life. Tagore's world, 'where the mind is without fear, and the head is held high,' does not have to be a fictitious aspiration out of reach for us all. By living in God's image in every aspect of our lives, it is truly an attainable goal."

—MARCY AND DR. ANTONIO JIMENEZ

Founders, Hope4Cancer Treatment Centers,
Dr. Jimenez is the Medical Director of Hope4Cancer and
Author of *Hope for Cancer: 7 Principles to Remove Fear* and *Empower Your Healing Journey*.

"In her soul-baring memoir, *Folly*, Kelsey courageously unveils her remarkable journey from the darkest places of suffering and despair to the profound transformative destination of redemption. What sets her story apart is her beautiful portrayal of God's grace in the midst of unspeakable trauma and pain. As her story unfolds, you see the hand of God strategically moving to restore the things in her life that had been stolen from her as a young girl, innocently looking to fit in the world in which she lived.

Her memoir is a testament of hope in the middle of darkness. Through her storytelling, she skillfully demonstrates God's love has no bounds. He can transform our past hurts and pain by making a way for us to walk in wholeness and beauty. Going on this journey with Kelsey, you will come away with a new perspective on the brokenness of humanity, our subsequent sin nature, and the redeeming power of God's grace. Her book is beautifully written and will have a powerful impact on many."

—CONNIE HAGEN, M.Ed.

Author, *Drinking The Cup You Are Served*
Director of Women's Ministry, LifeFamily Dripping Springs

FOLLY

*The Memoir of a Call Girl
Saved by Grace*

KELSEY DANIELS

Fedd Books
P.O. Box 341973
Austin, TX 78734

www.thefeddagency.com

Published in association with The Fedd Agency, Inc., a literary agency.

Cover Design: Hailey Merlo Media (https://www.haileymerlomedia.com/)

ISBN: 978-1-964508-03-0

LCCN: 2024909628

Printed in the United States of America

To Lena Wadsworth. A friend to whom I will forever be grateful for and inspired by. My story does not exist without your faith, encouragement and the gift that is your pure heart and call to ministry.

TABLE OF CONTENTS

AUTHOR'S NOTE

Before you embark on this reading experience, it's essential to acknowledge that the content of this book touches upon sensitive and challenging themes such as abuse, mental health struggles, and trauma. As such, it may not be suitable for younger readers or those who may find such topics distressing. I approach these topics with honesty and with the intention of shedding light on the human experience, and to foster empathy and understanding around difficult discussions. As you navigate through the chapters of this memoir, I encourage you to proceed with caution and self-care.

The first ten chapters lay the foundations for my initial belief systems, but light breaks at chapter eleven and continues to rise. My goal with this note is to encourage the reader that hope is on that horizon, and as the story unfolds, you will begin to bear witness to the transformative power of faith.

Folly
noun /ˈfälē/

A lack of understanding, sense, or
rational conduct; foolishness.

PROLOGUE

It is a common misconception that call girls move about cloaked under the shadows of night. At least it was for me in the summer of 2021, as I was typically operating under the thin veil of mid-afternoon to early evening. I also preferred the title of "companion." The days were easier back then. Before I knew the truth. Before it set me free. Back when my time was spent floating between trysts, all while existing merely as a bystander or character from an Edward Hopper painting. Many afternoons in my late twenties were spent just like this one in San Antonio—lounging around hotel rooms and getting paid thousands of dollars to sip champagne in my underwear. Tash Sultana played delicately in the background, and the linen hotel room curtains both blotted out the midday sun while also coaxing the room into the golden glow of high noon.

It's true that when you are living a life of sin, life itself seems to carry on without disruption or interruption. As if the devil himself places enough trust in you to continue to keep his operations up and running without any help from management. Still, as I lay half-naked on a copper-colored leather couch looking out onto the River Walk, all I could think about was Jesus.

A man emerged from the bathroom running a towel through his damp head of hair before buttoning up his collared shirt and adjusting his tie. I had been seeing David for just shy of a year now, and even though he rarely visited for longer than 90 minutes, he always reserved and paid me for the full three hours. I was kicked back and lounging on that same copper couch when David began to shake his head in ironic and comedic disbelief at the sight of me, "You're a bad habit, you know that?"

I did. And I was. This lifestyle happened to be one for me. I toyed with the necklace I had worn that day. One that David had given to me a few months earlier, which had been accompanied by a pair of Manolo Blahniks and a note that read, "You're my favorite part of the day."

David pulled his sports jacket from a hanger in the closet before redirecting his gaze back at me. His voice was bold and riddled with sincerity.

"I saw on your website you raised your rates. Good for you! You are worth all of that and more. Work smarter, not harder!"

We exchanged glances that conveyed admiration, a sense of security, empathy, and a great deal of trust. Work smarter, not harder. *Funny,* I thought, *isn't that exactly what I am doing?*

I walked David to the door, where he kissed me on the cheek before beholding me for more than a few seconds too long. As if he were taking in the last few glimpses of a sunset before nightfall. He made me feel beautiful, smart, accomplished, and somehow, even more importantly, valuable. It was a key reason why I craved this world. Why I could never imagine leaving.

"Until next time," he said, lingering. I figured his mind must be playing a tug of war with itself. Struggling between the fantasy of staying a bit longer in my suite that looked out onto the water and the responsibility that was the *everyday reality* that he needed to enter back into.

Once he did leave, I hopped in the shower with plans for spending the rest of the afternoon down by the hotel pool, in the company of the Texas sun and a few skinny margaritas. I took a washcloth to the fogged-up bathroom mirror and then took one long hard look at myself. It was the first time in my life I not only didn't hate my body, but I thought I might love it. I had lost twenty pounds since moving to Texas, and between the biweekly hydrafacials, eyelash extensions, and other investments in my appearance, I had begun to like the girl in the mirror. I had a calendar filled for the next month and had just ended that week with an income of $15,000.

I was finally in control of my life, and I was starting to believe that maybe— just maybe—I might actually be worth the $1,000 I was charging per hour.

It was hard to imagine that less than two years prior to that afternoon at that five-star hotel in San Antonio with David, I was standing outside a two-star hotel in Illinois, where I had just received a text from a 312 number that read, *Outside gray Buick.* The text had prompted me to toss back the remnants of my prosecco, not yet having developed the palate nor the pockets for real champagne, as I made my way through the revolving lobby doors and out into the fall of night.

I had not met the man in the Buick. The entire situation I found myself in was really some back-alley rendition of the Milgram Experiment meets *Charlie's Angels.* Nonetheless, outside the cool midwestern air grazed the parts of my skin left uncovered.

The Buick was pulled up alongside the fire lane. Its crimson taillights revealed the rising exhaust, while simultaneously acting as the only source of color outside the spectrum of gray and blues under the mask of moonlight. I knocked gently on the passenger side window, understanding that this was how about one-fourth of all *Law and Order: SVU* episodes started, before bringing my eyes down to window-level. An arm emerged on the other side of the tinted glass, and it popped open the door from the inside.

"Hiiya, Sam!" The driver said, as the scent of stale tobacco slapped me in the face. Samantha was the name I went by in those days.

"Come on in!"

I pulled open the Buick door to notice a back seat filled with crumbled up McDonald's paper bags and empty plastic bottles of Diet Coke.

Mike was a man well into his sixties, which churned my stomach to the highest degree, when he began eyeing me like Thanksgiving dinner. He had thinning brown hair that was greasy and slicked back. His skin was leathery, indented with nooks and crannies like that of an English muffin, and he wore a large, flattened gold ring on his pinky finger. The tips of all his fingers were stained a spicy mustard-like yellow, which made sense given that his entire car smelled like an ashtray. His large pot belly rested only inches away from the steering wheel, which made me nervous, as each time he laughed, I feared he might, on accident, honk the horn. I proceeded to hand him a small stack of bills.

"310?" He asked.

"285," I corrected. I had done the math six times on my phone back in my hotel room just to be certain.

"Thirty percent of 950 is 285," I said firmly.

Mike pulled his phone out of his breast coat pocket. The font size of the text message was so large it allowed me to see the names of five other girls he was collecting from tonight. Next to each name, was a dollar amount, along with his take from every transaction.

"285 it is!" He exclaimed. As he peeled away a fifty from the stack and tucked it into that same breast coat pocket.

"So, how was your first day?" Mike asked.

My brain was fried, but I flipped on the switch like I always had. The part of me that could function without cognitive thought and was pleasant and agreeable. Still, my head seemed like it might implode.

The clock on the dash read 10:30, and that day seemed to hold more hours than twenty-four. Ten hours before that moment in the Buick, I was shuffling my feet across the worn-in hotel room carpet inside, doing my best to ignore the giant chip in the French pedicure on my big toe and dismiss thoughts of self-hatred.

I clung to my phone for dear life, checking it every so often, just to be certain I didn't miss a call. You know, in case the vibration or the audible ring failed me. I had been pacing back and forth for the past ten minutes and dressed for the past hour. Then, a thought occurred to me: Why was I so nervous? Was this even the first time I was doing this? In a way, it sort of seemed like I had been doing this my entire life. Then the phone rang.

"I'm sending him up. Don't forget to call me once he leaves. Have fun, doll!" The woman on the opposite end of the line relayed. The words were encouraging, almost sweet. Like the agave I use when I make margaritas.

I opened the door to a handsome man with olive skin and green eyes. I welcomed him in with a big smile as I stepped behind the door to conceal my body and the black lace kimono that was draped around it. Even after the initial hug and thanking him for seeing me while I was in town, he remained silent.

He walked past me and further into the room. His back was the only thing giving me any sort of attention. Then, the thoughts rolled in. *He thinks I'm ugly, I am too fat. I am not what he expected. Why did I think I could come here and make money? What if he tells the agency that I am unattractive?*

Finally, he asked me, "What are you doing here?"

My stomach did a backflip, and a rush of anxiety welled over me. Did I know this man? Did he know me? Have I seen him before? I laughed, like he had just told me a dad joke.

"What?"

His hands were tucked into his dress pants pockets, and he took a few steps closer to me. He asked the question again, this time a bit louder.

"What are you doing here?!"

And again, I laughed at the joke and offered him a glass of bubbly or sparkling water I had chilling on ice. Once more, he took a few steps closer, removed his hands from his pockets, and then began moving them up and down in line with my figure.

"What are you doing here?!! You're beautiful!"

I still didn't understand.

Chapter 1

POPCORN CEILINGS

My first memory and my first basis of truth are the same nine words.

"You need to care what people think about you."

A sentence sandwiched perfectly between a set of quotation marks and thrown from my mother's lips outside of my preschool. The words stuck uncomfortably to me, like sand inside a wet bathing suit. It was the autumn of 1997 in Connecticut, and the preschool lawn was still fresh with the morning dew. Auburn and rust-colored leaves blew across it, morphing into eggshells that, from that day forward, I would walk upon.

I grew up in a small house in a tiny town outside of Hartford that had a cherry tree in the side yard— a tree that never produced fruit good enough to eat. Shortly after budding, the tree would bloom only to sprout small, dark pieces of fruit speckled with rot, punctured and tunneled through by worms and other insects. The rotted fruit would then quickly wither and fall to the matted clay-like floor beneath it. This was the place where I could often be found flipping over rocks, examining the cracks in the bark, and dreaming.

The arguments of my parents often broke through the screened-in front door and cracked open windows that cut short the daydreams. Still, I recall imagining myself exploring the pyramids of Egypt, wandering the once Hanging Gardens of Babylon, and roaming the banks of the Nile River before drifting down it.

The Nile River is symbolic of life, harmony, fertility, and abundance. Only on this day, as I pictured the ancient river and heard my mother's instruction replaying again and again at the forefront of my mind—"You need to care what people think about you"—the Nile seemed to only carry me that much closer to death.

Only once did the old man next door interrupt my daydreams. I was seven years old when he led me out of my parent's yard and away from that sour cherry tree, through his backyard, down the hatchway, and onto a plaid couch where he exposed himself. I recall feeling confused as to why he had a snake in his pants.

That's when I heard my mother's voice yelling for me and, afterwards, scolding me for wandering into the neighbor's yard. I didn't much like playing outside after that.

Later, while my mom's hands were submerged in soapy dishwater and holding that night's dishes, I tugged on the back of her shirt to tell her what had happened. It was then that I realized she was crying, following another argument with my dad. As such, she shooed me away.

It was the day I realized I was burdensome, that I should just keep things to myself. It was the day of my first secret.

I was sixteen the second time I encountered *that* Nile. This time it took the form of a long crack in the popcorn ceiling above me that eventually split into two, just like the Blue and White Nile that come together and act as tributaries for the main river. I searched up and down that crack in the ceiling. I viewed the room around me through a near sedated, mental fog. My mind was scattered, like a deck of cards, fifty-two pick-up style, and dispersed throughout the room. *How did I get here?* I asked myself.

I retraced my steps, as if in search of misplaced car keys, gathering the bordering pieces of the puzzle to lay the framework and work inward to complete the picture.

Jack was a senior and had called my house every day for the past two weeks. So, when he had asked me to skip seventh period study hall that day to go with him to Subway, not going almost seemed like it might be a dealbreaker. I told my friends Nora and Isabel that I would be back in twenty minutes, which would leave us plenty of time to review before our individual Spanish presentations.

I never skipped class. I prided myself on attendance and had a debilitating fear of being late. But Subway was just around the corner, and I would be back in twenty minutes. Except, Jack didn't drive to Subway that day. And when I noticed he began driving in the opposite direction, he ignored me when I asked if we were still going.

Instead, we arrived at his house. A small yellow house on the corner with a large oak out front.

The driveway was cracked and raised in places as roots from neighboring trees breached the surface. As if they were intentionally acting as barriers and hurdles to stall my way across it. To deter me from walking through that front door. Jack said he needed to grab his practice gear from inside and suggested I come inside and not wait in the car.

Inside, I noticed the stack of dishes in the sink after he pulled a Gatorade out of the refrigerator. After, his eyes became a different type of kaleidoscope-dark, and shortly thereafter, I was under *the Nile*. Recalling the dirty dishes in the two-bay sink stacked with breakfast bowls that still contained pools of milk and remnants of Cheerios. Underneath *that* Nile I remembered the distinct line that separated the living room carpet from kitchen tile. The distinct line that separated me, standing in one room and him gulping a Gatorade in the other. I rushed to fill in the blanks and solve the missing pieces as to why I was there in that yellow house—why his body was suddenly on top of mine.

When I look back on this moment, I see myself hovering. Floating above my body that inhabits the bed below me. A body, wherein now, I have lost any sort of attachment to. I never actually see what is being done to my body, only that my mind seems to be caught in a perpetual state of catch-up.

The walls around me, that now hold secrets, emit a high-pitched white noise, a buzzing static like that of a beehive. Even on dry land, all my senses appear to be submerged underwater. The color within the room fades before dissolving into a two-dimensional drawing as I continue to seek solace in *the Nile* above me.

Then, suddenly, I am standing in the front of a room, and thirty pairs of eyes are locked onto my person. The world around me feels colder. Harder. The time and space between being inside that yellow house and standing motionless in front of a classroom of my peers has gone unrecorded. The expectation of me and the task itself, also momentarily forgotten, carried up and away like a Japanese lantern, taken by an unforeseen wind.

Spanish. This was my Spanish presentation. I could not muster words to come forth in English, let alone translate or recall anything I had prepared for this moment in Spanish. *Say something! Speak Spanish!* The only words present in my mind strung together were English. And those words were, "Everyone knows what I just did."

Jack stopped calling my house after that.

The following morning, I joined my parents in the kitchen, wondering if they might notice something different about me, if there was some sort of maternal "knowing" that lit up or went off when your daughter gave it away. I sat at the kitchen counter, avoiding eye contact, which wasn't unusual for me.

My dad read the paper as my mom spread butter over a piece of Rye toast in silence. Life was always hurried and rushed back then. I learned quickly that not only money, but time seemed to always be in short supply. So were words. Conversations in those days took the form of arguments swatted back and forth between rooms like a game of tennis. While a family of five, we were really five strangers living under the same roof. Only on that particular morning there wasn't a shortage of time. There seemed to be more time than ever before. Still, I remained invisible. I questioned if anything around me was real. If maybe I had died in that yellow house. If maybe I had never actually left.

A week or so later my dad looked briefly over the top of his glasses and around the side of his morning paper.

"You're not eating?"

I actually hadn't eaten in days. At dinner, I spent the entire meal cutting my food into microscopic pieces and shuffling it around my plate. If I did take more than a few bites, I would simply discard it by throwing it up in the toilet upstairs and running the shower in the background to drown out the noise.

"I'm not hungry," I responded, hoping my mom would hear.

"Be careful," my dad said. "You're getting too skinny."

I looked to my mom to see her response, hopeful of her approval. It went unacknowledged as she spread strawberry jam over a piece of toast. Maybe she just didn't hear him.

It was in the backwoods of Cape Cod, where we would vacation each summer with our neighbors from across the street—a couple with two kids, a boy and a girl around my older brother's age—that I first threw up. Following a night of my dad cooking up a storm involving Alaskan King Crab legs with drawn butter, baked stuffed shrimp, and pasta salad, I had an issue buttoning back up my jean shorts.

"Honey," my mother said sweetly, "You are growing, but you are growing the wrong way!"

I waited until the adults had cracked open an after-dinner drink and took my travel toothbrush with me into the woods, in search of what might be an acceptable tree to discard of my dinner. It was there, shrouded among the pitch pines and black and white oaks of the maritime forest, that I would learn to very much enjoy having secrets. I was ten years old.

I was about twelve when my parents were punching away on their calculators while paying bills when my dad announced,

"Well, you all better get athletic scholarships because we cannot afford to send any of you to college!"

That day getting an athletic scholarship became my one and only dream, as I knew that was how I would get my parents' attention.

So, in the fall of 2008, I achieved my only dream when I was offered an athletic scholarship to join the University of Massachusetts, women's lacrosse team, graduating with the class of 2014. I verbally accepted the offer and committed to sign a National Letter of Intent the following fall.

Dozens of division one lacrosse programs had expressed interest, and many had extended me offers, but I still never felt good enough to be on the receiving end of those invites. While many athletes dream of finally touring campuses and meeting their future, potential college coach and teammates, the entire recruitment process for me was a horrifying ordeal. Everything that took place off a lacrosse field just didn't make sense to me. I could not carry on a conversation with anyone, let alone a college coach, whose sole job was to judge if I was a good fit for their program. The entirety of it all was my greatest fear and biggest insecurity.

Two weeks following the day at the yellow house, I attended my official visit to the University of Massachusetts, my future college. It was bitter, wet, and rainy that day as I shivered underneath my winter coat outside at the football stadium. I wasn't entirely sure what to pack, but I definitely did not pack enough layers. I was huddled together with a group of my future teammates listening in to a conversation. In those days, I was nearly mute.

"We are sorry, she is just shy," acted as the continuous apology my parents seemed to always be giving on my behalf.

I learned from a very young age that saying less was always more and that saying nothing was even better. I didn't have opinions or preferences of my own, as I always defaulted to the preferences of others. I lived in fear of judgment, criticism, and being scolded, as was the case at home. Life was a continuous assimilation to the environments I entered, and the opinions of others were all that mattered to me. I needed to be good. I needed to be quiet. I was determined to be obedient.

After that football game at UMass, I would go on to try alcohol for the first time, in excess. I quickly learned alcohol made me forget about the constant winter I found myself in. It also acted as the perfect social lubricant, allowing me to escape myself while seeming to grant me permission to become anyone else.

I don't remember where I woke up the following morning at UMass. The night after the football game and the morning of the send-off brunch, an event where all parents and players would be in attendance. I don't recall if someone picked me up somewhere or if I slept on the futon that was provided for me by my host. I couldn't tell you. My memory resurfaces after I had thrown myself into the shower and after I had realized I had forgotten to pack a hairbrush. I used my fingers to part sections into the clumpy mess that was my wet hair, attempting to give myself a beached wave-type look. It didn't work.

I continued to run my fingers through my wet hair as frames from my drunken actions after the football game collided with the ones that began to resurface from that day inside that yellow house. I had a craving to throw up. To rid myself of the alcohol that marinated in my stomach, yes, but also to act as a hard reset for some sort of mental, physical, and emotional homeostasis.

I pooled water into my hands from the running sink, slurping the room-temperature liquid in hopes it would dilute, if not erase, all memories of how I had just sabotaged my future.

I wore an off-the-shoulder shirt that revealed my black bra strap and dark jeans with rips in the knees. Both items had small holes in the seams from where I had ripped out the security sensors and shoved them into my purse at the mall, as was the case with my entire wardrobe. It was not until I was seated in front of the coaching staff that I realized how inappropriate my look was. In that room filled with beautiful people, surrounded by wealth and opportunity, I felt like a wet, stray dog.

We met with the coaches, who asked how the visit was and the foreboding question of whether or not alcohol was involved in our activities last night. I said there was not.

On the ride home, I thought of my future teammates and how they were dressed appropriately in sweaters and polos and carrying Longchamp bags. How did everyone remember to pack a hairbrush? I was also trying to figure out why my parents had been acting so oddly since arriving at the brunch venue. It wasn't until much later that I realized it was because they were smiling so much.

My mom turned around to face me from the front seat of the car, her eyes conveying excitement.

"We are so proud of you, honey!"

How could they not see I was just barely holding it together? It was the moment I had been waiting for my entire life—for my parents to take the time to see me. I wished I was sober enough to savor the moment. Instead, I took small sips of water, trying to convince myself I was not going to vomit all over the leather seats of my dad's beloved Volvo.

Later that afternoon, I had a Facebook message from a recognized name and face from The University of Massachusetts. The message read:

"Not a very good way to make a first impression! The way in which you handled yourself was completely inappropriate. A member of the guy's team, really? Good luck coming into your freshman year with the reputation you have now!"

I retreated into the bathroom where I splashed cold water on my face. I was unraveling. This wasn't happening. This wasn't real.

When I returned to the computer, my mother was hovering over it. She was bent at the waist and hands on her hips. Her face—inches from the computer screen. A bone-chilling, fully present, unparalleled shock and mind-numbing fear welled up inside my chest. Her words struck me there, as if by javelin.

"So, what are you, the UMass slut now?"

It was then that I decided, I guess, that's exactly what I am.

Chapter 2

OCCASIONAL ANGELS

2010

I couldn't attend UMass after that. I broke my commitment and scrambled at the last minute to find a school that would accept me. Searching my inbox for any conversations I could potentially strike back up with college coaches. The brook was dry. I applied to a handful of prep schools out of desperation, assuming I could do a post-graduate year, which would give me the second chance I needed. I was denied admission to them all.

My senior lacrosse season came around, and I was spotlighted as one of the top players in the state of Connecticut and targeted as an All-American. I was, without a doubt, a selfish player. My stats and performance were what drove me and, by default, led to attention and feelings of self-worth. Winning or losing didn't seem to play a factor in achieving those goals. Consequently, I had failed to consider the holistic nature in which the All-American award was given.

When I finally broke the news to my parents that I would not be named an All-American at the end of the season, they took the news worse than I did.

"I've already told everyone at work you would be an All-American. What am I supposed to tell them now?" my dad asked.

I didn't answer.

Days later, my dad announced, with the five of us divided up between the kitchen and the living room,

"Well! There won't be a vacation this summer since Kelsey decided to pass up all her scholarship offers!"

I had failed at reaching my goal and was now resented for it.

I decided to attend a small division three school in Massachusetts and play both lacrosse and basketball. Western New England, or WNE, is a picturesque college with an undergraduate enrollment of roughly 2,500 students. Red brick buildings matched the paths that led to and from them around campus. In the height of autumn, the leaves of the trees were the color of blood oranges, and students sported the school colors of royal blue and gold.

As a Division III institution, most of the money for team travel and gear came from fundraising. A few months into the fall semester, I was driving with two of my teammates to a charity golf tournament that would act as our biggest source of fundraising for the year. Crossing a four-way intersection on the way there, another car ran a red light and collided with ours in the middle of the intersection. My head slammed into the driver's seat headrest in front of me, and I was knocked out on impact. I awoke in confusion, to the pungent smell of sulfur and to the overwhelming impression that I would somehow get in trouble for not having worn my seatbelt. Dazed and confused, I fussed around for the belt as the door next to me opened, and I was scooped up into the arms of a stranger. In this man's arms, I was weightless, as light as a feather.

Occasional Angels

My entire life, I had felt burdensome and heavy, but this man, whose face I had not yet seen, allowed me to surrender to the feeling of fragility as he called me sweet, endearing names I had both heard and never heard before. He calmed me with assurances, took off his sweatshirt, and zipped me up in it, followed by his arms that wrapped themselves around me. I have no recollection of what the man looked like or if he ever even told me his name. Only that, in the arms of this perfect stranger, did I feel safer than I had anywhere and with anyone before.

Maybe it was the impact, the confusion, but I broke down and bawled. I wailed like a little girl as I sat on that street corner in the arms of what must have been an angel.

I suffered a concussion and was out of sports for nearly two months. I went from being in the best shape of my life to binging everything from alcohol to ice cream in the dining hall. Once I was cleared to practice, I pulled my hamstring right away, which set me back another two weeks. By that point I felt so far behind in conditioning and practices I didn't know how I would ever catch back up.

Each next practice and following play became the next chance at redemption. The next opportunity to prove myself became my obsession. It impacted my attitude, and I grew envious of my teammates that were performing well. I was convinced that I was the better player, and if I hadn't been in that accident, I would be seeing time on that court.

Eventually, my coach called me and two of my teammates into her office. The one thing the three of us had in common was that we were the last three people off the bench and occupied the last three seats, furthest from half court each game.

That day in Coach Cal's office, we were shown a replay of last week's home game. A game that I did not play in. The three of us looked on as we watched one of our teammates knock down a three-pointer. In the background, our entire team shot up from the bench in praise. Except the three of us in that office.

I remembered the scenario vividly, as it was the first time I had debated not standing in celebration for a basket. What I wanted to explain to my coach was that we had stood up *four* times before that in a matter of twenty seconds! That there had been multiple steals and baskets in a short amount of time! Weren't there roll-over good jobs, like when someone sneezes more than three times in a row?

I was aware of my poor attitude. I had always been hard on myself, and I was abnormally disappointed in my skills and my performance at that time. It's not that I wasn't happy for my teammates; I had never rode the bench before, and my performance was my life. Somehow, in not playing, I lost what little hold over myself and the small amount of self-worth I had managed to keep hold of all those years.

My brain still felt like it was on fire from the accident. I had constant headaches and at times felt rage boiling up inside of me. I sought out opportunities to drink whenever I could to dissociate and distract myself, from myself. I went on a date with a football player who had asked me out a few times. It was rumored around campus that he came from a very religious household, was a virgin, and did not believe in sex until marriage. For some reason, that made me feel comfortable enough to invite him over to my dorm to watch a movie one night, where he assaulted me.

I was stressed out, checked out, and refused to slow down and take the time to be still, to think, to talk to anyone. I wasn't a good teammate or roommate.

My freshman-year roommate was a gift from God. She was everything you would want in a friend and had all the qualities you would want in a roommate. She was everything I wasn't at that time: kind, patient, warm, generous—an all-around good person.

My shyness now came across as bitterness and having a chip on my shoulder. I was consumed with the single event that seemed to have sparked and unraveled my future. That day inside the yellow house. All I saw was how my promiscuity had overshadowed my identity as an athlete, leaving me miserable at a small school where I had expected to be a decent-sized fish in a relatively small pond.

Lacrosse season finally came around, and we were winning. More importantly, as I saw it back then, I was playing well and scoring a lot. At the conclusion of the season, my parents suggested I consider transferring since the whole "basketball thing" didn't work out. I had every intention of going back to WNE for my sophomore year, mainly because I had loved my lacrosse season and was hopeful for the basketball season the following year. Still, I figured there was no harm in shopping.

That summer, I drove to The University of Connecticut with my mom and met with their coaching staff. Exiting the field house after an introduction and tour, my mother and I made our way back to the parking garage past the famous Gampel Pavilion, where the basketball team plays.

It was a sickening sort of humid that day. I remarked to my mom,

"I'm not sure about this," in reference to the school, the transfer, if I was gay or wanted to still inhabit life on this planet, etcetera, etcetera.

She stopped point-blank on the sidewalk and said,

"You're kidding." Her voice and face were riddled with disappointment and irritation. "Why did you have me mail out those highlight reels to coaches? Why did we bother coming here today only to waste their time?"

I knew my mother had my best interests at heart. I also understood that she wanted so badly to give me and my siblings everything she never had.

She once told my sister and me that her only dream growing up was to one day have a family and a home of her own. I never fully understood what a foster home was when I was younger. Only that my mom and her five siblings grew up in many of them over the course of their childhoods. They were often separated from one another for long periods of time on end.

Growing up, I would catch my mother's gray-blue eyes fixate on the steering wheel in front of her or on the kitchen counter top, so she would have a moment to breathe. She would leave the present moment and go somewhere back "there," her lips teetering a fine line between quivering and not, before snapping herself back to the present day and rattling off the laundry list of errands she had left to do before we headed home. I now recognize this trance-like state my mother would sometimes drift into, although I didn't back then. Past traumas that serve as a buoy, tethering you to a time and place, preventing you from ever fully escaping your past or drifting too far.

My mother lost her father in a plane crash while she was pregnant with my older brother, a plane he was piloting with her stepmother as the passenger. My mom's biological mother, with whom she holds only a few memories of, passed at 38. Given the drugs and alcohol in her system at the time of her passing, it was ruled a potential suicide, although no one knows for sure. A noticeable shiver would be sent up my mother's spine whenever my dad would drop chicken breasts battered in egg wash, flour, and breadcrumbs into sizzling oil on the occasions he made chicken parmesan.

"I do not think those burns ever went away," my mother once said.

Her stare lowered to the floor, as if something there held her attention. One morning during her childhood, she was playing with her biological and foster siblings when her foster mother tossed a pot of sizzling cooking oil out the open kitchen door, which caught one of her foster sisters right as she ran past. It's why she has never been overly enthusiastic about doughnuts, as that was what her foster mother had made in the oil that day.

My mom loved us kids in a way I'm not sure she ever experienced herself. If one of us was sick, without hesitation she would make homemade chicken noodle soup in the crockpot and often stay up all night next to us. Throughout my childhood and up until my sophomore year in college, she never once missed a game. It was common for her to wake at four in the morning to get a workout in before work, just so she could depart work early enough to make it in time for the games.

Still, that steamy and damp day at the UConn campus, I was overcome with obligation and guilt. Overwhelmed with the understanding that my parents must know what is best for me. Even though I was ambivalent, I figured I had been given a second chance at what I thought was my dream. I enrolled at UConn for that fall semester. I would finally make my parents proud.

Chapter 3

2011

I emailed my freshman year coaches to inform them that I would not be returning to WNE. I convinced myself it was a clean break, but in reality, I still had no idea how to speak or interact with adults.

There were a lot of differences between the Division I and Division III programs. The first being that at the Division I level, your sport is your job. I was excited about this. It was what I signed up for. The hours between ten in the morning to two in the afternoon, during the week were dedicated to workouts and practice. Other team-related activities that fell outside of those hours were game film, team study hall, and mandatory eight-minute ice baths after practice in 48 degree water. Three or four of us at a time would submerge ourselves up to our sports bras in the icy tubs, clinging to the side of the galvanized steel for emotional support. I loved the pain and the discomfort. It acted as a painful reminder that I was an athlete. My life now meant something.

Each fall, our coach's way of enticing us to come into the season prepared and in shape was to withhold any access to our team locker room or team gear until the majority of the team passed fitness testing. Our team locker room was to be "earned" in the fall. Until then, the doors would remain locked, and we would be dressed in the previous year's clothes. Or, if you were an incoming freshman—or a transfer like me—you were dressed in random t-shirts flipped inside out that did not display any words or logos aside from the Nike swoosh.

In the interim, while waiting for access to our locker room, my teammates and I toted our lacrosse sticks all around campus. Multiple pairs of footwear, turf sneakers, and trainers were looped and weaved into the hooks in our backpacks, dangling outside of them. We would hold up t-shirts, hoodies, anything to try and build a wall standing shoulder-to shoulder as we changed in hallways, outside the field house, or in random bathrooms within the sports complexes.

At times, we would work out for four hours and not have the opportunity to shower until we had time to trek back up to our dorms later that evening after classes. In more ways than one, I constantly felt filthy, but soon that just became a habit and then the lifestyle.

At our first couple of fall ball games, I was in a midfield rotation and seeing decent playing time. During one of the games, a long-ball was thrown to me during transition. I leapt in attempts to catch it but missed it by at least a foot.

"Daniels!" My coach shouted from the sidelines. She waved me over. My substitute was already in the sub box, toeing the side-line and hoisting her stick up in the air. I sprinted through the sideline, slapping the stick of my teammate. You always run through the line.

My coach didn't allow us to call her "coach." We were to call her by her first name, Alexis. It took some significant time for me to get used to that since I saw her as the person who held my fate in her hands, not a friend. Apparently, when Alexis approached me, I took a step to the side. Almost insulted, she asked me if I had a "bubble issue." I hadn't realized I had done anything. I was panting and still catching my breath. Confused, while mentally freaking out that she now thought I was weird, I assured her there was no issue. It was then that she instructed me to take off my gloves.

"I don't like the grip you have on your stick," she said.

She seemed to believe it was the reason I had missed the pass in the first place. And she was right. Still, for some reason, I thought she was joking, and I laughed. Again, she looked at me with raised eyebrows to note she was insulted. I immediately ripped the gloves off my hands and shoved them into the side pocket of my backpack, where they would remain until the spring season.

I did not know how to play lacrosse without gloves. I had never played without them, and I saw this as the ultimate setback. I had always been a heady and superstitious player. I wore the same headband, laced up my turfs and cleats the same way, and I always drank a red Powerade before each game.

This season, I was suddenly forbidden from wearing my gloves, and gone were the days of red Powerades.

At WNE I had work-study and was given a check every other week for odd jobs I held on campus. Division I athletes, however, were not allowed to hold jobs. Our sport alone kept us preoccupied for upwards of thirty hours a week, on top of classes and studying. A few of my teammates and I at UConn would take turns discreetly working coat check at one of the bars on campus, where we would sit in a closet and collect and then redistribute the coats back to the drunken college kids for some cash under the table. But the opportunity only came around every so often. All to say, that semester, in more ways than one, I felt I was at a disadvantage.

Our coaches referred to the culture of our practices as an "all-out dog fight." Our coaches believed in holding each other accountable both on and off the field. Correction and confrontation were encouraged, which usually just manifested themselves as passive-aggressive, player-to-player comments.

We had a positional coach who loved to pick on the weakest links. That first fall season I didn't start off in her doghouse, but later that fall, I definitely found myself there. I was an athlete. I understood how to take constructive criticism from coaches—to a degree. I heard; I listened; I was obedient, and I did my best to make the correction or adjustment. I wanted them to like me and play me, so I adapted as best I could.

What at first was, "Got it," and "Okay," in acknowledgment of coaches and players offering guidance, soon just became overbearing. It seemed excessive. Many, myself included, felt the need to defend and stand up for ourselves, to explain, to talk back, which then was cause for concern, as a freshman or sophomore standing up for themselves to a junior or senior was unacceptable a majority of the time. If a teammate scored a goal, it was standard for the goal to be celebrated. However, it wasn't uncommon for a teammate to tap someone's stick in recognition, only to then let them know,

"Hey, nice shot, but I was open on the other side of the net, so pass it next time."

That turf field was the Galapagos Islands, and Darwinism was the scientific theory behind our dogfights. It was incessant gaslighting by players in front of coaches, which is exactly what was wanted. To divide the alphas of the pack from the meek.

There was sometimes not enough time to run to the bathroom between "lift," our strength and conditioning sessions, and practice. One of our captains once asked on behalf of the team if we could have a bathroom break about halfway through practice, to which our coach replied,

"You can sh*t in the woods for all I care!" Everyone just sort of took that to be interpreted as no, and practice carried on.

As one might imagine, the best players were always the ones who thrived in silence. Their performance spoke for itself, and their inability to show any emotion associated with a correction didn't egg on the bullies.

The lacrosse field had been the only place where I had held confidence and trusted my own judgment, but soon the turf became just like the rest of the world. I second guessed everything; I doubted my game sense and questioned my athletic vision and ability. I wanted to play well and score, while also wanting to pass to the upperclassmen, so there was less of a chance I would get called out or put down in front of the coaches. I grew completely self-conscious, nervous, and anxious. Gone were the days of operating in a state of flow.

As the leaves fell from the trees on campus, indicating the early stages of winter, so came with it my first full-blown wave of anxiety and depression. While lacrosse is a spring sport, we were outside in the tundra practicing in Connecticut in mid-January. As long as the weather hovered around fifteen degrees fahrenheit *(including windchill)* we were playing outside, layered up on the turf and wincing whenever snow or the bitter wind blew through the wind tunnel that was Storrs.

One practice, I was rounding the twelve-meter arc, having just lost my defender and ready to receive a pass on the move, when I caught the ball, and was then completely trucked by my defender. The whistle blew, signaling a foul. I got up, annoyed, and went back to the start of the drill. The whistle blew again as I cut to lose my defender before, again, rounding the twelve-meter arc.

Catch it, don't drop it. Catch it. Catch it.

Catching the ball on the move, my defender met me with a quick stick to my hip, pressing against the bone, before she made the first swing, attempting a check. Protecting my stick, I pivoted, changed directions, and looked for an open teammate when *whack,* her stick caught my stick, my goggles, my ear, and the back of my head. The whistle blew again.

"Again!" Alexis shouted. "Watch your stick," the last part spoken as almost a formality.

Again, I lost my defender, but the ball hit the side of my wide-open stick. I rushed to pick up the ground ball when my defender checked my empty stick, scooped up the ball, and ran out of the drill. Alexis blew her whistle.

"Again," she said. Less enthused.

I was more than frustrated. I dropped the ball, yes, but the rest could have been fouls. This fourth time, I had an extremely difficult time losing my defender and getting open. All to say, I ended up catching the pass but lost it after one final check to my stick and also my head.

Three checks to the head in practice was not common. It also was not uncommon. I was miserable, but this is what we signed up for. I was born and bred to be obedient and to push past pain. If this game and level of play was easy, everyone would do it.

It wasn't too long afterward that I began missing unguarded, open passes. Then, I was tripping over my own two feet on the turf. A frustration-induced rage soon brought with it tears that I did my best to prevent from coming forward. I had gone from being a stoic, near emotionless athlete to now doing everything in my power not to cry on the turf. With this newfound anxiety came hypersensitivity and the paranoia that everyone hated me.

"What is going on with you!?" Alexis asked, as she took a seat on the edge of her desk. It was delivered more like a rhetorical question than a question denoting actual concern. *Don't cry. Don't cry.* I told myself.

My elbows were resting on the tops of my legs as I buried my face in my hands. I didn't even want to look in her general direction. I was completely ashamed.

"I feel like I am going crazy," I said in between choked-up sobs. To which she matched my intensity and said, "And I am beginning to think you are!"

Chapter 4

2012

"I'm sorry, what?" I asked as my gaze broke free from the large oak tree outside the office window. My mind, at that moment, reinserted itself back inside my body.

"I asked how classes are going." A woman said. She was seated behind a desk on the other side of the room. Her hazel eyes were hidden behind rectangular framed glasses, and her dark curly hair was bunched together and held back by a single large clip.

"Fine," I responded. I began meeting with Dr. S in the spring semester of my sophomore year and had been meeting with her for about a year by this point. Dr. S was unlike anyone else I had encountered while at UConn. She was calm and patient and always seemed to be wearing at least part of a smile. There was a severe mismatch of energy, and being in her relaxed and reserved presence only made me feel that much more anxious.

I was a neurotic, hypervigilant mess in general, especially in those meetings. I would cling to my coffee cup and shake my leg uncontrollably, glancing over at the clock on the wall every few minutes, not wanting to overstay my welcome, or even worse, be late to my next obligation. I don't remember much of what was said in those meetings, only that I lived in constant fear that any and everything said was being relayed back to my coaching staff. As a result, I never said much. When I did try to speak, I fought the urge to cry uncontrollably.

I showed up disheveled to those morning therapy sessions. My hair pulled back in a messy bun, having done little more than brush my teeth and maybe wash my face that morning. I had put on close to twenty pounds since transferring to UConn, so my appearance was an additional source of shame. I am five-foot-seven, and that semester, I weighed about 150 pounds. My speed had always been my secret weapon and my innate ability I could fall back on. Yet now, given the weight gain, even that was gone.

It was not common for athletes, at least at my university at that time, to see a therapist. To see a therapist was to admit you were mentally weak, which was a different type of suicide in its own right. As a result, I had ruled depression out as a diagnosis for myself. I was an athlete. Athletes are not depressed.

One session, Dr. S. asked me if she thought my quality of life might be better if lacrosse was no longer part of it. Without thought, I snapped back at her, "No! That's not even an option." And it wasn't.

Being a lacrosse player was not a choice; it was who I was. It was my identity. It was all I had. However, in the past year, my skills had declined so significantly that the coaches had just stopped yelling at me altogether. I was simply ignored. Now, after a year, I longed to be yelled at again. At least then I would know I was still worthy of investment, that there might be hope for me.

Still, I couldn't picture my life without being an athlete. I was with my team and working out, sharing meals, and practicing together every single day. I rarely went out on weekends. Sometimes, I would get ready with my roommates only to be hit with a wave of depression before we were about to leave. I felt fat, or I hated my clothes. Soon, the occasional thoughts of self-loathing played on repeat, forever simmering on the back burner of my mind.

"I'm dumb. I'm fat. I'm stupid. I don't belong here. I'm not good enough to be here. My coach wishes she had never brought me onto the team. I wish I knew how to die. I'm so ugly."

My sister, Eliza also attended UConn at the same time that I did. Eliza and I were polar opposites in every way. She was always smiling, making friends everywhere she went, and had a spunky, uninhibited sense of childlike joy. The last thing she cared about was pleasing others for the sake of being liked. She was too busy being herself, having discovered a love for music and a passion for caring for animals. As part of her work-study on campus, she worked in one of the dining halls where she would clock in close to five in the morning, filling trays of French toast and scrambled eggs. Her light brown hair was covered by a hairnet, and she had a river rock-like shine behind her eyes.

Then, one day, the light behind her eyes faded, and the smiles stopped. There was a hardening of her heart that made even her everyday movements around the dining hall appear slower. A rage boiled up inside of me when I was told she was date-raped by a co-worker. In those days, I always felt like I was asking for it, but my sister was calculated and innocent. She didn't drink alcohol and didn't go to parties.

My sister, along with three other women from campus that year, filed a lawsuit against the university on the grounds that their cases and claims were handled with negligence. One of the women claimed that a campus police officer responded to her report of assault by saying, "Women need to stop spreading their legs like peanut butter, or rape is going to keep happening until the cows come home."

The women were represented by a well-known civil rights attorney, which gave the case even more media attention. Overnight, I went from being my sister's biggest confidant and throwing a fountain soda in the face of the man who assaulted her, to essentially placing greater distance between her and me. I could not understand why she wanted the world to know about a moment that broke her, or why these women wanted to broadcast these horrible moments and memories. I truly believed back then that men were just men. They do and take what they want and we, as women, just need to learn to adapt and work around it.

Somehow, the women bringing awareness to the systemic issue and their own assaults, stirred up an unnerving and agitated confusion within me. More denial. More detachment. More dissociation.

After my Friday visits with Dr. S, I had my favorite class, Societal Deviance, with my favorite professor, Dr. Miller. This was the second course I had taken with Dr. Miller. The semester prior I received a C- as my final grade in his Introduction to something or other class, but I came back for more because I was mildly infatuated with him.

He did this cute thing where he meandered over to the classroom door, counting down the seconds on his watch to when class would start and once it did, he would lock the door behind him. The previous semester, I had to run across campus sweaty from practice and toting all of my gear to try and make it to class before he would lock the door. I was late twice.

That semester of my junior year, however, I came right from Dr. S's office to Dr. Miller's class. So, while I was never out of breath, my eyes were typically still puffy in the aftermath from all the crying that spewed forth during therapy.

"Sex, drugs and rock n' roll!!" Dr. Miller said with gusto at the start of class.

The projection screen lowered, and he tinkered with his thumb drive before making his way over to the classroom door and counting down the seconds on his watch to lock it behind him. Dr. Miller was unlike any other professor I had ever had and was everything I was not. Confident, in control, and he held power and favor. His lectures consisted of schools of theory or charts revealing statistics, as he spoke freely referencing life stories and tales that brought them to life. He was a storyteller masquerading as a lecturer, and it was the most engaged I had been in my entire college career. It is also one of the few classes I actually remember.

"What would you say if I told you that college women were hanging out with older, successful men and getting compensated for it?" Dr. Miller asked. My ears perked up like a German Shepherd, and I sat up a bit straighter in my chair. He went on to explain in loose detail the trend of college women getting wined and dined by men and having their tuition paid for.

As someone who had zero dollars in their bank account, the idea of being able to join my teammates at Starbucks or afford a monthly tanning membership seemed more than appealing. He then asked the million-dollar question:

"If sex is implied, and these women are being compensated, is it prostitution?"

I scanned the room for indications as to what others might be thinking. The answer was obviously no. A prostitute was an older woman who wore fishnet stockings and a second-hand bra while posted up at a run-down motel. I envisioned an ashtray that needed to be emptied on the nightstand and a pile of blow on the bathroom counter.

Dr. Miller picked up a dry-erase marker as he began to do the math on the whiteboard at the front of the room. Muttering, "Three hundred dollars a trick, let's say she sees two men a day ... takes a day off here and there ... holiday, kids' parent-teacher conference, works 300 days in all." It was then that he drew three giant circles around the number 180,000, which was written in red on the board in front of me.

"She is still bringing in six figures plus—whichever way you slice it," he said.

I couldn't wrap my head around it. In all my time waiting tables at a pizzeria during my breaks from school, I had never collectively held more than $200 in my hands at any given time. I continued to cross-reference the lifestyle these women must have led. One filled with drugs, domestic violence, and diseases. I pulled an Elle Woods at that moment, following her logic that "Exercise gives you endorphins. Endorphins make you happy. Happy people just don't shoot their husbands." I rationalized my own version of it right then and there, that if college women are going on dates with older men, it must be normal. And if it is normal, it cannot be prostitution.

I was so depressed at that point I had little to no interest in dating, let alone sex. But if it was a prerequisite to getting paid, I didn't see the harm in using it as a means to an end. How hard could this be to execute? I went back to my apartment and decided to teach myself a new skill. I was going to learn to navigate the dark web.

Weeks later, I walked into the nicest restaurant I had ever been to, an Italian restaurant with tables lined with white tablecloths and two forks on the left side of the small bread plate. I slid into a red leather booth as the host graciously placed a menu in front of me as I waited for my date to arrive. I tried to recall what he looked like in his online pictures. *Marathon Runner and Iron Man competitor, business owner, enjoys skiing and sailing.*

A man entered the restaurant, and although I was certain he was not my date, a confusion came over me as he began to approach me in the booth. My stomach dropped once I realized that the oldest man I might have ever met was, in fact, my date. *Is this really what 45 looks like?*

"You're even hotter in person!" He exclaimed as he took off his coat and handed it to the hostess without giving her a second thought. I smiled through two-fold embarrassment. He proceeded to snap his fingers at the server and hold up two fingers in the air.

"Two chardonnays!" he said from about ten yards away. I had never been more thankful to be dining at an empty restaurant.

His eyes leeched onto my legs as my attention was drawn to the saggy skin around his jawline, then to the deep lines that ran horizontally across his forehead. They appeared to deepen as he inched closer to me in the booth. His hair was thinning and appeared a combination of gray and white, while veins—both navy and violet, bulged from underneath his sun-spotted hands. We engaged in a bit of small talk before he reached his hand under the table and grabbed my quadricep without warning. I both flexed and shuddered in surprise. He then moved his hand down my leg past and into my boots that covered my calf muscle.

"Oh wow, you are an athlete!" He exclaimed.

I wasn't sure if this was normal, but it definitely was not how Dr. Miller had described it. Or at least how I had interpreted it. I figured lunch would be over soon and focused on the money I was confident I would be receiving.

That day was the first time I had ever ordered grilled fish in a restaurant—or any fish, for that matter, outside of the sushi restaurant across the street from campus or the mystery poached fish often served in the dining hall. It was the most beautiful salad I had ever seen. The drive was already worth it, and it was a meal I had no interest in throwing up.

He asked me questions I had no answers to. What my major was, what my career goals were, what I wanted out of an arrangement. I told him whatever it was I thought he might want to hear. That I was in business school and that whatever his ideal "arrangement" looked like was fine by me! Also, I would like to eventually go to law school. None of that information was true, but it all seemed far better than the truth. And even though I had no clue to use an alias at this time and still introduced myself to these men as "Kelsey," this fake backstory stayed with me as I recycled it back to all the new men I would eventually meet.

I skewered a small ball of fresh mozzarella and half a cherry tomato onto my fork and placed it in my mouth when the man leaned over and whispered into my ear,

"Why don't you go to the bathroom and take your panties off. I like my girls to be a little more on edge when they are eating."

I began coughing, nearly choking on a caprese bite, which I tried to play off as a laugh. Lunch came to an end just as the snow began to fall. He invited me back to his place where he was confident "we could find a way to keep each other warm."

I thought I might throw up that salad after all. Back in my dorm room, I reviewed his profile and pictures, realizing that all his uploaded profile photos were pictures of the same man I had met, only all of them were pictures taken of Polaroids. Pictures of pictures that were probably taken in the '70s. I was not paid, but I was catfished before it ever became a mainstream word.

Chapter 5

GAS STATION WINE

2012

I didn't recall slamming on the brakes of my car, or seeing the "Wrong Way" sign as I drove down a one-way highway merger.

"What the f-ck is wrong with you?! Are you blind?!!" shouted a woman in muffled hysteria through her windshield. Her car bumper rested inches away from mine and given how I had almost just killed the both of us, the two middle fingers she was giving me seemed appropriate.

The clock had yet to strike noon that day in Providence, and yet there was already an entire bottle of wine coursing through my bloodstream. My left cheekbone was tender to the touch from the friction it had received earlier from a box spring mattress, and I was just noticing the large rips in the tops of my black stockings that rested just above the middle of my upper leg. *What was I doing here?*

Less than two hours prior, I was stepping out of my car over a frothy puddle of toothpaste and mouthwash I had just gargled and spit out onto the pavement. Tory had suggested I meet him for coffee at a motel right off the highway in Providence. It was a ways from Storrs, but he promised to give me $300 for making the trip, so it was pretty much a no-brainer.

Inside the motel, I walked past children scooping Fruit Loops into styrofoam bowls, women spreading peanut butter on toast, and old men stockpiling hard-boiled eggs and sausage links onto paper plates.

Off in the corner, a man dressed head to toe in black athletic gear sat with his back to the entrance. I was concerned I was overdressed, but confused as he had instructed me to wear a dress and stockings. All thoughts regarding my outfit, however, left the building once Tory gave me a tight hug and my eyes locked onto his large, off-yellow, horse-like teeth that displayed graying around the gums. His eyes were dark and beady and seemed to be outlining my body while he held a coffee tumbler that he periodically took large, audible gulps from. Three or four at a time.

He rattled off all of the things he had bought for his former sugar baby and all the places they had traveled to together. He expressed interest in wanting to share those same experiences with me—skiing in Aspen and snorkeling off the coast of Mexico—before telling me he had a present waiting for me in the room. A present? For me? I guess I could get past the whole "teeth thing."

He requested I take the stairs, so as not to raise any unwanted eyebrows, and to meet him in the room. I complied.

I tried not to stare at his teeth as Tory welcomed me into the frigid room. The cold cut through my stockings, causing my freshly shaved legs to prickle upon contact. A horizontal gravity grabbed hold of me like quicksand, pulling me further into the confines of the motel room and over to the window, which seemed to do little to no good at stopping the winter from seeping in. My eyes gravitated over to the faded maroon-patterned bedspread that had clearly seen its fair share of action.

Tory then pulled a bottle of white wine out from his backpack. A "$5" sticker was stuck to the neck of the bottle. You would have thought it was a Birkin bag by the way I lit up over its reveal. All the men I met on the website claimed to be seeking "just one girl they could spoil." So that's what I believed. I wanted Tory to know I was the girl he should choose.

He retrieved two cups wrapped in plastic from the bathroom, filling the first and handing it to me as I waited for him to pour himself one.

"Oh no, no. I can't. I have to get back to work after this. I got it for you! To help you relax and unwind from the stress of classes."

I took a small sip from the cup, but he looked displeased, so I tossed back the rest of it.

"That's my girl!" he said, bringing the bottle again to meet the cup and fill it. He waited until I had finished the second cup before grabbing my backside and pulling me in for a sloppy, stale-coffee smelling kiss. I tried to hold my breath while still pretending to be into it. *$300. $300 $300.* I repeated in my head.

It was sometime after the fifth cup that my body was thrown on the bed, and my face was pressed into that same ugly maroon-patterned bedspread. One of my arms was pulled behind me, and the other grabbed at the roots of my hair. The full measure of his body weight was on top of me as half of my body hung off the bed. My eyes narrowed in on a small patch of light that showed itself on the wall to my right. *$300. $300. $300.*

"Wow! You're fun! Let's do this again sometime!" Was the last line Tory said before exiting the motel room door.

I was unsure of where he might have left the money for me. For some reason, I thought he might have hidden it, like some type of game. I hobbled to the bathroom in discomfort, using the wall as a means of support. My right hand clenched my lower abdomen as I searched under the unopened bar of soap and used towels, becoming increasingly aware that I might need to use the bathroom. I was determined to find the money before I did anything else. I opened nightstand drawers, going as far as to flip through the Bible and the Book of Mormon, thinking maybe he could have hidden the bills within its pages. Still nothing. I lined the toilet seat with paper and hugged my chest down toward my knees, wrapping my arms underneath them for comfort, security, and warmth. Maybe men just don't pay girls on the first date.

I drove back to see Tory in Providence two more times after that. The third and final time I worked up the courage to ask for gas money. He had yet to pay me a dime. Tory answered by explaining how he had been preparing a giant Christmas surprise for me. But if I was feeling impatient, he would be willing to give me a couple hundred dollars the next time we met instead. A Christmas surprise sounded much better. I said I would wait.

It was around this time one of my former high school teachers began messaging me on Facebook. For a handful of years, our only contact was when he sent me Merry Christmas messages or wished me Happy Birthday. At some point, messaging had shifted to texting. I had mentioned I was struggling with lacrosse, and he offered to come up to campus and take me out for a drink to talk. I wasn't sure how to feel about it. How I *should* feel about it. I was still only twenty—did he know that? I wasn't entirely sure if it was normal for students to go out with their former teachers, but I figured it must be if he was asking me.

Craig was in his mid-forties, drove a Nissan, and was parked outside the foot of the freshly salted steps that led up to my apartment sometime later. We drove a few towns over to a tavern that didn't card, where we sat at the bar top and ordered beers.

I felt ugly and naked, and tears of frustration lingered behind my eyes the entire night, just waiting for their curtain call. I didn't think he cared so much as maybe he just felt bad for me.

Craig came to visit me more and more often. Drinks at the local digs quickly turned into dinners and drinks, and I figured this was what dating might be like. After a night filled with margaritas, we pulled into the parking lot of a local town park. I knew what we were doing was inappropriate, but I liked the attention. I liked having this secret.

Craig pulled a bottle of vodka out from behind the driver's seat, and we took turns taking swigs from it to slice through the awkwardness. Ten minutes later, the Nissan was lit up with brilliance in the form of flashing red and blue lights. Craig cursed, rushing to zip up his pants and stash the bottle of vodka while keeping tabs on the state trooper in the rearview mirror. The trooper asked for Craig's license and registration.

"Miss," the trooper said. "Are you here on your own free will?"

I laughed, thinking it was a joke, before realizing it wasn't. I told him I was.

We were told the park closes after sunset, let off with a warning, and Craig drove me back to campus. I didn't understand why the trooper had asked me if I was there willingly. The sentence genuinely didn't make sense to me.

The next time Craig picked me up from campus, we skipped dinner, and he drove me straight to a motel that accepted cash and allowed him to pay by the hour. The bed was a spring mattress covered with a near-transparent white sheet that was tucked under a thin gray quilt and covered with foreign hairs. Given the unsanitary set-up, it was hard to believe the room also contained a hottub, which, after cosuming a pint of vodka, I willinging hopped into. It was something about having been in a similar environment with Tory that gave me confidence to step into a role and a character. One who was compliant and, more than anything, willing to please.

We went back there often. It could have been as little as five times or as many at fifteen. All of it blends together as just one very long wrinkle in time. I was starting to like this side of me that held a man's attention and was wanted in certain places, at certain times and wanted, well, just in general.

Chapter 6

JERSEY TURNPIKE

2012

In those days, I struggled with my beliefs. I would pray nightly to a higher power to end my life. I would bargain and plead for it to be given to someone more deserving, like a child with cancer or someone fighting to live in the ICU. I was exhausted during the day but feared going to bed at night. I had anxiety-induced nightmares that would often cause me to wake up in a cold sweat having soaked through my t-shirt.

I had been prescribed antidepressants that left me in a muted haze. I roamed campus like a zombie, my face crestfallen, eyes sunken in and with deep plum-colored bags underneath them. Binge eating and purging offered me a fleeting and illusory sense of control amidst the chaos while I continued to scour the dark corners of the internet for men who might pay me, as Dr. Miller had mentioned in class. Craig wasn't paying me, and while I liked the attention, I was growing bored of being fed vodka and just driven straight to that hourly motel. All I really wanted was some spending money to go out to eat with my teammates.

One morning, huddled in the front seat of my sister's Toyota Camry, I watched as early morning workers emerged from inside a gas station carrying the pink and orange printed Dunkin' Donuts cups and paper bags.

"Come or don't come. It's up to you," The man on the other end of the line said. He had a thick Jersey accent and seemed to be trying to sound more Italian than he might actually be. "But I am telling ya, you won't find a better guy than me on the site."

He introduced himself as Anthony, a Princeton graduate and a business owner. He proclaimed himself to be handsome, fit, and single. Without seeing a picture or knowing much more than that, I merged onto the freeway and made my way to the Garden State.

I embarked on a four-hour drive where I was promised $500 upon my arrival. After reaching the hotel, I waited anxiously in the lobby for around thirty minutes, constantly refreshing my email for updates.

A man in light-washed jeans and a Hawaiian button-up eventually caught my attention and nodded in the direction of the elevators. Anthony didn't fit the Hollywood handsome stereotype, nor was he conventionally good-looking. He had shaggy brown hair about two shades too light for his orange-tinted fake tan. His unusually wide chestnut loafers gave him an almost aquatic-like appearance, and he had poor posture and a slight hunchback, resembling that of a gorilla.

Together, we ascended up and away from the lobby level in the glass elevator. A mix of excitement, fear, and vertigo took hold of me, reminiscent of pre practice and fitness test jitters.

"You're hot. Love the boots," he said. His smile hadn't dropped since we arrived in the elevator, and it had a bizarre, Alice-in-Wonderland-Cheshire-Cat sort of way about it.

He scanned the keycard and pushed open the door, which quickly swung backward; I caught it before it hit me in the face. He made way for the bathroom with the plastic drugstore bag, and I sat down at the foot of the bed. That's when I realized I was sober. That, unlike each time with Tory and Craig, I did not have a bottle of vodka or wine to consume to escape myself or the moment. Anthony emerged from the bathroom smelling like mouthwash and self-tanner and finally removed his sunglasses.

Between the room's low lighting and the curtains that had been pulled compeltely shut, his once brown eyes now appeared entirely onyx. He sized me up like an anaconda about to strike its prey.

$500. $500. $500.

Fifteen minutes later, Anthony was running a comb through his wet hair, having just stepped out of the shower. "You're fun! Let's do this again sometime!"

I was hearing that line a lot lately, but it somehow meant more coming from a Princeton graduate. He extracted a small stack of bills from his leather wallet, which maintained composure from the crease as he propped them up on their sides.

After he left, I threw back the covers I'd been huddled under for warmth, picked up the bills, and ran my fingers across them as if it were my first encounter with a U.S. dollar. I counted them three or four times—just to confirm my hazy reality. All I could think at that moment was,

"That was the easiest money I've ever made."

I flirted with the idea of stopping somewhere around Greenwich to split up the drive. Sushi sounded like a plan. Like Gollum in *The Lord of the Rings*, I continued to think about *my precious money* inside of my bag as I descended down the elevators. I was different when I arrived back at the lobby level. I did not feel ashamed for acting like a slut. On the contrary, for the first time in a long while, I was proud of myself.

I hopped back into the Camry and merged onto the freeway, only to be pulled over fifteen minutes later on the side of the New Jersey Turnpike, using what little willpower I had to not kick the now flat tire attached to my vehicle. I couldn't afford to scratch my first-date boots. My only pair of boots.

"F—-! This is exactly why everyone hates New Jersey!"

I yelled at the top of my lungs and shouted up toward the heavens. Once again, God was punishing me for being a slut.

"Why have you always hated me!?" I shouted.

Everything about the situation felt more dramatic than it actually was. A symphony of honks and beeps came from the never-ending fleet of 18-wheel tractor-trailers on the pike. I retreated back inside the Camry to phone roadside assistance, who told me the wait would be an hour.

I soon noticed a gray Honda Civic pull up behind me from the rearview mirror. A man's eyes observed me from his car's center mirror as he adjusted it to get a better look. I'm sure a rational person would have thought they were at risk of being raped or kidnapped, but in my head, I said to myself, *"Great, I'm going to have to have sex with this man."*

Once your body is taken from you once or twice, just handing it over the next time and the time after that tends to be easier than fighting your way out of a situation. The man stepped out of the car as I repeatedly pressed down on the "lock" button.

"Do you need some help, miss?" He had stopped about twenty feet away with his hands raised. I lowered my window a couple of inches. "It looks like you have a flat. Would you like me to swap it out for you?" His voice was different, and the look in his eyes was strange and unfamiliar.

His name was Michael, and he changed my tire right there on the side of the turnpike as I thought through all the ways he might "suggest" I pay him back the favor. Instead, he invited me to lunch at a bistro a few exits up.

I agreed to lunch, and we pulled off the shoulder and back onto the highway. Only when he took one of the following exits I floored it further up the highway. I had been emailing back and forth with Anthony since the flat, who told me to meet him at an auto body shop a bit further up the pike. Soon, I was sitting in the passenger seat of a silver truck as someone patched my tire.

"It's a buddy of mine's truck," Anthony said.

I believed him. I believed everything he told me that day and thereafter. I believed him when he told me I was submissive and that I was more sexual than most women. I believed him when he told me that I needed to be dominated and was a girl that needed to be "owned." Also that he and I were not like most people as he showered me with compliments.

"I just want a cool, college chick, ya know? Professionals are disgusting and riddled with diseases."

I nodded along in the front seat. A hummingbird to honeysuckle. He invited me back to the hotel for lunch. I figured it was payment for the tire and didn't think declining would be an option. It was around two in the afternoon when I left that Newark hotel again for the second time. There was not another $500, and lunch was never served.

Chapter 7

AN EMBARRASSING WAY TO DIE

2013

I drove to New Jersey a few times a month, fitting trips around my lacrosse schedule. Anthony claimed to be well-versed in this world and more than willing to show me the ropes. He described our "arrangement" as having all the benefits of a relationship without any of the downsides.

I visited him at that same Newark hotel three or four more times before he suggested our one-hour meeting change to overnight and weekend stays in various cities. The amount I was paid was always $500.

He wined and dined me. He took me to restaurants, ordered me vodka martinis and always placed my dinner order on my behalf. We explored cities and streets I had never been to. He shaped my initial understanding of the world and of my place within it. He filled the role of teacher, coach, parent, boyfriend, mentor, and savior.

He told me marriage was a sham and kids ruin your life, solidifying beliefs I already held.

"The women get lazy," Anthony began. "They stop wanting to please their husbands and as they get older, they get bitter. You can't blame the guy when he goes and finds himself a younger woman who wants to explore their sexual side."

It all seemed logical.

"Stick with me, kid," Anthony began. "Don't get lazy, and I will give you the world."

It wasn't long before I was instructed to delete my online dating profile and was required to get on birth control. Believe it or not, I had never taken it. I held a debilitating fear that any hormones would make me gain weight and slow me down for lacrosse. But if I was to continue to see Anthony, it was a requirement because he didn't like wearing protection. Neither did Tory or Craig, for that matter. For some reason, sexual health never seemed tremendously important to me. I was under the assumption that only prostitutes, or people that sleep around, get STDs. I made a doctor's appointment and complied with his demand while in sheer disbelief that of all the girls on the website, a Princeton graduate had chosen me.

Back on campus, I was so far down the bench I could nearly touch the goal line. I was a hot mess on the lacrosse field and what seemed like near catatonic outside of it. It was my junior year, and I was actually making it into less games than I had the year before. My parents still attended home games but made it clear that traveling to away games didn't make sense when I was not getting playing time. It reinforced the belief that unless I was exceptional I wasn't worthy of attention.

On top of it all, in season there were no days off. Our coaches had a rule that if you did not play in thirty percent of Saturday's game, you were required to participate in a circuit workout Sunday morning. I accepted the never-ending hell I was in as inevitable and inescapable. Soon, I started running to Anthony whenever my schedule allowed.

After only a few months of spending time together, Anthony told me he loved me, and I returned the words. Around this time, he also began to slowly introduce dominance. What started out as the occasional slap over time soon progressed. I had read about the term "grooming" in many of my classes, but I never saw myself as vulnerable. I was a D1 college athlete at a Big East university who thought she was in love. Nothing of what I was learning in school translated.

My birthday came around, and Anthony invited me to spend the night with him in New Jersey. I leapt at another opportunity to see him, and he even bought me a present. Cherry red, Beats headphones, just like the ones all my teammates had. It was the best gift I had ever received. Aside from that, it was the same old story of meeting at a hotel off the highway, having dinner, way too many drinks, and waking up to him already having sex with me while I was still unconscious.

When he went to shower, I searched the nightstands, past a half-empty wine glass, for the remote to turn on some background noise. That's when I heard the bill slide underneath the door.

"Anthony, I think they gave us the wrong bill," I chuckled. Almost mocking the hotel staff for their clear incompetence. "It's addressed to some guy named Daniel—"

The sliding wooden bathroom door suddenly flung open, and the paper was ripped from my hands. Droplets of water from his clumpy, poppy-brown hair splattered on me in the process. He vanished back into the bathroom, and I was left damp and bewildered. I retreated back to the bed. He returned with a towel wrapped around his waist as he rummaged through his bag with his back facing me.

"Is Daniel your real name?"

No response.

"I mean, I am biased, but I like the name," I said, jokingly.

"Stop talking." He ordered.

I had never heard his voice like that before. It was an effortless sort of authoritative demand, similar to someone just hanging the phone up on you or telling a dog to sit. I sat silently under the covers before he turned around and ripped them off of me. He grabbed my left ankle and pulled me toward the edge of the bed before rolling me over onto my stomach. I started laughing, thinking he was being playful.

"Stop it!" he said, in that same tone.

I bit my bottom lip in attempts to silence my laughs over whatever game it was we were playing. That's when my wrists were pulled behind me and tape was wrapped continuously around them. The laughing stopped once I felt as if my shoulders might actually pop out of their sockets. The tape was too tight, but the sound of its ripping continued as he stepped off the bed and ignored my requests to take off the tape that was hurting me. There was more ripping of tape before his knee pressed into my lower back and he grabbed a fistful of my hair and jerked my head around in one quick motion.

Craaacckk!

A series of snaps, cracks and pops, like stomped bubble wrap, sent a sharp heat up my neck and down my upper back and right shoulder. My vision grew spotty, then blurry, and for a short while was filled with incandescent colors. Prisms of emerald and lilac dangled like Christmas lights where the sun had snuck in around the curtains. Then something was lodged into my mouth, and it was sealed in place with another strip of tape. That's when I realized that the fabric in my mouth was my underwear from the night before. I hadn't thought about crying until that moment. I remember debating over whether or not it was an appropriate time to cry or if mentally I was still just "weak."

I eventually began to pull my wrists further apart so the tape would cut deeper into them, wanting to redistribute the pain and bring my focus away from where I was experiencing the pain the most. I longed to die, but not like this. Surely, this would be an embarrassing way to die.

Cause of death: Asphyxiation. Murder weapon: Last night's thong.

I stopped asking questions after that, and of course, I still referred to him as Anthony. To this day, I can not fully turn my neck to the right. I learned to fall in love with pain in that season, to harness its intensity and convince myself it would lead to feelings of euphoria as Anthony said it would.

Soon, I craved and welcomed the pain. The kinesthetic anguish allowed me to consolidate my self-hatred while also acting as a continuous reminder that I asked for all of this. That I should be grateful to have such a great thing going with Anthony.

The beatings I received gave me brief furlough-like detachments, allowing me to escape the reality that lay outside of the hotel rooms: forever winter, practice, exhaustion, more pain. I had already come to terms that reward and punishment in both of my environments, hotel rooms and the lacrosse field, often looked and were awarded the same. We were beaten down physically and mentally on the lacrosse field in attempts to reveal who would be the scrappiest, hit the hardest, and in a way, give their life for the cause. Who might receive the honor that it was to be seen, favored and chosen by Alexis.

Whether I was on the field or stepping foot into a hotel room with Anthony, my heart raced as if I were caged and about to be plummeted into an ocean surrounded by great whites. Only, over time, I learned that with Anthony, I should always assume someone had chummed the water first.

Outside of those rooms, Anthony held my hand walking down the street and showered me with "I love yous." He would tell me I was amazing when the servers would bring our dessert to our table. It was the part of our relationship that always left me second-guessing as to whether or not I overreacted behind closed doors. That maybe, just like on the lacrosse field, I was mentally weak, dramatic, or further losing my grip on reality. I convinced myself that I bruised easier than most and that my skin was just overly sensitive, hence the bruises and bite marks he left on it.

"Just a reminder of who owns you," he would say.

One afternoon, Anthony was running late and directed me to go up to the room and make myself comfortable. He mentioned having concealed a room key among the fake plants in the lobby. I followed his instructions, went up to the room, and set my things down on the desk. Before I had the chance to scream, a hand was clasped over my mouth, and a man wrestled me to the bed as he attempted to pull a nylon bag over my head, the type of material kids used to cover textbooks in school. I saw Anthony's face, so after a few seconds, I stopped fighting.

"It's me! Play along!" He said. "Fight back! Act like I am about to rape you!" I did as instructed.

He used to love restraining my wrist and ankles. Often, he would leave me still restrained as he showered or went down to the hotel bar for a cocktail or two.

"I'm going to leave you for the maid to find you. So hot," he'd say.

I spent the time anxiously awaiting his return by mentally drawing circles across the popcorn ceilings above me. I would count the bumpy, raised parts like dots on a basketball, attempting to do the math in order to determine how many the entire ceiling might hold, all as a means to occupy my time. I once broke out of the restraints, but when Anthony caught me seated on the edge of the bed on my phone, he didn't speak to me for the next hour at dinner. Lesson learned.

I would meet him at various casinos in Connecticut or Atlantic City where he would go on about his ability to count cards or take home any woman he wanted. He walked around like a king and expected me to treat him like a god. Each new encounter in Anthony's presence began to feel more and more like a privilege, one that could be revoked or rescinded at any possible moment.

On our first trip to Atlantic City, we were tossing back cocktails at an indoor hotel pool when he came up behind me and plunged his hand up the backside of my bikini bottoms. I froze. Could anyone see us? I stood motionless in the pool as he handled my body and began to have sex with me. I watched on as people gathered by the pool bar and kids splashed around in the shallow end. I was mortified. All I could think was that if we were caught, I would probably have to register as a sex offender. I hated my body for always working against me.

As many times as we went to Atlantic City, I cannot recall whether I drove or arrived by train or taxi for each new encounter. I have no recorded memories of travels in between arriving and departing. I really only remember the things that broke me or affirmed my identity.

During one of our trips to Atlantic City, I stepped away from the bar to use the restroom. When I returned the bartender approached me.

"He put something in your drink."

I was confused. I laughed. I didn't understand why he was looking at me so seriously or what exactly he was saying.

"Do you know this man? He put something in your drink while you were in the bathroom." The bartender repeated.

I looked to Anthony to tell me what I should do. He was silent. He appeared annoyed and uninterested. I laughed it off and assured the bartender he was my boyfriend and all was good.

I don't remember Anthony's excuse or if I even asked for one. I trusted him wholeheartedly, even though on more than one occasion he would just up and leave me at a restaurant, in the middle of a train station—really anywhere we might go. This taught me early on how to navigate the train systems, to broker deals, to give favors, to con my way into places and out of situations, and how to make a bagel last an entire day of traveling with a hangover.

I refreshed my email every few minutes, as I never wanted to miss an email from him. It was also the only way we communicated. He said it was more convenient than texting or calling, and I believed him. On the rare occasion he did call me, it was never from the same number. Anthony would abandon me somewhere, and then minutes later my inbox would be flooded with emails from him claiming how our time together had run its course. How I was just like every other woman—bitter and uninterested in making him happy. I was twenty-one at the time, and he made it very clear that I was close to aging out. He preferred his "co-eds" closer to 18, but I was fun because I could legally drink.

I was never entirely sure of what I had done wrong when he would get angry and leave me, only to then patronize me afterwards via email. I endlessly showered him with apologies in hopes to win back his favor. I would beg, grovel, and in desperation agree to his every demand. I was required to send him photos, videos, to have video calls, and to write erotic stories to send to him throughout the day. Unexpectedly, I found myself having acquired a third, full-time job.

The $500 that was given to me each time we got together was soon no longer "mine." I was instructed on how and where to use it. To buy outfits for him, lingerie, and to get my nails done. I was starting to realize that $500 after filling my gas tank and buying a new outfit really wasn't all that much.

When we would part ways the following morning, I always had a debilitating hangover and severe stomach aches, pains, and cramps that left me hunched over and in pain for days. I thought of it as a reminder of Anthony's love for me, his ownership of me.

Occasionally, I took the train from New Haven to meet him in one of the many cities along the Amtrak line. It seemed like it was always winter back then. I was also always underdressed for its elements in a pair of seven-dollar Forever 21 leggings, a sweater long enough to cover my butt, high boots, and winter jacket.

One morning, a female conductor was making her way through the cars. I held out my ticket to be punched when she asked, "Heading home? Back to school?"

I knew she was talking to me but was also unsure if she was. Just like how I heard what she had said, but I needed her to say it again so I could understand what it meant.

"What? I asked.

"Do you live in Connecticut? Go to school there?"

There were only a few lines exchanged, but after she moved on to the other passengers, I broke down crying. Back then, I didn't understand why, but now I realize it was because she saw me.

A separate occasion at the Newark train station, Anthony shoved the $500 nonchalantly into my jacket pocket as an announcement came over the speaker, announcing that all train services were suspended due to the approaching winter storm. I asked him what to do, and he pointed me in the direction of the car service.

"You'll be fine! They'll take good care of ya. Gotta run! Bring a friend next time!" as he made way for his parked truck.

Flurries had already begun to fall, and my hangover was coming in hot! I inquired about a ride with a man at the front desk of the car service. He informed me that they were closing and that all the drivers had left for the evening. The tiny bell mounted above the door frame had already begun to jingle, and I was halfway out the door when a man emerged from a side office.

"I can take you. Where are we going?" Occasional Angel.

Randall drove me the four hours back to campus as the snow came down and stuck to the road. We were in a large Chevy Suburban, and it must have been evident I was struggling since he stopped at a Dunkin' Donuts and bought me a water and a large plastic bag that my head hovered over and dry heaved into for the remainder of the trip back to Storrs. He quoted me $450 for the ride, so I removed a fifty from the stack of bills Anthony had given me and handed the rest over to Randall. I couldn't rationalize returning with nothing. I trekked up the snow-covered steps to my building. One more thing to be ashamed of.

Chapter 8

RETURNING VIDEOTAPES

2013

The summer going into my senior year of college, Anthony had planned a vacation for the two of us in Miami. Well, he was already going to a Spinning Convention, but he pitched it to me as a vacation. It was my first time flying first class, and Anthony ordered himself his usual frothy pink drink: "Madras. Shaken,"—cute, while I anxiously downed a bloody mary. Anthony had instructed me to meet him in the bathroom after takeoff and the seatbelt sign had been shut off.

"In what world does no one see us enter that bathroom together?" I asked, making light of the comment.

"Don't even fuc*ing start this crap," he hissed as he slurped his pink drink from around the obstacles of ice. "I really hope you are not going to be like this all vacation."

Before takeoff, he had asked the flight attendant for a couple of blankets, claiming I was cold. I wanted to believe it was a thoughtful gesture, and at first, I did. The cabin lights were dimmed for takeoff, and Anthony went about draping the blanket over me. He told me to loosen my belt buckle before he plunged his left hand down the front of my yoga pants, rubbing me aggressively. Painfully. Not subtly. I fixed on the seat back in front of me hoping that I was still invisible. I turned to see the couple in the aisle across from us where the woman's face displayed utter repulsion.

Just surrender to it. I thought. *It will be over soon.*

I slept about eight collective hours for our three-night stay. I would wake up from a deep sleep to discover things being done to my body while I was unconscious. The second morning in Miami, I took a risk. I told Anthony I was in pain and could not physically have anything done to my body that morning. I winced when I put on underwear, my bathing suit bottoms, and even while taking a shower. Everything hurt.

He was silent as he stood up from the bed and walked over to the window. He ripped open the blackout curtains as if he were snapping a wishbone with two hands. A clear-cut, definitive tan line separated a white backside from a burnt back, arms, and legs. He stood there for a while as I showered him with apologies. The tops of palm trees were in clear view from the bed, and I knew withdrawing the statement was the only way to fix this. I reminded myself that I was the luckiest girl in the world to have him. That without him I was nothing.

After his spinning classes, we met back in the room where he picked up my Vera Bradley duffle and threw it on the bed.

"Pack your things. I called you a car. It'll be here any minute. I moved your flight. You're heading back today."

He went on about the lavish vacation he had taken me on and how I had been disobedient. Ungrateful. Unwilling to fully please him.

Returning Videotapes

"There were two girls hitting on me in class. Great bodies. Younger. Why shouldn't I spend the rest of my time with them?"

I threw myself at him, agreeing to anything and everything in hopes he would not send me packing. A few minutes later, my bathing suit top was wrapped around me like a gag.

We touched down in Newark and parted ways like we had in the past. Our flight was a round trip from Newark to Miami, so it was on me to find my way back to Connecticut. Only, this time he didn't pay me. There was no $500 after this trip, and I had about twenty dollars to my name. I figured I was being selfish. The trip was a present in and of itself.

I bought water, a bagel, and a train ticket back to Connecticut where I had left my car at Union Station, where it had been parked for three nights. I didn't have enough money in my bank account to leave the gated lot outside of the parking garage. There was no gate attendant on duty, so I checked my mirrors and made note of the security cameras as I stepped out of my car and lifted the gate. Luckily, it stayed open as I raced back to the driver's seat and zipped through the parking lot as I checked all mirrors for the next twenty miles, paranoid that I was being tailed.

After returning from Miami, my parents gave me the silent treatment for nearly two weeks, despite my efforts to reconcile by leaving souvenirs for them on the kitchen counter. They had forbidden me from going on the trip with someone they hadn't yet met. But by that point, I had done a lot of things without their permission.

For the past couple of summers, I had waited tables at a local pizzeria, but that summer, I had decided to coach club lacrosse instead. There were a couple practices during the week and tournaments every other weekend, so in between training for lacrosse and frivolously checking my email to see if I had heard from Anthony, that was the crux of my summer.

FOLLY

My teammate at UConn, Riley, coached a separate club lacrosse team, and we found ourselves at most of the same weekend tournaments.

Riley was a year above me, and while she played four years on the lacrosse team, she would be back at UConn that fall to finish up her credits to graduate. Riley stood just north of five feet and had straight light brown hair that rested just above her shoulders. Her pale cheeks were riddled with freckles, and I have yet to find anything within nature that replicates the color of her blue eyes.

So, in the summer of 2013, we met up in cities up and down the East Coast, strolling through the shops of Stowe, eating slices of pizza, and swigging craft beer in New Hampshire Ale Houses. She was also very curious about my relationship with Anthony, so I told her everything, from my very positive and *groomed* perspective. I finally had someone to talk about my closeted life with.

I met Anthony in Atlantic City that summer. The following morning after our arrival, I woke up before him and snuck off to the bathroom for some water. Secretly, I hoped I could somehow avoid the mandatory morning sex. I quickly drank two glasses before filling up a third when he appeared in the doorway. He reached out to grab me, and as he did, the glass either slipped or was knocked out of my hand. Either way, it shattered to bits as it hit the floor, and he pressed me up against the sink before throwing me to the floor.

Through delirium and still somewhat drunken blurred vision, my palms and knees caught shards of the fragmented glass. Compulsively, I grabbed used towels from under the sink to clutch and shield my hands as he handled my body. It was then, as my knees collected bits of glass and skidded on the wet floor, I realized that I didn't want to be there anymore. Fear struck me, and I finally asked myself —*What am I doing here?*

That day, like a demented country song, I cried hysterically on the bathroom floor. And he loved every minute of it.

Viktor Frankl has a quote that reads, "Between the stimulus and response, there is a space. And in that space lies our freedom and power to choose our responses. In our response lies our growth and our freedom."

In those days, that space didn't exist for me. Entering that space required an awareness of the ability to choose. To think, to make a decision. To have an original thought, or to put into practice exercising independent thought. In those days, I did not make decisions. I followed instructions, I abided and bended to authority, and I functioned on cruise control.

A separate morning, I awoke disoriented, as Anthony's silhouette came into focus, and I felt warm liquid pooling around my legs and feet. The smell of urine hit my nostrils along with a debilitating nausea as I attempted to untangle myself in the wet bed sheets.

"That is disgusting!" I yelled.

I rushed to the bathroom and threw myself into the shower as urine streamed down my legs and ankles.

I never fully understood the power of spoken words back then, that every time he would make me shout, "You own me! You are my master!" I believed it more and more.

He also loved to choke me. Once, after repeated taps to his hands indicating "that's enough" went unacknowledged, my body was thrown into full-on panic and survival mode. My legs flailed underneath him as I tried to shake myself free. He fed on the fear in my eyes, and I searched again for a savior within the art on the walls, the desk lamps and the empty cocktail glasses scattered around the room.

Just when I felt myself having crossed the threshold between life and slipping under, accepting the fate of death, he backhanded me in efforts to shock life back into me.

From that day forward, I attempted to "tap out" much earlier than need be, allowing myself time to stage a similar show, without actually having to experience that again. There was only one time the suffocation came in an alternate form. While my wrists and ankles were bound, Anthony emerged from the bathroom with a soaked hand towel and a large Evian bottle. And yes, even after he water boarded me, I kept running back to him.

Back on campus one evening, a knock came to my door. One of my roommates, Claire, expressed her growing concerns regarding my relationship and recent behavior.

"Last night, we were all watching a movie together as roommates," she began. "And every time I looked over at you, you were refreshing your email! Your eyes were locked onto your phone the entire time. He has a sick hold over you that is not healthy!" she exclaimed.

Anthony had warned me no one would understand our relationship, and at the same time, I attributed the fact that I got out of bed on the weekends now to be entirely his doing. It was the first big blow-up fight with Claire that was never fully resolved.

The fall semester of my senior year, Anthony booked us a suite at his favorite hotel in Westchester, New York: The Ritz-Carlton. That trip was different from start to finish. He greeted me at the valet, welcomed me with a kiss, and even took my bag for me. It was the only time he had ever booked us a suite, and upon entering it, a bottle of brut was already on ice, accompanied by three glasses resting on the glass coffee table.

"I decided to splurge for ya," he said, wearing that big sly smile he always did and chewing gum obnoxiously on one side of his mouth in tandem.

That afternoon, we walked into an Irish sports bar where Anthony ordered us cocktails, shots, and a house punch served in a giant scorpion bowl, garnished with maraschino cherries, purple orchids, and a handful of colorful bendy straws. The bar floor was covered in a thick layer of peanut shells.

"I love you. You know that, right?" he asked.

Back then, I truly thought he did. We had recently been talking about different exotic destinations to host our destination wedding. We tossed back our shots before he deceivingly took hold of my hand.

"Hey, say tonight at the bar we meet a single girl in a black dress checking us out. We chat her up and invite her back to the room with us. What do you say? Wouldn't that be hot?"

Anthony was always rattling off sexual fantasies that I was *expected* to help him "cross off his bucket list," but I didn't want anything to do with a threesome. I was just barely twenty-one and thought I was in love with someone who cared about me. I didn't want to see him with another woman, nor did I want to be with one. I told Anthony maybe someday it would be an option, but that I wasn't really interested in *that* particular fantasy.

"I don't understand you, Kelsey!" he snapped, ripping his hand off mine. "I do so much for you! I fly you first class to Miami; I take you to nice places! Do you know how much this room is costing me? Do you know how much I spend on you? And you say you love me? *Pffft.* "

I didn't want this to ruin our evening. It was looking like it might be our best date to date.

"I treat you like a princess! Maybe this has just run its course if you're no longer interested in making me happy."

I figured the odds of us randomly encountering a woman in a black dress at a bar, let alone one who would want to come back to our room with us, were incredibly slim.

So I said, "You're right. I'm sorry. It would actually be super hot."

Anthony rushed us down the street, reiterating that we were going to lose our reservations. Parts of my ankles had been rubbed raw and blisters had already begun to form from the power walk back to the Ritz from the Irish bar. Inside the hotel elevator, he pushed me against the wall and shoved his hand up my dress, then pushed me away once the elevator stopped a few floors up.

An elegantly dressed couple stepped in. They were both beautiful people, and the sight of them reminded me that my outfit collectively had probably cost me shy of $100. I looked over at Anthony in his khaki pants and fuchsia short-sleeved button up and wondered if he was as much of a fraud as I was. He didn't really seem to fit in here either.

The elevator doors opened to the most beautiful restaurant I had ever seen. It was golden hour, and through the dining room rested a 180-degree view of downtown Westchester. The sun streamed in, revealing fingerprints and other impurities on the glass and stemware and particles of dust on the dark wood tables, but the sight of it all must have been the first time I ever experienced stillness and some type of bliss.

Anthony walked right past the host and to the bar, which confused me because I thought we were late for our reservations. Next to us at the bar top sat a girl with dark hair, a mouth full of braces, and who was dressed in a black sundress and a pair of Old Navy flip flops. She instantly made me feel better about my own appearance.

"So, what do you think?" Anthony asked, nodding over his shoulder in her general direction.

Certainly, he was joking. I made some wise remark about not being into brunettes, and he responded by tightly squeezing my hand under the bar.

"Don't you dare f*cking embarrass me," he hissed.

"I don't want to see you with another girl! What are you talking about, you're my boyfriend!" I pleaded. I was trying not to cry or have another anxiety attack.

He told me he loved me again and catered to the romanticism of it all, how he really just thought it would just be fun to play some drinking games together back in the room and hang out with her. I just didn't understand how the most romantic getaway he had planned for us now involved a heavier-set girl with braces.

Before I knew it, the three of us were drunkenly stumbling into the elevator and then back to our suite, where we popped open the conveniently pre-ordered bottle of brut. It was a great coincidence that there just happened to be three flutes!

I remember feeling like the outsider in the room. Like their plus-one, as they each instructed me on what to do and with whom, as Anthony posed me for pictures and at times had the other girl take some. I lost myself in my drunkenness and reminded myself that love comes with compromises. Plus, he had said he wouldn't have sex with her.

I was so drunk that I was stumbling and tripping over the furniture. At one point, I nodded off and woke up on the bed to the two of them having sex on top of me. Inside that room doused in pure white and gold, everything going on felt dark and evil. I pulled on my dress, grabbed my wedges and purse, and left.

Chapter 9

SEA OF BLACK

2013

I had left the room without a plan. I was too drunk to drive, and there was no possible way I could afford a room at the Ritz. I waited nearly an hour in the lobby in hopes that Anthony would come and get me. When he finally did, he just told me I was being jealous and irrational. That I had seen what I wanted to see and had overdone it on the shots earlier.

Together we headed back up to the room where he told me to wait in the hall so he could collect our things.

"What?! Why don't you just tell her to leave!?"

He said he didn't want to be rude and that he had booked another room in the event we met a girl at the bar and I got jealous.

It would take me years to uncover the nuanced memories of that day. Like when the door opened and I saw through the crack the girl dressed in the hotel bathrobe and wearing a giant smile upon seeing him while a giant cart of room service, that looked as though it had already been eaten, rested at the foot of the bed. For nearly a decade I would continue to believe that it was just happenstance that there were three champagne glasses, an extra room booked, and that we were late to a dinner reservation on a night where I didn't eat dinner. They seemed to have eaten together in the room I thought was reserved for him and me.

Anthony scanned the keycard to our new room, pushed open the door, and again, I caught it before it hit me in the face. It was not a suite; there was no champagne, and he wasn't done with me yet.

When Anthony finally ended our relationship, it was through a sudden and abrupt email. After nearly a year of compliance, he severed all ties. He wanted another three some, and I was traumatized from everything that had gone on in the room. I was not sure how long I was passed out for or if things were done to my body while I was.

Still, in desperation, I called and texted every burner number he had ever contacted me from—nothing. During this time, I cried out to God and gave Him another chance to prove His existence. To prove to me that He didn't hate me and to bring Anthony back into my life. Nothing.

If it was not for all the obligations aligned with lacrosse, I would have stayed in bed for a week. Of the five of us seniors in the graduating class, I was the only one not named captain. I was unsure if I was hurt by it or if I was too busy grieving the loss of who I thought was the love of my life to care anymore.

I went on a hunger strike and threw myself into my workouts. I lost fifteen pounds in two weeks, gained my speed back, and was playing significantly better. I tried to have a good attitude and be a good teammate, all while shopping online to find men who would be interested in beating me up. I needed a distraction to take me away from who I was and what my life had become.

In our last fall lacrosse tournament of the season, I played fairly well. Alexis called me out at the end of the game for my hustle and how hard I worked. It gave me hope for the spring season ahead.

Riley also spent a good deal of time at our apartment on campus that fall. It was not uncommon for my roommates and I to venture into the living room on a Sunday morning to find Riley and her freckled face folding laundry on the couch or watching TV with an iced coffee in one hand while she bounced a lacrosse ball against the ceiling with the other for entertainment.

Other times, Riley would burst through one of our bedroom doors and hurl herself onto one of our beds, only to begin jumping up and down on her knees shouting,

"Adventures with the Princess! Adventures with the Princess!" in a surprisingly convincing Russian accent.

I wanted to hate her on those days she woke me up, but Riley had a child-like spirit about her that made the initial "red" I was seeing turn to mush after I realized that of all the beds she could have chosen to jump on that morning, she had chosen mine.

We would go on daytime adventures to Dunkin' Donuts before taking her forest green Jeep Cherokee for a drive through the backwoods of Connecticut. We would be dressed in our everyday outfits of issued sweats layered with flannels and beanies.

In the driver's seat of her Cherokee, I packed a lip of tobacco for the first and last time. We were randomly drug tested as athletes, so anything aside from alcohol was out of the question. But when Riley offered me to partake in her newest habit, it seemed like a type of recklessness that just might be safe enough to try. A recklessness that soon left the Cherokee pulled over and me bent over on the side of that back dirt road, sick as a result.

Riley was the type of person that when you were in conversation with her, you were the only person in the room. She was the type of person who would pack Tupperware to take home sushi from the Asian buffet the next town over, and also the person to deny the existence of it to the manager when he asked her what was in her backpack. Riley was so passionately curious about everything, and she made myself, as well as others, feel seen.

We broke for winter break and in between getting in pre-season shape and shifts at the pizzeria, I continued to meet men online. I met men at the Connecticut casinos for cocktails to discuss "arrangements," which usually meant I drank a few martinis and made out with them at the Craps table. Sometimes, they led me upstairs even though the only compensation I ever received from men was in the form of dinner and margaritas.

Dr. S. once told me to have lower expectations, to assume that I would not see playing time on the lacrosse field, so in the event I did, I would be overjoyed, instead of constantly let down. I put the same theory into practice when I met these men. If they paid me, I was worth it; if they didn't, I was still just me.

One December afternoon, I made the hour-plus drive to a picturesque, storybook Connecticut town to visit a man named Dominic for the second time. A thick blanket of unblemished snow covered the city streets while various storefront windows advertised a tasteful mix of fonts and scripts. The coffee shops, bookstores, art galleries, and bistros, in all ways, felt charming and elite. The entirety of the scene itself would have made for an ideal backdrop for a Norman Rockwell painting.

The smell of garlic and rosemary drew me up the freshly salted walkway and into a near vacant Italian restaurant. Dominic and I were led to our table, where we dipped focaccia in olive oil blended together with dried spices and split a bottle of Chianti. Then my phone rang. It was from a teammate who never called me, so I took the call outside, figuring it might be important. Through muffled tears and sniffles, the girl on the other end of the line said,

"Riley's gone." And just like every other time when something didn't make sense, I responded with a laugh.

"What?"

Riley had hit black ice on her drive back to campus, which resulted in a fatal car crash. I was mad at God that He had taken someone who was loved and adored by all those around her, especially when I was open and willing to give up my own life if in fact He needed to take one that badly. It was Riley's death that somehow sparked the realization that I wanted to attempt to live. Riley's funeral was held on New Year's Eve. A day where instead of coming together with my team as a pod of red, white, navy and gray, we emerged from our respective cars and entered the funeral home in a uniformed sea of black.

After paying our respects to the family, a few of us gathered together to share, through tears and laughter, our favorite memories of our late teammate. While this was taking place, one of our teammates, Amanda, could be heard sobbing and shouting from the other room.

"Why is she gone? Why is this happening?!! She was my friend!"

Numb to my own emotions, Amanda's cries to me just seemed like a cry for attention. This would be my first lesson in understanding the cliché that all people grieve differently. Amanda's screams and shouts interrupted the stories being shared among the seven or eight of us. Talking behind peoples' backs had really just been a survival mechanism since grade school. If I feared judgment coming my way, I redirected it elsewhere. This situation with Amanda was no different; she seemed to be staging her own show, and I agreed to the statement when a few others mentioned it.

That night my teammates and I dressed in flannel t-shirts and backwards hats in honor of our late friend and teammate, Riley. We drank out of sadness, out of tradition, and celebration. Later, I returned back to my apartment on campus to a near-empty townhouse. Reaching for the doorknob to my room, I discovered it was locked.

My roommate Claire then emerged from her bedroom.

"Don't be mad," she said, sounding as if she were already trying to deescalate a not-yet existing situation.

"Why is my bedroom door locked?" I asked her.

That was when my door unlocked from the inside to reveal Amanda, wearing my clothes and having already helped herself to my bed. An argument ensued over it all. Amanda called me out for talking behind her back. I told her to both get out of my clothes and my bedroom. The entire thing went from zero to sixty as the screaming match leaked out into the living room. Amanda threw darts in the form of words like "crazy" and "psycho," going on to say how she and Coach Alexis talk all the time about how 'crazy' I am in her office together.

I dared her to call me crazy one more time, and if she did, I was going to knock that smug look right off her face.

Then, annunciated and in slow motion, Amanda said, "You are fuc*-ing cray-zee!"

Cue catfight.

I took a step toward Amanda, but she grabbed my hair and pulled me to the ground as she delivered punches to my face from on top of me. One of my hands was raised to block them, and the other tugged on her shirt, well—my shirt—to get her off me. Claire was now crying and screaming as she tried to intervene and pull Amanda off me.

Two weeks later, I sat at a circular table and was joined by all three of my coaches. I never admitted to hitting Amanda, even though, after realizing I was being formally charged with assault and battery, I wished I had. Amanda had submitted pictures of bruises and cuts that I in no way could have given her and rips in her clothes that I supposedly performed—clothes that she had not even been wearing, as she had helped herself to my closet that evening in addition to my room and bed.

Lifeless, I stared at the wall, watching my future and my only dream melt down around me like crayons left out in the sun.

Alexis talked with my dad, who was also seated at the table. I wished I had the guts to shout at him,

"Why aren't you defending me?!! Why aren't you fighting for me?" I had nothing left to give to this world that deemed me guilty until proven innocent. I still believed that God hated me but also that I was to blame for my own undoing.

The walk out of the field house that day was the worst of all the walks of shame.

"We are told that hard work will pay off one day, but sometimes that's not always the case," said my dad.

I couldn't believe what I was hearing. My entire life I was told that if you work hard, you'll be rewarded. But now, I was told that none of that even mattered, that my life was one giant lie that officially held no meaning. I made an agreement with myself that day to avoid whatever it was the world told me I should do or want. Up until that point, I had been obedient and worked hard, but look where it got me. Anthony was right. I did not fit into this world. I belonged in the dark.

I was instructed to move out of my townhouse. Flashbacks of my coach calling me the team cancer resurfaced as I packed the contents of my room. I was told I would "ruin the team cohesion" if I were to stay. All my contents fit into a few boxes that I placed in the backseat of my sister's tiny Toyota and returned my team gear and clothes to the athletic facility. I change my mind—that was the worst of the walks of shame.

I arrived at a separate townhouse around the bend where I would spend my last semester of college. I placed my moving boxes on the small wooden desk in the corner before laying my bedding down atop the tiny twin mattress. I leaned back against the side of my new bed, thinking about where I was, how I had arrived there, and everything that had led up to that moment. Then, I let go of it all and tears finally released from behind my eyes. The time had come to now grieve all that had been lost.

Chapter 10

BLUEBERRY PANCAKES

2014

I was stripped of my position as an athlete and, consequently, the infrastructure that had been put in place to help me succeed. I needed physical therapy on my hamstring but was no longer allowed in the complex. I needed the therapist I had been seeing for nearly two years to navigate this change, but I would have to switch to one not affiliated with athletics.

I had officially been abandoned by everyone in my life.

In all our time together, I never showed up to Dr. S's office in anything outside of a pair of sweats. But at our last appointment I wore jeans, boots and a sweater, and I had taken the time to straighten my hair—not a spec of issued athletic gear on my person.

"This is the best I have ever seen you!" Dr. S exclaimed, unable to contain her smile.

Her reaction gave me a sense of normalcy. As much as I didn't want to admit it, it was the best I had felt in years, maybe ever. I could not recall ever existing without obsession over some obligation I needed to uphold, worries about performance or a person I needed to please.

That day, I volunteered information to Dr. S, knowing it could no longer be used against me. I told her vaguely about Anthony and how our relationship had just ended, to which she replied, "Well that is great, as it was an incredibly age-inappropriate relationship!"

I didn't know what an "age-appropriate relationship" looked like. Anthony had told me he was 37 but given the thin layer of white roots that grew in on our last day in Miami, I would guess he was probably in his fifties.

I filled the four-hour gap that would have otherwise been reserved for workouts and practices with extra classes and courses I had always wanted to take but never could due to scheduling conflicts, courses like American Diplomacy, Public Policy and, of course, an additional class with Dr. Miller.

The girls I had moved in with that semester were wonderful and all members of the field hockey team that had won the National Championship earlier that fall. Curious about their success, I asked Harper, one of my new roommates, how they managed it all. Not only were they victorious on the field, but the field hockey team was notorious for all being great student athletes, a team with a tight-knit camaraderie, and they were well-liked by the other athletic teams.

At one point or another, two of my three new roommates had lived with members of the lacrosse team, so, in turn, they knew a bit about our team's inner workings.

"The difference between lacrosse and field hockey is that if drama reaches our coach, there is a big problem. Astronomical. Gargantuan. We settle our business between ourselves, and if absolutely necessary, we will get a captain involved. Our coach treats us like adults and expects us to act like one. Your staff seems to want to give you all the illusion you are adults, while fostering animosity and encouraging you all to rat on each other," stated Harper.

I was in disbelief at the truth behind everything Harper had just said. She had just summed up a dynamic in a few sentences. A dynamic I never really took the time to understand or pull apart. It was not uncommon for teammates to rat out others on my now-former team for things like breaking the team drinking rule in order to win favor with the coaches. Risking or sabotaging team chemistry wasn't tremendously important, especially when the rule breaker played the same position as the rat.

"Of course, no team is perfect," Harper went on. "But we respect one another even if we don't like one another. We lift one another up, and on every occasion, I see lacrosse ripping each other apart." I had never thought of it that way before.

Furthermore, since I was still technically an NCAA Division I scholarship athlete, I was told I was not eligible for work study, so I got back online and began meeting men for drinks and coffee on the outskirts of campus for $100 to begin to build my bank account.

I had been meeting up with a young lawyer I had met on the site who advised me not to go to the police station to talk to anyone about the fight in the initial stages of the investigation of my assault and battery charge.

"Won't not showing up, like, make me look guilty? Like I am hiding something?" I asked.

"No, the exact opposite. If you show up, they will interrogate you without a lawyer, and if you crack, then you will look guilty."

I guess he had a point. I could not look an adult in the eye, let alone have a conversation with one without hysterically crying. How would I handle myself in front of a police officer who believed I beat up my teammate? Then again, maybe this guy was a lawyer in the same way Anthony was "37" and a "Princeton alumni."

My hearing in front of a judge fell on my birthday, where I continued to accidentally fill out my birth year on various forms instead of the current year, "2014," out of sheer habit. My day of birth felt like a plague and while I never celebrated it, I decided that day I would just erase it.

Back on campus, I would occasionally venture out with my new roommates to a nightclub a few towns over, a place that advertised house music, strobe lights, and five-dollar drinks. The first few weekends I received high-fives and praises from half the football team and a few others for giving Amanda "exactly what she deserves." I wasn't mad about that part.

The owner of the club, Vinny, was a heavy-set Greek man with thinning black hair, an austere demeanor, and a face that made him appear consistently grumpy. He knew some of my new roommates' friends and showered us with free shots.

Before long, Vinny and I were fooling around in the back rooms of the club, and I was drinking for free. I looked forward to going to the club now that I was the middleman facilitating free drinks for my new roommates.

After a while Vinny began bringing me home from the club or picking me up on nights I hadn't even planned on going out. He didn't pay me like Anthony, but I liked the attention. It was something to do.

Vinny and his brother Nico had a band of brothers who could be found with Bud Lights in hand and eyeing the new "talent" of college girls that made their way into the club after eleven.

Officer Bennet, a state trooper, also frequented the club. He possessed a charm and wit that made me blush like a schoolgirl. He asked me to refer to him by his first name, Ross, even though he was always dressed head to toe in uniform. He inquired about my days, my hopes, my dreams, and how my classes were going, sharing secrets and light-hearted gossip about the club and his usual haunts around town.

One evening, he insisted I take down his number, offering to be a resource if I was to ever find myself in a bind. The gesture meant a lot to me, and it all seemed cordial, so we exchanged numbers.

Later during the week, I received texts from both Vinny and Officer Ross Bennett, showering me with compliments and asking about my weekend plans. So, that weekend, I went back to the nightclub with my new roommates. I had developed a habit of branching off, loving the version of me that was independent and uninhibited. After a couple of drinks that night, I asked Officer Bennet, "You know I am sort of hanging out with Vinny, right?"

"Oh yeah," he began. "He's cool with it. He knows we are just having a good time." I wasn't sure what he meant by it, but I wasn't going to read into it.

One evening, after a few rounds of tequila shots and vodka cranberries, Vinny asked me to meet him outside around the back of the club. I scampered out the side door in my tank top and hot pink skirt through the snowfall, doing my best to shield my hair from the elements.

He waved me over to a garage filled with a handful of cars covered in tarps. We fooled around in the garage before I rose from my knees and brushed the garage floor gravel from off them.

"You're awesome," Vinny said, through a giant grin as he re-fastened his belt.

Shortly afterward, Nico popped his head in from a separate side door across the garage, and the two men exchanged nods. It was weird, but again, I didn't read into it.

My buzz was wearing off, so I suggested we go back inside to the bar, but Vinny wanted to "chat" in the garage a bit longer. Soon after, Vinny's portly friend Brian entered the garage.

"You remember, Brian, right?" Vinny asked.

I had chatted with Brian a few times, and we had even shared a cigarette a few weeks back on the nightclub porch. Yes, I remembered Brian.

"I figured you and I always have such a great time, you wouldn't mind having a good time here with Brian."

It didn't seem like a question, but was it a request? I was nowhere near drunk enough to even try to understand what was happening. I felt awkward and unsure of what to do, but without much thought, I found myself just leaving.

A week or so later, Vinny texted me, telling me to be ready to be picked up by eleven. My face was washed, and I was dressed for bed, but I proceeded to plug in my curling iron and reach for my mascara.

The nightclub had hosted a party that night and was closing up shop early, but Vinny asked if I wanted to join the staff out for a midnight breakfast. I was in.

We drove to a building that looked as if it had been foreclosed. It had gray paneling and a collapsible, accordion-style gate that was clamped together by a large padlock. Vinny pulled a chain of keys out of his back pocket, fishing for the right one to unlock it. Nico and Officer Bennet pulled up shortly thereafter.

The building was freezing, as if the owners had left the heat on only just enough to keep the pipes from bursting. The restaurant itself resembled an old-school diner, complete with red leather booths and laminate white granite tables. The four of us took a seat on one of the booths, and Vinny reiterated that the staff would arrive there any second. Then they would start serving up omelets, cooking bacon, and flipping blueberry pancakes.

I don't recall having any drinks that night, so the four of us sitting in that booth, void of music or conversation, was exceptionally awkward. I excused myself to the bathroom in hopes that when I returned, the staff might be there, or at minimum, there would be conversation.

I fixed my eyeliner in the bathroom mirror, washed my hands, and pulled a few sheets of brown paper towel from the dispenser on the wall. That's when the bathroom door opened, and Officer Bennet stepped into the women's room.

"Wrong door, officer! The men's room is across the hall," I said sarcastically as I reached for the inside door handle. His calloused hand, however, caught my wrist before I was able to. In one swift movement, my left hand was twisted behind my back, and I was pushed up against the bathroom wall. I thought for a second he was messing around, even though he had slammed me into the wall and his grip around my wrist grew tighter. That's when I heard the sound of clanking metal on metal and felt his hot breath in my ear.

"You said no to Brian, but you will never say no to me."

I never did get those blueberry pancakes.

The time and space between the clanking of belt metals and me pressed up against the door of Vinny's car has gone unrecorded, but I remember the sound of my sobs competing with the pellets of rain that came down in sheets all around us, the type of rain that makes a statement each time it smacks the pavement. Vinny was silent as tears and snot poured down from my face.

He dropped me off outside my townhouse, and I stumbled inside. I was not close with my sister, Eliza, but for some reason, she was the only person I could think to call. It was late, but she answered right away. I tried to make sense through quivering lips of distress. I didn't understand why this time was so different, why out of all the encounters up to that point, this one did me in.

"Kelsey, you need to call the police!" Eliza said, with concern and with sincerity. My eyes then grew drier and fixed themselves on the floor beneath me.

The hysteria retreated, and the connection was made as I allowed the phone to slide down my cheek and drop to the floor before barely releasing the whisper, "I can't. He *is* the police."

I took a shower and awoke to about a dozen missed calls and texts from my sister. I wrote her back and said that I drank too much the night before and had made the whole thing up. I apologized for bothering her so late.

About two weeks later, Officer Bennet showed up at my townhouse. He asked to talk in private, so I led him into my room. He shut the door, unlatched his utility belt and placed it on top of the books on my desk. The initial stages of marking his territory. He was the warm, charming person I talked to so many times at the nightclub. He asked me about my week, peppered me with compliments, ran his fingers through my hair, and stated that he wanted to talk about a few weeks back. I didn't know what this was. I began to think maybe I misinterpreted our encounter in the women's room. But soon, again, there was the clanking of metal on metal, and this time his hand was pressing down over my mouth.

They all showed up after that. The entire band of brothers. When I wasn't being picked up to go to the club, I was instructed to leave a rock in the front door of the townhouse to keep it propped open. Officer Bennet, Vinny, and some of their friends had an all-access pass.

They came over mostly during weekday nights, alerting me via text and always reminding me to follow "the rules."

The meetings always ended the same way. Me, on my knees, posing for the camera and instructed not to move until I heard the second door close. First my bedroom door, then the front door of the townhouse.

Blueberry Pancakes

I was studying at the library one night when I received a text from Vinny and ignored it. The following evening, Officer Bennet was outside my apartment and instructed me to get in. He drove me straight to the back garage of their nightclub, where Vinny and Brian were already waiting for me. And even after I had learned that lesson, I was still completely blind to my own reality—I was being trafficked.

Chapter 11

LITTLE SANDY TOWN

2014

I met Brett on a dating app later that year. Brett lived on the main street of a coastal Connecticut town, decorated with seafood shacks, second-hand bookstores, and antique shops that lined the boardwalk. The path cut through high cat tailed grass within the dunes. The beaches were all private and exclusive to the town's residents. As such, the town was calm, remained endearing, and you never had to search for too long for a spot to lay your beach blanket. It was the type of town that was small enough to where you were a regular everywhere but large enough to where there wasn't a shortage of places to go or things to do or see.

Gradually, I stopped going to the nightclub altogether. Opting to spend my weekends with Brett in his little sandy town. Brett was seven years older than me, and his young-adult life took me away from life on campus. It moved me away from the pain that was seeing myself cropped out of the lacrosse team photographs printed on posters and fixed across banners throughout campus. All my years of hard work and dedication were quickly erased with a few quick clicks in photoshop. It was like I had never existed.

Having a boyfriend and trying to act normal at first was a fun ruse. I just wasn't sure how to keep playing the part. On more than a few occasions I would, out of nowhere, get claustrophobia within my own body.

I would find myself shouting, "Get off me!" and "I don't know you!" and "What are you doing to me?" as I pushed him off me, screaming and crying as I locked myself in his bathroom.

"Kelsey, come out, let's talk about it," he said, his voice concerned and compassionate.

It happened mostly after nights of drinking, after the lights had been shut off and the only sounds were the crashing waves on the beach and the rickety ceiling fan in his bedroom.

I would go from kissing my boyfriend to being ripped from the scene and lost in the shuffle. Washing in and out like the tide that left my mind scattered, like the residual trail of sea lettuce and Irish moss that washes up along the banks of the Long Island Sound.

Eventually, I just learned to sink into the confusion, to be okay with not understanding who was on top of me, where I was, or what would happen next. I became a Russian nesting doll of detachment, aware that Brett could probably only tolerate my "freakouts" for so long, and I didn't want to lose him.

I started avoiding Officer Bennet and Vinny's texts and calls. Whenever I didn't need to be on campus, I wasn't, and sometimes Brett would come and stay with me. Only once did they intercept me on a walk from the library back to my townhouse, bringing me back to the nightclub garage once more, where three of them had their way with me.

Brett's birthday came around, and I decided to hop back on the site to make some quick cash so I could do something nice for him for his birthday. I drove out to Mohegan Sun where I met a rather large man with a poorly fitting suit and a greasy comb over.

After the second martini, he suggested we go upstairs, and while I hadn't planned on that, I agreed. The elevator doors closed, and instantly my martini tasted sour in my mouth. It then occurred to me that if I had sex with this man I would be cheating—and I didn't want to cheat on Brett.

I told the man I was not feeling well and asked him for some gas money. To this, he replied, "I don't pay bitches for not doing anything."

Back at Brett's, he gave me the cold shoulder as he heated up takeout in the microwave.

I decided to come clean about where I had been. Figuring that once he knew I had turned down the opportunity to make money by not having sex with a stranger—just so I could come home to him—he would see it as some giant, romantic gesture!

His head lowered, and I could tell he was trying not to cry.

"Kelsey. This is not the kind of argument we should be having as a couple!"

I didn't understand why he wasn't proud of me. Then a darker thought crept in: *What if my brokenness was contagious? What if Alexis was right, and I was a cancer?* Our relationship fizzled out soon after. He started cheating on me, and I was still a train wreck.

After that, I secured my first bartending job at a fine dining restaurant and agave bar in one of Connecticut's premier shopping districts. Guacamole was made table-side, and all drinks received fresh limes to be squeezed by a hand juicer. I was living back at my parents' house, spending my days off soaking my hands in warm water and trimming my cuticles, which would turn black from the citric acid in the limes.

Often, during shifts, the drain behind the dishwasher would overflow, clogged with plastic straws, mint leaves, and lime wedges. The back bar would flood, leaving my shoes submerged in murky bar water, while I spent the night making drinks in soggy socks. On any given night, I was making roughly $200.

It did not take me long to realize that drinking was not only socially acceptable before your shift but near expected. A few of us who worked the lunch shifts would head to the Thai place across the street to spend our tips from lunch devouring lychee martinis and sharing a pitcher of red sangria.

Brett had since reached out and came to visit me every now and again while I worked. One night after drinking two frozen margaritas, a vodka martini, a glass of red wine, and an espresso martini with one of my supervisors, I made the half hour drive home and was pulled over and arrested for a DUI three miles from my parent's house.

Embarrassed, Brett picked me up from the slammer, spent the night at my parents' house with me, and drove me to work the next day. In the two years I worked at that bar, the only time we ever had a bar meeting was coincidentally the morning after my DUI, when I was suffering from a category five hangover. Brett waited until I had exited the car before he rolled down the window and told me he never wanted to see me again. And again, my belief was affirmed that people will abandon you when you need them most.

In the event I lost my driver's license, I decided to rent a room for $500 a month a few blocks away from the bar so I didn't have to quit. The owner of the home, an older woman, enjoyed blasting "Set Fire to the Rain," by Adele at three in the morning, which would jolt me awake. She claimed it helped her insomnia.

She had two overweight Shih Tzus who would claw at my door that I always kept shut. When the door was open, they would storm in and alleviate the discomfort located on their backsides all over my area rugs. They didn't last long. The rugs, not the dogs.

Even though I was drinking like a fish, that fall, I ran a half marathon and still enjoyed working out. It was the weeks that turned into months of not running five miles a day and snacking on churros behind the bar that led one of the female bussers to shout at me one day, "Girl! You need to stop eating! You used to be skinny!"

That was my cue to start throwing up again.

I somehow managed to not have my license suspended as a result of the DUI and also save $5,000.

For as far back as I could remember, I had wanted a Jeep Wrangler, so I showed up to the car dealership and asked to speak with someone about buying one.

"Is your dad or boyfriend coming to help you with this?" One of the sales guys asked. "Is your dad or boyfriend the one who wants to make a sale today?" I responded.

I didn't know how to drive a manual, but I figured between YouTube videos and a test drive with one of the used Jeeps in the lot—one that I had no interest in purchasing—I could pick it up quickly. I told the sales guy that my first car was a manual and that I just needed a refresher course. Tiny lie.

We took the Jeep to a grocery store's parking lot to practice shifting gears, working the clutch, etc. The process proved more challenging than anticipated. Back at the dealership, the salesman drew up the paperwork for me to purchase the used manual Jeep I had been test driving.

"I've had a change of heart," I said. "I think I want to purchase a new Jeep." The next day, I wrote a check for all the money in my bank account and was delivered the manual-transmission, two-door Wrangler and given the keys to my first vehicle. While waiting at the exit before merging onto the main road, I spotted all of the salesmen watching me through my rear-view mirror.

Don't stall. Don't stall. Don't stall. I repeated.

The last car drove past me, and I shifted from neutral into first gear to merge onto the main road when—*stall.*

From the rearview, I witnessed half the men of the dealership reach into their wallets and slap bills into one another's hands.

Afterwards, I drove the Jeep to my town park to practice working the clutch on hills. After ten minutes of repeated stalls and no forward movement, I broke down crying. I had just spent all of the money I had earned from slaving away at the tequila bar up to my ankles in murky bar water on a vehicle I didn't even know how to drive! My black-stained cuticles matched the leather of the steering wheel, and I was reminded of how pathetic my life was and how being a great athlete in a small town got you great headlines each time you were arrested.

I decided to try moving the Jeep one more time before heading home. I put one foot on the clutch and the other on the brake before moving it to the gas. No movement. It was only then that I looked down to see I had been in neutral that entire time.

Chapter 12

GLUTEN-FREE

2015

After a year spent muddling mojitos and serving up chips and salsa, I found myself pouring pints and shaking dirty martinis in a small-town Connecticut tavern. Opening a restaurant is a lot like going to summer camp, and in the fall of 2015, that was exactly how I viewed my life. One really long party or stint at summer camp. The Tavern was located in the type of town where when merging off the highway, you almost feel transported back in time, as if by DeLorean, to a world taken over by tobacco fields, auto body shops, pool halls, and a slew of mom-and-pop restaurants, most of which serve Denver omelets, ribeyes, and chef's salads from open until close.

The type of town where one might get themselves "stuck," having no real reason to ever leave, while also not having much of a compelling reason not to stay. The only thing changing at the diner the locals might attend every Monday, Wednesday and Friday for a decade was the Pie of the Day. And that was only in the rare event they ran out of cherry, which was always the Pie of the Day.

There was comfort in the standstill of that town. Existing there was like drinking a not-so-fizzy soda. One that was just flat enough to notice, but not so much so that you would send it back or not sip on the second if the server brought you a refill.

The Tavern was located inside a small eighteenth century home with a fresh coat of canary yellow on the building's exterior. A large oak tree sat out front, with leaves that fell to cover the second story porch in the fall and a trunk and branches that could be seen from every window inside.

The building itself was rumored to be haunted. Guests occasionally complained of cold spots in the middle of the dining rooms and glasses would fall from tables without reason. The laughter of young children was also said to be heard on the second floor. As the story goes, two young children died of polio in a far room. After repeated complaints of cold spots and laughter, the space was reverted from a separate dining room and into an area that housed buffet tables and party platters for events and where servers would polish and roll silverware.

During the opening months of the restaurant, our boss, Aaron, showed respect to the supernatural by placing out a glass of red wine and a cup of orange juice on the copper bar top before he closed each night.

"Only drops were left in them each morning," he would say, eyes widening as he retold the tale.

When I wasn't working solo behind the bar, I worked alongside a man named JR. JR was a tall and lean thirty-something man with coarse, dark Sicilian hair. Each season he would test out a new beard and mustache combination. On the first day of winter, he might stroll into the bar with a mustache like that of W.B Mason, matching the trucks that would drive by on the main road outside. Come spring, you might find him clean shaven, and once Thanksgiving rolled around, his face might reveal a very distinguishing goatee.

He listened to the guests intently and pensively as he used his index finger to push his wide brimmed glasses a bit further up onto the bridge of his nose. JR and I both had a dark sense of humor, and our relationship was rooted in brotherly and sisterly love. As such, he never missed out on an opportunity to fill my club soda straw with vinegar or to pile a puddle of scorpion pepper hot sauce in my veggie chili if I happened to leave it unattended.

The Tavern was a boys' club but was run by the few women that held it all together and had quicker one-liners than most of the guys. Servers would ask new hires to search for the "lobster gun" in the basement or to fetch new menus for the dinner shift that would obviously be in the "menu room." Pumpkin spice martinis were *obviously* served with a slice of pumpkin pie on the rim, so you'll have to ask the head chef for that. And before you clock out, make sure you check the kitchen for loose tiles. Here's a broom, use the butt end and tap them one by one.

Candace, one of the servers, began raving about how good the house salad was one day. That's when a male server leaned over the bar top and said, "That's because today I buttered her lettuce."

I asked him if he meant that he had substituted her mixed greens for butter lettuce, "No," he responded, grabbing the soda gun and refilling himself a Sprite.

"I actually took each piece of lettuce and put butter on it."

In all the time spent at The Tavern, however, the most noteworthy character was a blonde with bright pacific-blue eyes. Her name is Lena, and she is a pivotal part of this story.

At work, Lena's short buttery-blonde hair was tied up in a voluminous ponytail that sat on the top of her head. Her white t-shirt hung off her shoulder, and she wore, quite literally, her mom's jeans before "mom jeans," ever really took off. Lena had a down-to-earth, valley girl kind of way about her. Walking through rooms, she had a bounce in her step like you might see someone shuffle dancing in roller-skates on the Venice Beach pier. She referred to everyone, regardless of level of familiarity, as "babe" or "hun," softening the demeanor of whomever around her like ripened bananas left out on the counter for a few days—ones you intend to use to make banana bread. She enunciated words as folks do in the Northeast, but her delivery was patient and delicate like the sweet tea served below the Mason-Dixon line.

The first time we met, she walked right up to me with boldness and stuck out her hand with childlike enthusiasm. "Hi! I'm Lena!"

There was a brightness about her, which made even more sense the day I discovered that the name "Lena," means "light." Her confidence had a ripple effect that seemed to connect everyone she met. At first, I was unable to discern my emotions toward her. I longed to have her confidence and be more alive and extroverted like her. I questioned if maybe I had a crush on her or if I simply wanted her to be my friend.

One of our lunchtime regulars, Jerry, was seated at the bar top, eating a chicken cutlet sandwich one day when Lena pulled up a neighboring bar stool and began chatting him up. The conversation of summer plans came up, and when asked, Lena said she would simply be preparing for graduate school for the following fall semester. It only took the question of "What are you studying?" for Lena to casually lay out a detailed scope in both total humility and complete eloquence to blow Jerry away.

What school she was attending, where she did her latest research and on the topic of whatever it was. How she studied under the professor who specialized in something or other and how her interest was to pursue a career in academia. Her thesis was on this or that and how her true passion was yada yada, a topic in evolutionary psychology.

She peaked around the bar top before slowly pushing out her barstool and uncrossing her legs.

"Be right back, babes! I gotta check on my table!"

I opened the beer tap to pour a blonde ale for a guy at the other end of the bar, making sure to discreetly keep my attention on Jerry out of the corner of my eye.

"She— she— is completely brilliant!" he said.

My head continued to nod as I delivered the beer to the other end of the bar. "I had ... I had no idea—she," he began. Before changing directions all together. He needed to focus on the positive.

"William and Mary is a beautiful school! A great school!"

Jerry fell victim to what many had. What even myself had. Assuming that if you are working in a small-town tavern serving up chicken piccata and lemon drop martinis, you couldn't possibly be a brilliant psychological researcher with a plan, with a dream.

Before coming to The Tavern, Lena had graduated from University of Charleston and returned to Connecticut, only to then be bed-ridden for a year, suffering from a bad reaction to Lyme disease. As a result, she had become severely gluten intolerant. One of our weekend traditions together would be to split a gluten-free pizza at the end of our shift. The guys in the kitchen would shout, "Gluten-free! Gluten-free!" when they had a gluten-free order printed on the ticket or they simply wanted Lena to come back to the kitchen. It was a nickname as much as it was a dietary restriction.

Lena and I hit it off right away, and we began spending our breaks between the lunch and dinner shifts at Johnnie's, the dive bar across the street. Shots of Jack Fire acted as palate cleansers between our vodka-sodas while men in their fifties and sixties played Keno and shouted at the TV.

The Tavern was our own upper-scale version of Cheers. Frank was usually the first to arrive. A heavier-set man who would wear a white button up, slacks, and circular glasses. He chained-smoked cigarettes outside and sparked conversation with any and everyone. So much so, many just figured he owned the place. Next was Cheryl and Evan, who would roll in shouting their usual "Whoop! Whoop!" that half the bar would repeat back. Tuesdays were All-You-Could-Eat Taco night, and on Wednesdays, the town's co-ed softball team would clear us out of Budweiser. On Thursdays, a few of the town's under-the-radar kingpins would come in for Manhattans. They sat at a corner table in the lounge and once asked me to "surprise them" with a cocktail. "Do we want to stick with whiskey? Spirit forward?" I asked.

"Whatevah," one responded.

It was my one chance to set myself apart. So naturally, I reached for the Sour Apple Pucker and made the three of them neon green apple martinis as a joke. Only, they loved them. They stopped ordering Manhattans all together and always handed me a crisp Benjamin on their way out. A group of six big, burly men would occupy a table in the back where each and everyone would drink multiple rounds of apple martinis. My life was a complete joke, but I was having a good time. There was a dysfunctional, redundant lunacy about the place, and I loved it. There, I found family.

Chapter 13

THE GRAPEFRUIT SPOON

2016

Life at the Tavern always went one thousand miles an hour, and that included outside of it. I had a regular who lived in the plaza where The Tavern was located. He was moving out of his two-bedroom, two-bath that looked out onto a Christmas tree farm. I moved in the next month. It was perfect, and finally I had my own space.

A few of us from the restaurant would spend the dog days of summer throwing the top down on my Wrangler and making way for the beach, spending the day soaking up the sun and crushing mudslides and piña coladas at the local beach bar for a few hours. Then, we would rush back to my apartment, shower, get ready, and do a couple lines of blow—all before heading into The Tavern for the dinner shift.

The Tavern was always packed. Drink tickets printed so fast that they would topple over the bar and create a perforated paper garland. It was loud, bustling, and overall just insane. At night, I had "server dreams" due

97

to the anxiety caused by a million tasks that needed to be performed all at once and forever.

IPA for seat one and two dirty martinis—one Tito's, one Goose.

Line up four rocks glasses. Make and shake four margaritas at once.

Three with salt, one without, check the ticket machine—four tickets.

Pull the tickets. Take a dinner order for seats five and six.

Drop the margaritas. Pour two pilsners on the way back.

Sixteen wants their check. Run the card on two.

Next to him needs a refill in two minutes.

I'm out of wine glasses!

Only to wake up at three in the morning to realize I never grabbed that extra side of ranch.

Still, the service industry isn't for the faint of heart. Every now and again you might find someone sitting on a keg or leaning up against stacked crates of vegetables in the walk-in cooler. A place of isolation to gather your thoughts or to forget them. A chilly confessional of sorts that also allowed for a quick escape from the demands of life outside of it.

After about six months of The Tavern being open, a server named Preston was hired. Preston had sandy brown hair, bright blue eyes, and by all accounts, looked like a Calvin Klein model. He could be spotted doing pull ups in between taking orders and running drinks and pasta dishes to tables. He never stood still, was always on the move, and he had the personality that could get the most unimpressed child to laugh and crack a smile. Sadly, he was also a recovering heroin addict.

It wasn't uncommon to work with people from all walks of life in the restaurant scene. In part, that's what made the dynamic so welcoming, so compassionate, so much fun. It was a place anyone was able to belong. In a way, each of us there was an island, somehow coming together under this old roof to form an archipelago of misfit toys.

It's an industry where "martinis" is a socially acceptable answer to the question, "So what are your hobbies?" And where you are constantly asked by patrons what your "real job" is.

Preston and Lena hit it off right away, which I wasn't thrilled about. I didn't want to lose the friend I had just made, and Lena was the type of person that seemed absurdly out of everyone's league, even just mine as a friend. Preston was the type of person to show up an hour late to meet Lena and I for lunch, only to come prepared with gifts to win back our affection. Drinks from the gas station, flowers, candy, scratch-off tickets, two-dollar bills, and even if we just ate lunch, takeout sushi from our favorite spot up the road.

Lena spent more time with Preston, which opened the floodgates for me to spend more time with Aaron, my boss, who happened to be twenty years my senior. We would spend days together shacked up in hotels imbibing on tequila neat and doing cocaine off any surface. The room would be scattered with takeout trays of olive oil-based pastas and a near empty box of bell pepper and mushroom pizza we would continue to snack on for days. Jason Bourne movies played in the background just loud enough to hear the gunshots and car chases but not loud enough to hear any of the actual dialogue.

I thought we were in love and was convinced we were soulmates. It was not a transactional relationship, as much as it was a convenient one. Dating the boss was my latest secret, while at the same time, I was convinced this was the best life had to offer.

I worked four nights a week, and on Thursdays, I worked a double, arriving promptly just before 10:30 with a Dunkin' Donuts coffee and a full grapefruit in my purse. There was a beauty in the stillness of the restaurant on those mornings. Clean surfaces not yet touched by man and a space in both place and time where the world neither demanded, nor expected anything from me. It was a time where I was in control.

I was cutting the morning fruit and stuffing bleu cheese olives one Thursday when Aaron walked into The Tavern and handed me a plastic drugstore bag. I reached into the bag and pulled out an odd-shaped utensil that I eyed with confusion.

"It's a grapefruit spoon!" Aaron said. "I always see you struggling with the knife and spoon. Now you don't have to."

I did my best to maintain composure as my eyes grew glossy. Everything within me at that moment was trying not to cry over a utensil. It was the best gift I had ever received.

Lena attended graduate school at William & Mary that following fall semester and moved on from that small tobacco town like I always knew she would. Life was different after she left. Days of splitting bottles of wine before work, venturing to the beach, and $200 lunches were now performed solo.

Lena had inspired me to go to graduate school, so I studied for the GRE and was accepted to a state school next spring semester. After that first semester, however, I was somehow presented with an offer to use my last year of eligibility to play Division II lacrosse at a school in Massachusetts. I couldn't believe I would finally be given the senior season I never had. I accepted the offer, and between the athletic scholarship and my bartending money, I was able to pay each semester out of pocket and walk away with a master's degree in psychology and zero debt.

I had a regular named Tim that came in three to four times a week. He was a man in his mid-sixties and was always wearing jeans and some sort of exotic-patterned shirt. "It's Italian." He would say, grabbing it just below the shoulders and pulling it a bit off his skin.

The Grapefruit Spoon

He lived in town and drank multiple double vodkas on the rocks, and after three or four of them, he would start grabbing other articles on his person and begin broadcasting their expense.

"See this shirt? $1,200." "This watch? $35,000."

The other regulars would nod their head in a 'good for you' sort of way. I liked Tim. He was always very nice when he slipped me hundreds and wasn't saying sexually explicit comments about me to the other regulars.

For my two years in graduate school, Tim began to promise to buy me a nice watch at graduation.

"Tim, that's incredibly sweet, but I could never accept that from you," I would say. I didn't want to know what I would have to do to "keep" said watch. I already knew most things in life were not without cost. When I was behind the bar, he was just another generous man, but he absolutely looked at me in a way that implied he wanted to keep me locked up in his house and slip me crackers in the crack underneath the door when I got hungry.

"Nope! Nope! I'm going to get you a watch. That way, you'll always have time for me!" He would say it with a salesman-y pitch and always hit me with a finger gun at the end to drive home the message.

My graduation day came around, and as promised, Tim showed up with a small gift bag. I was flattered, and I was shocked. A man who had delivered on his word. Aaron eyed the situation from around the corner as I opened the bag to reveal nothing other than a small box with a watch inside.

"So you always have time for me!" Again, with a solo-finger gun. I thanked him from across the bar before begrudgingly coming out from behind it to give him a hug. He asked me out to dinner which caught me off-guard.

"Uhh—sure. Sounds like a plan!" I said, under duress.

I took my present and my phone and made my way into Aaron's office. I quickly Googled the brand of the watch to discover that it was sold for the average price of $26. After a year of this man telling me he was going to get me a luxurious present that I did not ask for, nor want, he presents me this. That's how much I'm worth: $26. I did end up going out to dinner with Tim and mainly because I had an agenda. We ate, drank, and ordered dessert. Then, when the opportunity presented itself, I started to cry.

"I'm just so far behind in my rent! I can't catch up," I went on. I agreed to let him drive me home where he stopped at his house on the way. I waited in the car, and he returned with $1,500 to give to me as a means to put toward my rent. He drove me back to my apartment where I thanked him for a lovely evening and went inside—alone. I ripped off the watch and threw it in the trash. The $1,500 was a much more appropriate graduation gift.

That Christmas Eve, Aaron and I spent the day at an Irish pub drinking Guinness and having Irish cream poured into our mouths. I had to work later that night and was running late, so I laced up my Chuck Taylor's and sprinted out my front door and down the driveway. That's when I wiped out on the pavement coated in black ice.

"Mother fuc*er!" I shouted at the top of my lungs. I hobbled down the hill with a twisted ankle and my now wet jeans that had ripped at the knee to make my shift in time.

It was about two in the morning on Christmas Day when I awoke, groaning in agony. My ankle was the color of a plum and the size of a grapefruit. Aaron drove me to the emergency room and waited with me in the lobby.

"That whore is ruining Christmas for your kids!" I heard blaring through the phone that was pressed up against Aaron's ear. I never fully understood Aaron's relationship status. Mostly because I didn't want to. I had just assumed that if he was spending all this time with me, it sort of just spoke for itself. It was then, as my ankle was propped up and covered in an ice-pack at the ER, that I silently prayed.

I prayed for my ankle to be broken. Totally broken. Shattered. Not sprained. I needed it to be broken. I needed to warrant him being here.

I deleted social media after that. My inboxes flooded with handfuls of women from his on again, off again girlfriend calling me all the names in the book. All names I had heard before outside of one that hit really hard: "homewrecker."

Chapter 14

ROCK THE KASBAH

2017

In between tending bar and graduate school, I took as many international trips as I possibly could. I went to Peru for ten days where I ate all the ceviche in Lima, befriended alpacas, and saw the sun rise in the apex of the mountains at Machu Picchu. I was convinced at this point in my life that all I wanted to do with my life was to tend bar and travel the world.

When I returned from that trip, I decided to head to my parents' house before heading home. The house was empty, but as I dropped my bags at the front door, I noticed a shaggy goldendoodle pressed against the furthest point of the couch in my parent's living room. Her eyes were riddled with fear and her body paralyzed by terror. *Don't worry, I get it.*

When asking later why my parents decided to get a dog, they proudly announced how after I was dropped at the airport, my mother had begun to hysterically cry. When my dad asked what would make her feel better and get her to stop crying, my mother dropped the act and asked, "Can we get a dog?" I had always felt like a vehicle, a means to an end. This time was no different.

I traveled to Greece, Iceland, Spain, and Austria before visiting both Cuba and Morocco with my friend Brianna, whom I had met my last semester at UConn after moving in with the field hockey team. Brianna, also a national champion, had an edgy, bohemian style about her. She wore Birkenstocks before they ever made a comeback, and her arms, wrists, and shoulders were decorated with small tattoos. Her long, dirty blonde hair, now concealed with a headscarf, always maintained the perfect natural beach wave. Her sharp green eyes bore a thin ring of yellow around her pupils. She is the type of girl who is unaware of how smart, beautiful, and all-around wonderful she is.

Together, we spent ten days in Morocco, shopping for magic carpets and drinking mint tea in Marrakech. We explored the blue city of Chefchaouen, treating ourselves to midday hammams and getting lost in the marketplaces. The scents of saffron, apricot, cinnamon, and leather consumed the streets as we spent the last days of summer underneath the North African sun. Men charmed snakes out of wicker baskets and placed monkeys on our shoulders as we walked through the old town square. There were little to no women our age wandering about the cities, and while correlation doesn't equal causation, the catcalls were still never-ending.

One evening past sunset, Brianna and I made our way through the city streets back to our Airbnb. During our walk back, a boy on a bike began heckling us and circling us like a shark. We ignored him at first and picked up our pace. Brianna grew increasingly concerned and agitated, while I didn't see it so much as a big deal. Men were men. After repeated shouts from Brianna telling him to back off, she balled up her cross-body satchel around her fist and whipped it at him on his final move toward us.

"Get!" She shouted. Chasing after him like a pesky seagull stealing snacks from your blanket at the beach. She wound up her bag like a slingshot again, and hit him a second time.

"Brianna!" I shouted, appalled.

Back then, I thought I was understanding and compassionate toward some of the traumas I knew Brianna held, in addition to my sisters, as a result of mistreatment from men. Still, I held the belief that there was no changing the minds of men, let alone their actions. They take what they want, and we as women just have to work around it. Anthony had already taught me how the world works, and being available to men at any and all hours, even when you didn't want it or were uninterested or unconscious, was all part of my job as a woman.

On our last day in Morocco, Brianna and I got our wires crossed and had drastically different departure times. I gave her a hug goodbye, left my luggage safely stowed away at our accommodation, and went off to explore the cultural mecca that was Marrakesh.

The catcalling was a bit worse, or maybe just more noticeable now that I was wandering alone. Nonetheless, I remained unfazed.

A handsome man who must have been in his early thirties with a five-o'clock shadow, green eyes, and golden skin like honey had abandoned his stand advertising four-wheeling excursions through the desert and caught up to me. He engaged me in conversation as we walked the city streets, and soon, he invited me to his house for lunch. I turned down the invitation but did ask him to point me in the direction of the post office. I planned to mail out a few postcards before my departure. He walked me there and again invited me to lunch, claiming that his mother was preparing a fish tagine and that she loved having guests in her home.

"It would be a great honor to my mother if you would join our family for lunch! She is a beautiful cook!" He exclaimed.

A knotted feeling of obligation rose up inside me, the nagging reminder that nothing in life is free. That if I didn't agree, I was contributing to the rude American stereotype. Before I knew it, we were leaving the medina and wandering into the fortress-style kasbah, venturing deeper and further into the matted-clay labyrinth, as he continued to reassure me every ten or so minutes that we were almost there.

I ignored the twisting in my gut and dismissed the grand majority of what many might refer to as "intuition."

"Just a few more minutes," he repeated. "You are going to make my mother's day! She loves hosting visitors!"

By that point, we had been walking, making twists and turns for over half an hour. I made mental notes of the turns we took through the collapsing corridors. Doing my best to commit to memory on which corners held the metal or leather goods stands or the paintings and small murals depicted on the walls of each junction. The once bustling marketplace grew noticeably more desolate and impoverished the closer we drew toward its core while I grew all the more uneasy.

We entered a small home with a dirt floor entryway, and my guide led me through the main room into a small bedroom and invited me to sit at the edge of the bed while he fetched his mother. However, I was not alone in the room. And the man who had led me into it hadn't so much as bothered to acknowledge the groggy woman—who could not have been older than eighteen—that lay under the covers of the same bed in which I now sat.

My host exited as two young boys, roughly fifteen, entered the room. Their faces were scowled, and they leaned up against the wall in front of me with their arms crossed. Large knives were tucked into their waistbands, and they snapped at the girl under the covers when she complained to them of something in Arabic. One of the boys snapped at her, and in submission, she laid back down.

After ten minutes or so, I just grew bored of waiting. I waited until the girl complained again and caught the attention of both the boys; one of them made his way toward her. With my back to the three of them, I heard a loud smack. A sound that I recognized as an open palm to face.

Outside, the man with the five o'clock shadow ended his phone call at the sight of me.

"It was my mother!" He began. Tucking his phone into his back pocket and pulling a joint out from another. "She is just leaving the market and will be home to cook for us in a few minutes!"

I had no reason not to believe him, and I was happy to have been given an update. I tried to remind myself I was blessed to be having such an immersive, cultural experience while on my trip and to be afforded the opportunity to make some new friends in the process!

Out ran the two boys that had been watching me. The man with the five-o'clock shadow shot them both a cold glare before quickly mollifying his expression once he sensed me looking. He shooed the boys inside and began to spark a flame from his lighter to light the joint. I didn't smoke weed, but out of obligation and courtesy, I was prepared to.

After multiple attempts to spark a decent flame, he cursed in Arabic before handing me the joint and asking me to wait while he went inside to fetch a fresh lighter. I was alone on the stoop when an old woman hobbling down the vacant alley grabbed my attention. Walking my way, she stopped about ten feet from me and shot me a stare that in some type of way pierced my soul.

One of her eyes was glazed-over from a cataract, and upon the sight of it, I was jolted into consciousness. A whisper then came forth from the deepest recesses of my mind, compelling me with an unbidden urge to flee.

I set the joint down delicately on the stoop. Slowly, I began to walk backwards, before turning to speed-walk, then run, and soon sprint my way out of the kasbah. The sounds of the Medina grew louder and thicker the further I distanced myself from the eye of the kasbah and that cataclysmic milky eye of that old woman.

Back in the states, it had been a while since The Tavern had felt like camp. Each week was a near carbon copy of the last. A place I had once viewed as a state of play with each passing day now more closely resembled a prison. I was a vase of wilted flowers, stuck in a perpetual state of stagnant water. It had been nearly three years now pouring beers and cutting fruit for garnishes on Thursday mornings. The only thing that seemed to change was that the thought to have my knife "slip" while cutting bar fruit had become all the more pressing. Slicing my hand open would guarantee me the rest of the day off, where I could retreat to the dark and be alone.

The thing was, I never took days off. I loved the money. Money was freedom, and money was power.

Aaron used to always tell me that he drank to forget, but I drank to outrun myself. To place a greater distance between the sober version of myself, who struggled and faced rejection and abandonment, and to embrace the party-girl persona that men found appealing. When I was drunk or high, cocaine or alcohol served as the perfect scapegoat. I could convince myself that it was external influences that were to blame for my failures and short-comings, not my inherent self.

Walking back up the hill to my apartment one evening I turned to take a loving look at the place that had brought me out of myself. I held

Rock the Kasbah

The Tavern's yellow exterior walls with a long gaze like a drawn-out, therapeutic drag from a cigarette, still blind to the notion that I had landed myself back inside another yellow house with a large oak out front. None of me realized that I had both literally, as well as subconsciously, replaced one yellow house for another.

Most of me knew that if I did not leave then, I would be stuck there forever, that I would never have a real reason to leave, and that I also lacked any real compelling reason not to stay.

Chapter 15

MAI TAIS & MOB TIES

2019

I needed to get out of Connecticut. Austin, Texas was a city that just seemed to pop into my head. Walking through the airport terminal on my first visit, an indiscernible feeling came over me—one that I today recognize as a supernatural peace. For the first time in my life, I realized I was home.

I moved to Austin and spent the first two weeks sleeping on the hardwood floor of my new downtown apartment. I used the same coffee mug for coffee, water, and six-dollar Trader Joe's wine, as I couldn't rationalize purchasing normal glassware until I landed a job. I walked up and down Rainey Street with a manilla folder holding a handful of my resumés. I wore the nicest dress I had that might be able to withstand the Texas summer and my only pair of sandals. Later, I returned to my apartment with pretty much the same number of resumés I had when I left.

The majority of the responses to my "Can I speak to a hiring manager" were met with, "It's July. No one is hiring in Texas in July!"

To lock in some sort of income, I began live streaming on Cam Girl websites where I basically stripped and used sex toys for tips. I would make as much as $800 in a day or as little as $80. By week three, I finally landed a bar gig at an icehouse, where I started serving frozen Mai Tais and pineapple daiquiris out of an open garage door window in 110 degree weather. The air conditioning behind the bar escaped out the open garage door window, and as such, my makeup didn't last much past ten minutes into my shift. I quickly understood why I was the only female bartender on staff and why the job had become available.

Neither the Cam Girl work nor the icehouse were sustainable forms of income, let alone glamorous work. It had been years since I had been on that sugar baby website from college, and I figured I might as well give it another go to add a third stream of income.

I connected with an attorney who I later met at a downtown hotel lobby bar, where he slipped his yappy dog a Xanax, and we enjoyed martinis. During martini number two, he electronically sent me $1,000. If there was one man like him, surely there were more!

Only, aside from Mr. Xanax, most men would not even consider paying anything north of $200 to meet. The current pool of men suggested I sleep over, have unprotected sex with them all night, have another go-around before the coffee was brewed, and send me home with the promise to consider a second date if, after some thought, they felt we "clicked."

I met men for dinner who somehow felt that dinner was compensation in and of itself. And even though at that time I could barely afford dinner, the last thing I wanted to do was to waste my time hanging out with these men for free. I was not going to allow myself to be treated like I had back in college, even if I was a sucker for some bubbly and a seafood tower.

One man from the website told me that no one in their right mind would be willing to pay more than $200 to hang out with a woman of my age. I was twenty-seven at the time.

Most men on these sites seek out women between the ages 18-26. Anything over, and you are yesterday's baked goods. It was becoming increasingly clear that the men on this site were not looking for women; they were looking for young, desperate girls they could exploit. They were looking for vulnerable women like me in 2013.

A bar guest of mine at The Tavern once said,

"There are two industries that will never go out of business: the pizza industry and the sex industry."

I believed it back then, and with each passing day in Austin, I grew to believe it more. I pulled away from that site and the predatory men that lurked and loitered on it and decided to advertise myself on various adult job sites, thinking that before my bar shifts, I could clean a house in my underwear or sell pictures of my feet. My phone and email were soon lighting up with inquiries from porn production companies and adult film stars. I video chatted with a producer who really sold me on the industry, mainly the $600 a day I would be compensated for filming porn. In Connecticut, I was used to making $300-$500 a dollars a night bartending, but at the icehouse, I was pulling that amount across three or four shifts. This opportunity arriving at my doorstep felt like a blessing, so the following week, I was booked on a flight out to Los Angeles to film my first adult film.

I hadn't much thought about God outside of the handful of nights I cried myself to sleep in Austin. Now that I was directly embarking on a life of sin, I was abundantly aware that I was nowhere on God's radar. That ship had sailed the first time I found myself under the Nile. However, two nights before I was meant to board my flight to LA, I miraculously came down with the flu. Again, God hated me and was punishing me for being a slut.

I emailed the producer to tell him I would no longer be coming due to illness and was now out $150 for the STD test I was required to take and bring with me. I nursed coconut water and snacked on overpriced artisanal crackers from the market at the end of the block. As I lay in the bed that had finally arrived and looked out the window of the high rise I could not afford, I found myself mesmerized by the cranes that reconstructed the Austin skyline before my eyes, past the floor-to-ceiling glass.

It was then, I was reminded of Dr. Miller's class and his infamous Sex, Drugs, and Rock n' Roll lecture.

Anthony's words, "Professionals are disgusting," dragged themselves across my mind like a nail to a file. I asked myself if that was even true while I began to dissect what was so inherently wrong with attaching a dollar amount to my time. Here I was, going on dates with strangers, bending to their every will, putting myself in danger and health in jeopardy, and never knowing if or when I was allowed to leave. I almost never knew if I was going to be compensated, and more often than not, I wasn't.

I thought back to that stereotypical image I had always held of a prostitute: a cracked-out woman dressed in fishnets in a dumpy motel. I realized that minus the fishnets and the fact that I preferred to snort my drugs, maybe I was already her. Maybe I had been her my entire life. A slut, a whore, a cancer, crazy, a homewrecker, and now I would be an escort. Also, maybe I could get behind fishnets.

So, once again, I opened my laptop and went scouring a different part of the dark web. I came across a Reddit board during my research that spoke to some of the boundaries many professional courtesans stated they put into place, all of which made absolutely no sense to me.

Things like, if you stay overnight with a client, you are entitled to, at minimum, seven to eight hours of uninterrupted sleep. Second, if a man tries to have sex with you without protection, it is within your rights to leave, as that is incredibly unsafe. And lastly, the one that blew my mind: if a man has sex with you while you are sleeping, or any form of unconscious, it is sexual assault.

Weird. I just thought that the last one was a standard Saturday morning with Anthony.

I posted my first advertisement under the alias of "Samantha" and listed myself at $300 an hour. I was officially an escort. I couldn't tell you who my first client was or my second, third, or fourth. All of them blended together in those initial days as I welcomed strangers into my barely furnished home. I started shutting off my phone at night in those early days, as most of the inquiries and *unsolicited pictures* received arrived between the hours of eleven at night and five the next morning.

"You up?"

"How much for twenty minutes?"

"Sup, wanna hang?"

"MSOG?" An acronym for "multiple shots on goal."

I saw clients whenever I could. After work, before work, and at any and all hours. I was making more money as an escort in an hour than I was at the icehouse in two shifts, so I eventually gave my two weeks and began looking for another bar job. I ended up interviewing at the cocktail bar of my dreams and picked up four shifts a week, making cocktails like Paper Planes, Vieux Carrés, and gimlets with the bar's house-made lime cordial.

I was first cut one night and was driving home around 10:30 at night when my phone began to ring. A picture message shortly followed of a business card positioned next to an identification badge laid out on a table.

Bobby informed me that he was not only a pilot but also a member of an elite crime family, hence the last name—*Gotti.* I wasn't sure if I believed him, but, quite frankly I didn't care. I could use $600, as he wanted to see me for two hours.

I quickly showered and hopped in an Uber. I stopped at a gas station to pick up a case of Coors Light, per Bobby's request, and arrived at midnight to the negative two-star hotel by the airport.

"I always repay my debts," Bobby said, in a breathy, Tony Montana sort of way, as he held out a ten-dollar bill for me to take. The beer came closer to fifteen dollars, but it wasn't a big deal. Bobby told me that he didn't carry large amounts of cash on him but had said that he typically put "his girls" on his company payroll. So, as instructed, I showed up with my account and routing numbers and the expectation that three-thousand dollars would hit my account sometime next week!

I stayed with Bobby for *three* grueling hours where he wanted nothing more than for me to give him a back rub and walk around the room in my underwear and heels while he sat at the desk watching YouTube videos of plane landings and pilots communicating with Air Traffic Control.

I took an Uber home and threw myself in the shower, in an attempt to scrub off the greasy, patchouli-scented hotel lotion from my hands that had been cramping up all night. I had a newfound respect for massage therapists. Between the late-night Ubers and the beer, I was out about $100. It would all be worth it come Monday when that direct deposit hit.

A few nights later, I met a man named Justin at his downtown condo. We opened some wine on his balcony, and he placed $200 under my wine glass.

"I'll give you the rest later," he said. It seemed fair.

I brought protection with me after reading I probably should, but Justin assured me that we didn't need it, that he had only ever been with his girlfriend, and they had just broken up; that he was as clean as a whistle! Okay! If you say so!

I stayed for two hours, which should have been six-hundred dollars, but somehow, I only left with three-hundred. I figured that drinking wine on his balcony probably just didn't count toward my time. I saw him the next night, and the night after that for four hours each night. We went for dinner and out for drinks, but again I was only given $300 each night. Justin was younger and far better looking than any of the other guys that had visited me at my apartment, so I wasn't going to be fussy about the small things— like money. I didn't believe I was even worth $300.

The following week, Justin asked if I would help him move some things to a storage unit across town. He didn't have a car, and I was, of course, happy to help him lug boxes in the 105-degree heat before dropping him back off at his condo.

"I was planning on paying you tonight," he said. "You're coming over, right? Midnight?" I nodded in full agreement. Back at my apartment, I ran a shower and sat myself down at the base of the tub. Finally, I asked myself the question: "*What the fuc* is wrong with me?*

Chapter 16

JUST AN APPLE JUICE

2019

I had ruled out participating in porn all together but was still receiving multiple inquiries from the adult jobs site, and Mitch was one of those persistent fellas.

"How would you like to fly to Chicago and make ten grand going out with successful men for a week?" I had yet to read anything by Gary Chapman, author of *The 5 Love Languages,* but in the fall of 2019, that line was definitely mine. Mitch spoke with a slow Midwestern draw and instructed me to send him a copy of my driver's license, as well as the dates I would be visiting and to call him once I had settled into my hotel in Illinois.

I took a few days off from the cocktail bar and found myself in the suburbs of Chicago a few weeks later, where Mitch instructed me to await a call from a woman named Dakota.

"You ready, sweets? He's here. Can I send him up?"

Dakota had a raspy, Estelle Leonard-like voice. I pictured her seated at an old desk, real *Mad Men* style, with her feet kicked up on top of it and crossed at the ankles. I envisioned her holding the cord of the mint green dial by phone in one hand as she took a drag from an obnoxiously long cigarette with the other.

My stomach was tangled up, braided, like a loaf of babka. I was staring at the chip in my French pedicure and shuffling my feet across the carpet before opening the hotel room door to my first client, a man with olive skin and green eyes who called me "beautiful" and had left me confused. I was listed for $300 an hour and had agreed to a 70/30 split. I was responsible for all of my own operating costs and was to be dressed, ready, and "standing-by" from eight in the morning to around 10:30 at night.

Exiting Mike's cigarette box of a Buick after my first night's "drop," I made my way to my room and got ready for bed. The last step was to retrieve a spare pillow from the closet, I had stowed it away for safekeeping. I threw the rest of the pillows on the floor in dismay and curled up on the far corner of the bed. I made more money on that first day in Illinois than I had in a week at the cocktail bar. I thought about all the money there was to be made tomorrow, and the two days after that, before drifting off to sleep.

On the morning of the third day, Mike picked me up from my first hotel. We were headed to the grocery store and then to my next hotel.

"Mitch doesn't like the girls to leave the room," he had said the night before. So I was expected to stock up on food so I didn't have to for the rest of my stay. I asked Mike if he wanted anything from inside the store.

"Just an apple juice," he answered.

This grown man whose drink of choice was apple juice was the same guy taking ten percent of my money. My life was a joke.

"Focus," I said under my breath. *"Beet and turmeric, something green, gross, kombucha—tastes like straight vinegar, what is wrong with people?"* I thought. My mind continued to shift in and out of focus and flashed to and fro with hazy snippets from the past two days.

"What are you doing here, Kelsey?"

I froze. A voice that seemed to speak into my left ear. Soft, but bold. A question that also seemed to insinuate something else. A whisper, but at the same time a firm interruption. The entire situation somehow felt like being pushed into a pool as I went through all of the self-defense mechanisms in five seconds. I knew exactly why I was in Illinois. I was finally collecting on what I had been robbed of for years. I was there because it was time to pay the freaking piper! The only issue being that now I was fairly certain I was schizophrenic. I headed to check out without any apple juice.

I spent the next two days shacked up in a different two-star hotel room. The lights and the room were void of warmth and comfort and laced with conversations that held no meaning. Conversations I wanted no part of, as it was much easier and more tolerable to throw my body at the man so my mind could escape. I was still convinced I loved the physical aspect of it, that I was more sexual than most women, along with everything else Anthony had told me I was and I had accepted as fact.

On my fourth and last night in Illinois, I had a repeat client, a man named Ted, who I had seen for an hour the first day. I willed myself to remember anything beyond the basic things I had committed to memory from our previous discussion days earlier, as I hadn't expected to see any of these men again. Construction and poker. Lots of poker. Talk about poker. We walked together under the star-bent midwestern sky as I tried to figure out why Ted, for some God forsaken reason, wanted to spend his reserved 90 minutes of time taking me out to dinner instead of inside the confines of my hotel room.

The smell of chicken wings steeped into the night air like a tea bag, sourced from the sports bar across the way. I would have much rather been naked and back at the hotel, where I had a bottle of prosecco on ice and home-court advantage. Back in the room, I would not be worried about getting in trouble with the agency for having left it.

When Ted had asked me earlier if I had eaten, it almost seemed like a trick question. Like it might be code for something. I shuffled through my mental Rolodex that was all of the code words and acronyms I found myself punching into Google before being redirected to Urban Dictionary.

BB, BBBJ, MSOG, GFE, PSE, DATY, Incall, Outcall, the list goes on and on. Shame on me for thinking that an email I had received from a man expressing interest in taking me to Greece for his birthday had anything to do with Mykonos or Santorini. It was not until he replied back stating that he preferred to not wear a raincoat while on vacation that I finally got the hint.

We were mid conversation when Ted pulled open the sports bar door from behind me. The lights from all the TVs mounted on the wall and the cacophony of noise stunned me still.

The drunken men cursing at the football games seemed too loud. Abnormally, obnoxiously loud. Breaking the sound barrier loud. My hands had instinctively covered my ears while my jaw was clenched shut as if preparing for pain, for a hit. Then—silence. Like the muffled noise of someone trying to speak to you from above water while you are submerged in it.

"Samantha? Sam?" Ted asked.

My mind thwarted me back into the present moment.

"Coming!" I responded.

Just An Apple Juice

Four days in a dark room servicing men had taken a toll on my psyche. I had lived in the bar scene, and I was just barely holding it together at that sports bar. I felt detached from the world, which seemed foggy, like I was viewing it through old contact lenses. A heaviness poured down over me as I focused on how my feet felt when they hit the hard floor. I questioned if I was fully awake.

We were led to a sticky booth on the far side of the restaurant, where a few minutes later, our server arrived at the table. I panicked. I had forgotten how to order, what I usually ordered or how I 'should' order. I looked to Ted to tell me the answer. He ordered a vodka soda, and that's when I remembered, that's what I usually ordered too.

"I'll do the same," I responded.

Then Ted asked me if I liked nachos. *Did I like nachos? Was it appropriate to order nachos?* I stared through the menu. *Do the other girls order nachos?* That's when the entire bar shouted in unison following a Bears touchdown, which caused me to jump out of my skin. The server was still looking at me, and all I wanted to do was vanish into thin air. *What was I doing here?*

I flew back to Austin with $2,350 in my pocket. Well—$1,600 after expenses. Not bad for four days' worth of work.

Chapter 17

CULT CLASSIC

2019

Lena was living in Boulder pursuing her PhD when I went to visit her that fall. She had been sober just north of two years, which, at the time, was terrifying because I worried she might not like sober me. I barely liked sober me! I also had no idea how I was going to not drink for the three days I would be staying with her in Colorado.

When Lena first told me she had given her life to Jesus, I figured she was now going to church on Sundays, and I just thought, *"Better her than me."* Yet as I sautéed garlic, oregano, and canned tomatoes on her stovetop, and Lena sprinkled walnuts and distributed silvered pears over a bed of spinach, I grew all the more suspicious. Together we were preparing a meal for a local women's shelter. Something Lena volunteered to do a couple times a month.

The house was cold, and not entirely from the late-fall winds that snuck in through the front door each time one of her roommates came or left but from Lena's humming that came forth in accordance with the worship music that played in the background. It was more than uncomfortable; back then, it was plain weird. Lena's new behaviors just continued to add to my theory that my friend had been brainwashed. That the "church" she was giving ten percent of her *barely existent* income to was in fact a cult. At that moment, her kitchen seemed to more closely resemble an asylum.

I stirred heavy cream into the tomato mixture before adding penne pasta, and I thought back on the story Lena had told me over a year ago as we walked the wooded trails of Connecticut.

When Lena had moved to Virginia for graduate school, Preston, the former server and closeted Calvin Klein model, had gone with her. Sometime after her first semester, Preston had, out of the blue, gone missing. It was then that Lena began to tear apart her apartment for clues, only to discover syringes stuck in the spines of her textbooks and lodged within the piping under the sinks and toilet, all before uncovering a bag of his heroin hidden in the freezer.

Later that same afternoon, Lena found herself sitting on her couch with a kitchen knife in one hand and that same bag of heroin in the other, torn with the decision of whether or not to take all the heroin and split open her thighs. Instead, the idea to call a church and ask for help seemed to be a pressing and impeding thought on her mind—one that she continued to dismiss but couldn't seem to shake. Lena did call a church that day, and she did speak with a pastor. She drove, as she tells it, still drunk, to that same church and found her way into the office of that same pastor and the head of women's ministry.

"You do not need to be perfect to come here," the pastor said. "You come here to get well. To foster a relationship with Jesus."

I hadn't known that Lena's drinking had been as bad as she described it. But then again, "casually drinking" takes on a different meaning when you work in the service industry, and I was still drinking heavily then.

Cult Classic

We spent our time together in Colorado hiking the Flat Iron Mountains, ordering lattes at boutique cafés, eating sushi, and window shopping down Pearl Street. Mostly though, Lena told me all about Jesus. She poured out the gospels to me and answered all my atheistic, agnostic, Old-Testament-condemning God questions with eloquence and confidence.

Lena also told me how she planned to leave her PhD program at the end of the semester to become a full-time missionary in Africa. Since I had known her, all she had talked about was one day becoming a psychological researcher, making ground-breaking discoveries about the human brain. I couldn't help but feel that she was about to throw away her future, that she was sacrificing a set plan to pursue a "God" who, based on my own experience, I knew would eventually disappoint and abandon her. I didn't know how to break my sweet friend's heart and tell her that.

At the airport en route back to Austin, I thought about how my friend was absolutely in a cult as I downed a bloody mary. While at the same time, I could not deny the change I saw in her, about her, and all around her. Even if her humming freaked me out, there was also a renewed softness about her demeanor. A joy in the smallest of actions, as I had witnessed her sprinkling walnuts over a salad. An aura of elegance and an alignment with her intentions. The way in which she seemed to, in all ways, synchronize and be in ultimate harmony with the world around her. Even the words she spoke and the stories she told were soft and silky, like the glaze over a doughnut.

It was hard to come to grips that the friend I used to party with had just told me that a life with Jesus was better than any drunk, high, or plans she could have for herself. I had a wonderful time with Lena in Colorado, but seeing how "clean" she now was only made me feel all the more dirty. Lena was back in my life, but just as she had been during our time at The Tavern, she was still destined for greatness and called to bigger, better, and greater things than her current environment held. And, with that, I knew it was only a matter of time before our friendship fizzled.

Back in Austin, I dropped down to part-time at the cocktail bar. I was now operating at $400 an hour, and I wanted to make myself as available as possible to take on clients. It was around this time I received my first inquiry regarding a 48-hour date from a handsome forty-something-year-old man who worked in technology. I figured the request was a joke, only to discover that "James" had every intention of paying me six-grand to spend the weekend with him at a Texas resort. My first thought: that maybe I was *his* last resort. That the first few handful of preferred companions, escorts, or whatever their preferred verbiage, were already booked for that weekend. Sure, I had daily rates set on my website, but I never figured someone would actually inquire about taking me up on them!

A couple of weeks later I found myself playing golf, frequenting the spa and hot tub, and playing poker while sipping scotch by the resort fire pits at night with James. It was the best weekend I had ever had up to that point. James seemed genuinely interested in getting to know me, and I loved that I didn't have to be my usual self. We were undistracted, without agenda, and it provided me glimpses into an unfamiliar encounter with intimacy.

We were nearing the end of our two-day getaway when he asked me if I wanted to extend our time together. And, if so, to tell him what he owed me to make it happen. I was very confused. Didn't he understand that I was dirty? Did he know that I was a whore? I wasn't the type of girl who was asked to go to resorts for the weekend; I was the girl who turned tricks in hotel rooms. I agreed to the date extension but didn't feel as though I warranted another three grand, as that was my 24-hour rate at the time. I told him two grand instead. I arrived back at my apartment after three days of relaxation, conversation, and an $8,000 payout.

This new taste of money only eroticized the possibility of what this job could become if I kept going. If I gave myself permission to embrace the part of me I always kept in the dark and instead, bow out and away from any sources of light.

I had been seeing a real estate broker by the name of Wayne for an hour twice a week or so. An hour that over time he pushed closer and closer to 90 minutes. Wayne didn't understand time limits as a boundary, and I was always too timid to speak up. I didn't know how to say or imply I wanted him to get the heck out of my apartment without being rude about it or risk jeopardizing the few grand a month I was racking in from him as a regular.

I decided to negotiate a monthly rate of $3,000 in an attempt to solve the issue of him overstaying his welcome, only to realize that the deal was skewed significantly in his favor. Whatever. At least my rent was paid each month.

Wayne had been separated and living the bachelor lifestyle downtown for a while. I usually suggested we meet at his place so I could control the timeline. Wayne later told me he was a sex addict, playfully mentioning that seeing me twice a week wasn't helping his addiction.

"Sex addiction is just a term that 'nonsexual people' like to place on those of us who have higher libidos," I responded. It was a line straight out of the Anthony handbook, and, as such, it was something I firmly believed.

I was later invited to a home in Nashville by a gentleman on behalf of another gentleman named Chuck, who sought my companionship for 24 hours. The organizer explained how this was a more or less a guys' trip, and there would be other men and "providers," an additional term commonly used in reference to the work I did—in attendance. I figured it wasn't a serious inquiry, but in those days, I entertained most requests and tried to capitalize on all that were fairly basic and to the point.

The organizer responded back with all of Chuck's "details" in addition to the address of the property. Let's see: a random mansion, with a bunch of forty-something-year-old men I didn't know that I would have to hop on a flight to get to? None of that mattered and was all irrelevant information to me. All I saw was an opportunity to make $3,000 and fly to Nashville with all expenses paid. I told them where to send a deposit and marked my calendar once the payment was received.

I arrived at the elegant, old-country style estate as my driver looped around the circular, faded brick driveway with a small fountain at its center. It reminded me of the riads in Morocco. Inside, I was greeted with a glass of bubbly and an ivory envelope with the letter "S" for Samantha written on it that was waiting for me on the large marble table in the center of the foyer.

"Welcome! I am happy you accepted our invitation!" A man said.

My things were brought to the room Chuck and I would be staying in as he gave me a quick tour and we got to know one another. Later, I was introduced to the other men and women in attendance, where I now set out to face my biggest fear—befriending the other women.

Bottles of champagne and white wine rested in a large silver tub, stationed at the end of a ten-foot-long wooden table that was covered in everything you could have possibly imagined that might go on a charcuterie board. Meats and cheeses, pickled vegetables, stone fruits, dark chocolate, Marcona almonds, honeycomb, and every type of olive and cracker found on God's green earth.

We changed into our bathing suits and headed out to the hot tub. All four of the women in attendance outside of myself seemed to have met before, implying that this was an event that took place more or less once a quarter. They were incredibly warm and inviting and seemed genuinely happy to meet me, versus viewing me as some type of threat or competition.

It was a nice change of pace. After a few glasses of champagne, I needed to use the ladies room. I leaned over and asked a curly haired blonde in a bright blue bikini if I was "allowed" to.

She chuckled at me lightheartedly saying, "Of course you're allowed to. Do whatever you want. You're not a slave here."

The comment shook me, and I had to ask myself if that is how I really felt. Only I didn't. I wrapped myself in a towel and scampered to the restroom, returning afterwards to a bacchanal that had dramatically evolved since I had left. Bikini tops were sprawled around in different directions, and the staff that had been refilling the bubbly and passing out martinis had since gone inside. Outside, Chuck flashed me a smile and waved me back over to the hot tub. This was who I was now, and I was pretty sure I loved it.

A few weeks later, I met with a man named Dean, an executive of sorts with a head shaved bald and an affinity for comic books. After five or six dates he expressed interest in wanting to date me in "real life." I wasn't sure how the dynamic of our relationship would change or where the line would be drawn that might distinguish what was expected of me as Dean's "girlfriend" versus simply providing Dean with the "Girlfriend Experience." But I decided to give it a shot anyway since he expressed interest in helping me start a career and he happened to be a well-recognized name in Austin.

Dean didn't drink, so without alcohol I was trapped in myself. We went to comedy shows, sporting events, took his boat out onto Lake Austin, and played tournament-style ping-pong downtown. Even though I didn't feel any sort of attraction toward him, he was fun to pal around with, and I imagined this was what normal couples must do.

After a month or so of us dating, I realized that the only real difference between Dean seeing me professionally versus now, personally, was that he called me "Kelsey" instead of Samantha and I was no longer getting paid.

Once at dinner, I offered to split the check, and he readily agreed. I had somehow gone from getting paid a few grand to join him at Top Golf to going Dutch at dinner.

Covid came around, and Dean asked me to stay with him until it all blew over. His house was a multimillion-dollar extravagant fortress, equipped with an arcade room, mini movie theater, eucalyptus spa shower, hot tub, four-wheelers, and a library filled with both books and vinyl. It was absolutely the ideal place to spend Covid. Only, I knew that if I were to accept the invitation, I would never be sure of when or if I was allowed to leave. I felt like a docile robot with half a personality. Moving in with him would only further blur boundaries and make me feel trapped.

I declined his invitation, and that was really the end of us. I debated backdating him an invoice for about $50,000. Instead, I cried over the rejection on my couch in my apartment and doused my drunken noodles in Sriracha.

Chapter 18

FIRST 'DATES'

2020

After two weeks of sheltering in place, my playground of Netflix, movies, and takeout quickly became a toxic cage. My cocktail bar showed no signs of reopening, and financially, I was a sitting duck. I thought of how if I were to die in that apartment, no one would find me for weeks. Not until my body began decomposing and the neighbors complained of the smell.

Every so often, I still cried myself to sleep, sending out one last sincere prayer to God. A God I believed to be real, but one I had never given a good reason to look at me. In prayer, through salt-water tears, I asked Him for just one person. I prayed that one person might come into my life that just might worry or care or find me before my dead body disturbed the neighbors.

I believed in the severity of the pandemic, but I still did not place much value on my own life. So the idea of gambling with life and death and understanding that with more risk typically came more reward, enticed me all the more. It sensationalized my closeted double life now that it was all the more forbidden. I had myself an inception of a secret—a secret within a secret and a double-decker of social deviance and recklessness. I had a plan and a means to provide for myself. I had a vision, and I was slowly building a sense of self-worth.

I stepped on the scale and read that I was the heaviest I had been since college lacrosse. I sat down and wrote out two lists. Things I thought I did well and things I felt I could do better at. That's when I realized the lists were identical and I was deceiving myself across nearly all areas of my life.

I cracked down, and I used this time to get back into shape and change everything about myself. I wanted to completely break ties with the trashy, prostitute version of myself that had dated men for free. I needed a new alias and to make some drastic changes to be worthy of eventually pricing myself at $500 and calling myself a "companion." So, goodbye, Samantha. Hello, Natalie!

I booked three professional photoshoots in attempts to upgrade my portfolio accordingly. After photographer and venue fees, outfits, etc., I invested roughly $10,000 but was certain I would see that all back in the form of bookings on my calendar.

I received my first gallery of pictures back, and I didn't even recognize myself in them. I couldn't believe the woman in the photos was actually me. I kept asking myself: *Is that really me? Is that actually what I look like?* What I saw visually did not align with that deep-seated belief that I was ugly.

I shuffled through an online gallery and witnessed a girl who looked confident and powerful dressed in lingerie, cocktail dresses, and red bottoms. I had been given a glimpse of a caged part of me that longed to break out while at the same time lustfully meeting that part of me for the first time.

First 'Dates'

"Natalie" was my very own Tyler Durden straight out of *Fight Club*. "Kelsey" had always failed, but "Natalie Nichols" would be a riveting success. Through the eyes of this newly improved and empowered version of myself, I envisioned achieving and receiving everything I had always wanted. Power, attention, and money—lots and lots of money.

When I had first begun to see clients, I had next to no protocol or procedure to determine who was invited to my apartment. If you had a fake name and three-hundred dollars, I was available. I did not perform any due diligence, as I did not want to have any excuse to rule out the next opportunity to make money.

To become a $500 an hour woman, however, would require me to set stricter standards and to raise the bar higher for the type of client I wanted to attract. That decision was firmly put into place after inviting a man to my apartment who tried to hypnotize me while he gave me a back massage.

I started requiring that the men provide me with references of other providers they had seen in the past six months who could vouch for their character, hygiene, and that they had a safe experience.

Renée was one of those women. I kept to myself in this world, but I had a good feeling about Renée. Our first conversation somehow carried on, and we quickly hit it off. We met for drinks the following week at a bar and grill in South Austin.

Renée is a woman in her mid-fifties and an absolute knock-out. Originally hailing from Dallas, Renée has short and choppy dirty blonde hair, striking green eyes, and a heart that rapidly revealed to me what southern hospitality looks like. Renée is a chic, former beauty and pageant queen, iron man competitor, and triathlete. She has a sharp eye for fashion and a passion for all things wellness and beauty.

She taught me about certain supplements to take to support brain health, liver detox, or collagen production, all while dropping liquid chlorophyll into my water glass. Then there was the first time she made me a grilled cheese sandwich, where she went on to use an entire stick of butter in the process. Soaking two slices of white bread purchased from the store with the crust already cut off, of course, in hot butter on the stovetop before adding in fresh mozzarella and heirloom tomatoes and basil from her garden. I consumed my chlorophyll and simply watched in amazement before she toured me through the third bedroom in her home that had been converted into the giant walk-in closet of my dreams.

Renée is the type of woman who would opt to dine al fresco as long as the temperature fell at or below 100 degrees. We spent countless dinners and brunches on the various patios of Austin, indulging in libations, often accompanied by her teacup Yorkie, Foxy, who came dressed in a golden collar studded with diamonds and a Prada or Gucci dog sweater in the chillier months that called for it.

Renée had been married three times. First to her high school sweetheart and then to two other wonderful men who had and forever would adore her. She was independent and a go-getter with a radiating personality that was both nostalgic and amorous, like summer rain. There was a sincerity and intentionality about her that rid the atmosphere around you of humidity and pushed aside the clouds and heaviness that was the neediness of men, which allowed sunlight to barrel through. She was a light in dark places. I loved Renée, and very quickly she became my closest friend.

While the two of us worked in the same industry, we did not operate under the same role. Renée specialized in erotic massage, which was something I never ever wanted to do. Which reminds me: I'm still waiting on that direct deposit from Bobby the mobster to hit. The difference in our job titles and descriptions made for a great partnership. When a client expressed a desire for a service one of us did not provide, we just recommended the other.

So, by the time a man named John came around inquiring about a massage, I politely pointed him in the direction of Renée, suggesting they would be a better fit. John had repeatedly inquired about same-day appointments, which I no longer accepted. I now needed 24 hours' notice to accommodate a date and was also now charging $500 an hour. John also refused to send me any personal information, which was also a new requirement of mine. A protocol I had implemented after a handsome, six-foot-something decorated college football coach had booked me for a two-hour date. However, when he showed up at my doorstep, he was *not* the person on the license that had been sent to me. I opened my door to a five foot five-ish redhead toting a backpack filled with sex toys. It was the first time I ever asked a man to leave.

With that, I immediately began to require screening information in the form of a person's legal name, where they worked, the position they held, and I needed proof of it all. I now knew exactly who I was meeting before each encounter.

As my self-respect slowly began to mature, I started taking a more vested interest in my safety. Except, with John, I ended up caving. I had a same-day cancellation and gave John the green light to come on over. I really wanted to end the day with four figures.

I opened my front door to the best dressed man I had ever seen: a handsome silver fox in a three-piece suit with crystalline-blue eyes. I welcomed John in, his cologne—a subtle blend of bergamot, cedar, and juniper—was equally inviting. John had reserved me for an hour. About thirty minutes of which was always spent getting to know one another.

"Oh! You like wine?" He asked. He had been looking past me at the large bookcase, which held a few wine and cocktail books.

"I was just at the wine shop before this. Let me run down to my car and grab a bottle for us to enjoy," he suggested, as he stood up to leave. Gone. Gone was my mask of confidence. *I'm ugly. He thinks I'm unattractive. I sound dumb. He's not going to pay me. A guy like 'him' would never be interested in a girl like me.*

I glanced over to the clock on the oven. I let him know there was about twenty-five minutes left in our date and asked if he was interested in extending our time together. "Sure!" He said, although unconvincingly.

He picked up his keys and wallet from the coffee table, and something inside of me shifted. An unforeseen second wind or the boost of found energy that kicks on during your final sprint after a long run. The phrase "Stand up for yourself!" repeated over and over again in my mind. It was encouraging, but I was already down on myself.

"I'm worthless. I'm fat. I'm ugly—Stand up! Stand up for yourself! Stand up! Stand up!" Somehow, the instruction cut through the thoughts of self-defeat.

"I'm trash—Stand up for yourself! Stand up! Stand up!"

And then I was. I was standing two feet away from him, and words were coming out of my mouth.

"That's fine, but before you go, I am going to need you to pay me for our first hour." He laughed it off and assured me that he would be right back. "Yeah, that is great and all, but I am going to need my fee for the first hour regardless."

My mind was just now catching up with itself. Mentally, I was freaking out, embarrassed and appalled by my perceived rudeness. I tried to maintain a face of composure as he looked through me, waiting for a tell or a flinch in my expression. Anything that might give him reason to not take me seriously.

"Alright," he said. Acquiescing and reaching into his pockets to retrieve his money clip. Loose business cards and five or six folded up hundred-dollar bills fell out onto the floor when he did.

He paid me $500 and sat right back down on the couch from which we had both just risen. When he finally did leave, I had a "good riddance" moment while also confused as to why he had no interest in doing much more outside of talking. Or why ten minutes after he had left, he was inquiring about another date. Who was this guy?

We met the following week for a scheduled three-hour date, which turned to five. I arrived at his hotel room where a bottle of Napa Cabernet, wine glasses, and a white envelope containing my fee were in full view. He was coachable. I could work with that.

There was a wall up within him that most clients I saw did not have. He was sloppy with the white lies that contadicted themselves here and there. But I had both accepted and loved that this entire operation was one giant eroticized smoke and mirrors. Here, I was confident, desired, and in control, and as for the men, they were once again bachelors, experiencing the excitement that accompanies meeting someone in an intimate setting for the first time. They were rule breakers, pursuing the unconventional and unorthodox. I was simply the co-pilot or plus-one to accompany them on the journey. A band-aid, ground-zero, or a stand-in for all things that seemed unrealistic, unavailable, or unattainable.

I was the drag of a cigarette they allowed themselves only when drinking. The extra slice of pizza, simply because it was the weekend. I was a representation of consolidated recklessness in the form of an empathic listener. One who was unrushed, undistracted, and solely focused on them.

The topic of Colorado came up during our second date, and I accidentally mentioned Lena and how she planned to become a full-time missionary in Africa. Something switched on in him just then. A drawbridge within that mental wall was lowered, and soon I was speaking to the man behind the curtain. I left that five-hour date with $2,500 and confusion as to why this man had zero interest, once again, in doing much else beyond talking.

I met John for lunch at a downtown restaurant a few days later. I learned quickly that John never looked at a menu, and when he did, it was just for optics, as he wasn't actually reading it. He would default to both the server and me to make any and all executive decisions.

"When you grow up in a family with six kids on a farm, you just eat whatever is in front of you, while it's there," he said.

His southern accent slipped out every now and again. Usually when he was attempting to come across as more down-to-earth and likable to maybe the waiter or younger man at the valet, although you could tell he put in work to try and rid himself of it.

John was the youngest of six boys raised on a farm in west Texas. He revealed to me that day that he believed heavily in birth order theory, as still, to this day, he claimed to be both the baby and his mom's favorite. Four to five in the morning wake-up calls were instilled in him from a young age as he put up fences, milked the cows, and did whatever else needed to be done on the family farm before the start of the school day. He claimed that even though he was raised tremendously poor, all of his brothers, in addition to himself, had become wildly successful. Why? As he puts it, it was because his parents were totally in love. Always holding hands, kissing in front of them, and always resolving arguments and fights with a hug.

I wasn't buying it.

His left ankle was folded over and resting on his right knee and navy socks with pink polka dots poked out from underneath his slacks. I was certain he was the only person in all of creation who could pull them off. We went on to spend many afternoons like this one. Immersed in deep conversations that so evidently showcased the polarization in our beliefs. Mine, at the time, bordering on liberal and feminist, while everything he said aligned with what one might expect a rich conservative man to believe.

I assumed that most people were having sex recklessly and for free, and as far as I was concerned, I was simply a capitalist and an opportunist. John disagreed with half of my statement, maintaining the stance that sex was something to be shared within the sanctity of marriage, positing that most people had values and felt the same. What world was he living in? Then it dawned on me.

"Wait, is this why you have no interest in sleeping with me?" I asked.

His head tilted back as he let out a few belly laughs. The genuine kind, where you catch glimpses of a person's true personality. Like taking a stroll around their home and seeing what books rest on their shelves. Learning more about them in a few seconds than any Q&A could ever reveal.

"Well, what did you think was the reason?" he asked, shaking his head and smiling in full entertainment.

I sent him a soft shrug. "I just figured you didn't find me attractive."

My first encounter with John was something like biting into a pitted date. But following our third encounter that day, that "date" seemed to have thus been pitted, melted down, and mixed with peanut butter to now more closely resemble something like caramel. He challenged my beliefs and always asked questions about my future. Soon, all other men failed in comparison.

Chapter 19

THE NEW SPOON

2020

The months blend together in Texas, especially during the summer of 2020 as I looked out onto Lady Bird Lake. Many of the local's still refer to it as Town Lake, and that day, like most, it was speckled with various colored canoes and paddle boards. The floor to ceiling glass of my apartment divided the world I created and existed in from that of where all others resided. This was the reality of the fortress I had built and the distance I placed between myself and others.

My only continued interactions in those days were my clients, my building concierge, and my personal trainer. Renée was the one friend I spent time with outside of the Benjamin Franklin's I would obnoxiously assemble into stacks of thousands to cover my kitchen counter and my robot vacuum that would bump into me every so often showing me affection.

I took appointments whenever I could. Each month I raised my earning expectancy by five thousand dollars, validating my worth and affirming my ability to cheat the system I had always seen as out to control and manipulate me. When I met or exceeded those financial goals, I was valuable; when I missed the mark, I wasn't worth what I was charging. I was ignorant, undesirable. My self-worth was directly related to if, when, and how often men booked me.

Each time I raised my rates, I attempted to prove to myself that I could live up to its assigned value, while on the most basic of levels I deemed myself to be worthless.

I loved "Natalie," the character I had created and who was pined after by many in the wide world of companionship. I liked her so much that I wished "Kelsey," the part of me that harbored shame and stewed in a residual pit of failure, would just be killed off.

One year prior to that day, I was crying myself to sleep on the floor of that apartment. One that was now fully furnished with accent tables, throw pillows and a dresser that had replaced the rows of moving boxes that had lined the walls and acted as a stand-in.

I had money; I was admired, and while not then, but very soon, my apartment would rarely be without a floral arrangement or a case of champagne. Being my own best friend would prove to be tremendously rewarding, even if at times I grew lonely in my isolation and through the division I made in separating myself from the rest of the universe.

John lived in San Antonio but was in Austin several times a month for business and now, more often, for me. He told me he was divorced, and I allowed my mind to wander. To accidentally lower a mental drawbridge that never should have been installed in the first place. I was no Julia, but he was definitely a 90's Richard Gere.

We met at another downtown hotel where I lounged by the pool as he carried on with his daily Zoom meetings. I was officially getting paid to drink margaritas by a pool. I was the smartest girl in the world. That night at dinner John had his ankle crossed over his knee again and was biting the edge of the "cheaters" as he looked off into the distance. He did this when he was in deep thought about how to frame certain questions he had for me, without wanting to overstep or come across as insulting.

John was always asking me about future plans, but the fact of the matter was, there was never a dollar amount I wanted to hit before retiring. Nor did I have a hard stop date on walking away from companionship. After all, I had only really just started! I had no plans of ever getting married and had absolutely zero interest in starting a family. There was no need for me to set a timeline. I was having fun and padding my bank account in the process.

I thought back to the man that told me no one would ever pay more than $200 to spend time with me at twenty-seven years old. Yet, here I was, now charging $500 an hour and my physical activities with John were limited to sunbathing and running my eyes down the "Wines by the Bottle" list.

I loved the way men looked at me when I was operating under this alias, like I was competent, entrepreneurial, and beautiful. I was now receiving some level of respect from men. I was finally being taken seriously.

"I have been thinking about going to law school," I said.

John thought it was a great idea. For some reason, he was under the impression I would be great at whatever it was I decided to do, even back then. It was John's stamp of approval and belief that I could be accepted into law school that had led me to believe that maybe I could.

A few days later, we were back at that hotel on Rainey Street. A three-hour date reservation this time somehow turned into eight, as we sat in our plush hotel robes and ate takeout sushi while the NBA played in the background. At the conclusion of our date, he pulled a large stack of hundreds from his money clip. I hated this part. He had paid me for the first three hours already, so the only thing owed was for the five-hour extension. I told him $1,500 instead of $2,500. He handed me the money and let me know that he would be traveling for the next few months. That this might be our last time together for a while. He really was a terrible liar.

We said our goodbyes, and I expected to never hear from him again. He didn't owe me an explanation. Whether it was that he just liked me too much or recently had a meeting with his accountant, it didn't matter. It was just the nature of the business.

The next morning, I had a text from John. He said he did the math and realized he had short-changed me. I explained it was my own error and blamed it on the assortment of nigiri coupled with Durant's hot streak that had led to my miscalculation. Also, that we were kosher. I wished him safe travels to wherever it was he was going. He wasn't okay with that answer. So I ended up meeting him back at that hotel later that morning where he handed me an additional $2,000.

"Interest." He said with a warm smile.

I didn't understand why this man was now over paying, especially seeing as he had no intentions of sleeping with me.

"Want to spend the day with me?" he asked.

Who was this guy? It was like trying to psychoanalyze Don Draper with nothing more to work off than the pilot episode of *Mad Men*. He counted out an extra two grand and handed it to me before pouring us each a cup of coffee from the pot that had been delivered to the room.

"I'll have to hit the ATM after coffee," he said, with another smile.

I met John for lunch a bit later. Lunch then of course turned into afternoon wine, which later turned into me heading back to the room to relax and watch *Ancient Aliens* as John took some work calls.

The New Spoon

Refracted light bounced off Town Lake and streamed in through the windows, illuminating John's blue eyes once he returned to the room. A noticeable shift in his demeanor contradicted the warm and inviting atmosphere inspired by golden hour that bathed the room in an amber hue.

"I have not been completely honest with you," John said.

The TV no longer advertised crop circle conspiracy theories, but instead Townes Van Zandt spun on vinyl. John didn't even need to say the next line, as I already knew what it would be, as "Waitin' Around to Die" played softly in the background.

"Well of course you are!" I said with a sardonic voice. Of course he was married. Once again, I had let my guard down and allowed myself to think, dream, and hope that a man like *him* would ever be available, let alone might be interested in a woman like *me*.

Nonetheless, this is what I signed up for. I enrolled in the charade that was a masquerade between two consenting adults. For me, it was that I was worthy of good things, and for the men, that they were not at a point in their lives where they needed to pay for a couple of hours spent in the company of a woman. It truly was a mutually exclusive hoodwink.

I retreated inside to grab a bottle of water and caught myself in an accent mirror above the record player. All I saw looking back at me was a prostitute pretending that she had not done this for free all her life, who was now trying to convince herself she was worthy of the fee she was charging. To convince herself—myself—that I held any sort of value. I was the dumbest girl in the world.

Two days later, John and I were sitting on that same sofa in my apartment where he had first tried to leave me. When John had ended things with me at the hotel a couple of night's earlier, he said that spending time with me did not align with his values. I do not think he understood how insulting the comment was, but I understood what he was getting at.

John was an elder at his church and a married man who identified strongly with his Christian faith. He was being sincere when he told me that sex was to be had between a man and his wife. I just didn't understand how he saw what we were doing as *that* much different. Even if we were fully dressed in turtlenecks playing chess, he was still with me behind closed doors, and I was still—let's call it for what it is—a hooker.

He wore a wedding ring that day, something he had never worn in front of me until just then. Tears subtly formed behind his baby blues, and he turned to me and said, "I am so sorry that I looked at you as anything else other than a child of God."

I wasn't sure how to respond. I had never seen a man cry before. I had never been referred to as a child of God before either. And for good reason: I was pretty sure I wasn't one.

"John, I'm a hooker. It's okay—I think I fall outside those parameters anyways."

"Stop calling yourself that!" He said, with almost a latent frustration.

The sun poured in through the windows, and the lake glistened on the other side of it. The room smelled of sandalwood from the diffuser in the corner and cinnamon from having just sprinkled it on top of our black coffees. That's when John again asked me about God, about Jesus, about marriage, and if I would ever pursue a different career. I was pretty direct in saying that none of the things he mentioned were for me. Then he asked me something else.

"Do you feel this way because you think you are unlovable?"

I didn't have a witty remark in the chamber this time around.

"I guess I have never thought about it like that before," I responded. And I hadn't, even though I realized it was exactly how I felt.

The New Spoon

Something about that morning, in the company of a man who wanted nothing from me, other than to bring me coffee and an apology, made that tiny apartment resemble something of a home that day and not just simply my office.

A few weeks later, we were back at the Hotel Van Zandt, only this time Leon Bridges played on vinyl and the wine read notes of clove, tart cherry, and black pepper. It was the dog days of summer, and as such, we watched the sun tuck itself behind the hills in the west from the comfort of our air-conditioned room.

The Austin bats ribboned their way across that tangerine and ruby sky, and it was at that moment that I realized everything about my life was the most perfect it had ever been. That somehow in the two of us knowing the darkest parts about one another, it made the world outside of us appear all the more beautiful.

"Are you ready for your present?" John asked.

I pulled the lid off of a medium-sized box and was struck with a foreign feeling, a brief confusion, and then finally—not knowing how to react, I simply shouted, "My new grapefruit spoon!"

Within that medium-sized box was a brown leather Bible. Written in golden script, a small, nearly forgotten word was inscribed in the bottom corner. A word that I had not seen in such a long time. *Kelsey.*

Chapter 20

GET THE DSM-5

2021

John and I had decided that night would be the last time we would see each other. He left an extra five grand on the coffee table in the living room. I only noticed it once I reached for the phone to call in-room dining. That night was a 'side of fries and the second most expensive bottle of champagne on the menu' kinda night. John could afford it. I turned on SportsCenter and drew a bubble bath, staring at the Bible on the coffee table. I didn't want to open it tonight. I wanted to get drunk and wallow around the executive suite in a bathrobe.

Two weeks later, Wayne showed up at my apartment to help me with my luggage. When Wayne first asked me to go away with him for the weekend, I said I would love to, while also casually reminding him that my three-day rate was then $12,000. To which he responded back with, "I can't afford that!"

To which I quickly replied back with, "That's not my problem!"

Money in reference to the trip was not talked about after that, yet I didn't have the heart to tell him I hated the shirt he was wearing, let alone tell him I didn't want to go away with him for the weekend. I didn't want to go away with anyone for a weekend, let alone Wayne and let alone for free! I wanted to hate Wayne for taking advantage of me like this, but I hated myself more. I had ended things with Dean because we were dating, and he was getting all the benefits while I gave away my time for free to someone I saw no future with. Now I was back in a similar situation with Wayne, and I was still incapable of establishing an immovable boundary.

Money continued to be a source of shame for me. It was at the root of every argument that took place in my household growing up, and Anthony had beaten it into me that it was unattractive for women to ask for money. I could be direct and talk business via email, but in person, I caved. I grew uncomfortable and agitated and wanted the conversation about it to be over. I truly believed that being taken advantage of was better than gambling with the possibility of abandonment.

I wanted to stay in Austin and enjoy my weekend in peace and solitude. Not only was this trip not making me any money, but it was also costing me opportunities to make it! That morning, I turned down a three-hour Saturday evening rendezvous, which only fueled my resentment toward Wayne.

I hadn't seen John since the night he had gifted me the Bible, but I reached for it on my bedside table to bring with me.

"Who gave you that?!" Wayne questioned with jealousy, noticing my name written in gold.

"A client," I responded, with zero attempts to hide my passive-aggressiveness.

"Are you sleeping with him too?!!"

Given the nature of my job, it seemed like an exceptionally asinine question. But then, like that first dose of coffee in the morning, it hit me.

"Actually, no," I said. "I'm not."

The Austin skyline pulled further away in the rearview mirror. If I wanted out, I needed to take action here and now. I decided to spark an argument to get Wayne to pull the car around. Without surprise, it worked flawlessly. That's when Wayne asked me, "Do you want to cancel the trip?" Freedom was at my fingertips.

"It's whatever," I said. Pulling my hoodie up over my head and curling up in the front seat. I cracked open my Bible and wanted to be left alone.

I could not recall ever reading a Bible. I was unsure if there was even one in our house growing up. Beyond Jonah and the Whale, the Twelve Apostles, the whole Jesus born in a manger bit, and certain stories Lena and John had told me, I knew next to nothing of what lay within its leather-bound pages. All I knew was that since I had cracked it open, I had become obsessed with reading it.

At Wayne's beach house, I would sneak out of bed each morning to brew coffee and venture outside to the porch to read my Bible and the few devotionals John had given me. I was also avoiding anything and everything that might be expected of me once I woke up. As far as I was concerned, I was not getting paid to be there, so in that way, I was not going to allow myself to be his beach cottage concubine. Plus, I was really thirsty to learn more about Jesus.

The second morning at the beach, I couldn't find my Bible and devotionals. I am a lot of things, but being disorganized has never been one of them. I soon found them tucked away in the back corner inside a kitchen cabinet. Wayne supposedly had no idea how they had got there, and I still thought men were pathetic.

I had been having back pain since the drive down to the beach. The afternoon of the second day, I was lying on the beach and couldn't move or get up. That night, I shot awake with debilitating pain from my kidney area and an inflamed chest cavity that felt like my rib cage was wrapped in fiery barbed wire.

Wayne drove me to an emergency room, where I was fed muscle relaxers and given an MRI. A $2,000 bill later only further fueled my resentment. I arrived back in Austin having no intention of ever seeing Wayne again.

Only, he continued to show up outside of my building and began cornering me at coffee shops, and when I was out at dinner with friends, pleading with me to talk. I placed Wayne on the 'no fly' list at my apartment, as he tried to gain access to my floor by convincing one of the new guys he was my boyfriend.

He sent me apology gifts in the form of flowers and handbags. I kept the handbags and forwarded the floral arrangements to the women in the leasing office. One Sunday, on my standard run around East Austin, I noticed his truck tailing me before finally pulling up alongside me. The car was moving at a glacial-like pace when he shouted,

"Kelsey! Can we just talk? I'm in love with you! I told my wife I am officially filing for divorce!"

This has to be a sick joke, I thought. I was constantly prepared to be kidnapped or thrown into the back of a van at a moment's notice—but this?

All I could think to say at that moment was, "I didn't ask you to do that! Leave me the f*ck alone!"

Wayne knew my name, where I lived, and now, somehow, all the places I frequented. It was now time to change the running route and just to be on the safe side, change my OpenTable password. Also, it was time to find a new place to live.

Country music had somehow taken a permanent backseat to worship music and audiobooks. More than ever, I was curious and hungered for knowledge, perspective, and truth. I talked with Lena almost every day and would bring her questions to ask God on my behalf, since I knew they were tight. Lena shared stories and parables from the Gospels; however, all I really saw when I cracked open my Bible was war, destruction, and God every so often deciding to "clean house" with certain groups of people.

"Stick to the New Testament for now, Kels," Lena would say. "God spoke to His people differently after He gave His one and only son to take on the sins of the world." It sounded a bit salesy, but I decided to take her advice.

I later told Lena, "If I could just have some proof. If someone could provide me with some evidence that God is real, I would totally be down to hop on this bandwagon."

"Kelsey," she said lovingly. "Why do you think it is called 'having faith'?" I hadn't really thought about it like that before, but I did see her point.

Late summer turned into fall, and although I hadn't spoken to John in weeks, I caved and invited him over one afternoon. An afternoon that he coincidentally happened to be in Austin.

Gin martinis were the drink of choice out on my balcony as we watched the bats release themselves from under the Congress Avenue Bridge. The warm breeze brought with it the smell of tikka masala from the Indian food restaurant across the way.

These were my favorite nights. Nights where it was just John and me, talking about Jesus, or something else, or nothing at all. One of those nights, John brought up the idea that I should consider attending a local church. Hard pass. Sundays were reserved for my run, which had since moved from the east side of town to around Town Lake, and I very much considered that my own form of church.

"Kelsey," his delivery was soft, just like the cashmere blanket that had been gifted to me by a client and was now draped over my couch—"You don't go to church because you have to; you go to find community and be around other like-minded believers."

Community? Yuck! It sounded more appealing when I thought it was just a prerequisite to knowing God. I ventured back into my apartment to pull two more coupe glasses from the freezer. I thought of how much I had finally done and achieved for myself despite God's abandonment. Of all the times in my life to start entertaining a pivot to righteousness and holy living, right now was terribly inconvenient. My life was one giant sin, but at the same time, I had never felt more in control.

I peeled two long sections from the rind of a grapefruit before expressing the oils over the martinis and dropping them into the glasses. I thought of that first grapefruit spoon and how it had long been discarded, and then of the second one—the Bible resting on my nightstand.

"I just remembered something," John began, as I made my way back out onto the patio. "I sat next to this wonderful man at a wedding about three years ago. We had such an amazing conversation, and I believe he is a pastor out in Dripping Springs. I will give you his contact information, and why don't you give him a call and tell him you will be attending service this Sunday?"

Surely, he was kidding. I was the antithesis of religion and the furthest thing from being welcomed there. But I was going to call up a pastor and ask him to put out the good doughnuts this Sunday and for good measure, to hose the joint down before I got there.

I didn't need community. I had always been a lone wolf and a black sheep. I had my Sunday rituals, I read my Bible and tried to pray to God, and I had never slept better in my life. I was all set.

A few months later, I had just walked a client to my front door and locked it behind him. I went through the normal motions as I always had when I took incall appointments. Strip the bed, start laundry, take a shower, remake the bed, etcetera. I settled into my fresh sheets and propped a pillow up behind me as I reached for and opened my Bible. I will forever remember the voice that split through the room like the crashing of waves, sending it rippling in a static-like frequency, while at the same time standing completely still. An anomalous silence, as if everything in all of creation that might make noise had ceased and bowed down to it.

"You sin in the bed you honor me in."

I felt the words in the innermost part of my marrow. An irrationality so profound it paralyzed me. Petrified me. I was an ant under a microscope while a part of me was stirred awake, shaken out of dormancy. *You sin in the bed you honor me in.*

The words were clear as day, but for some reason, I did not understand them. I looked down at the open Bible in my lap, then to the envelope of money on the table by the entryway. Then back to my Bible and back to the envelope. I thought about what my night had consisted of and what I was doing now before repeating the words over and over again, deconstructing the sentence to make sense of it in my head.

An ambient noise still lingered deep within my ears, as if a conch shell had just been pressed up against it and I was hearing what resembled the ocean.

"You sin in the bed you honor me in." It was not until that moment that I realized I was one huge contradiction. Also, I had never thought of it that way before. I felt fragile and exposed, convicted and ashamed, fully clothed, yet naked and afraid. Slowly, I peeled back the covers and stepped out of bed. Making my way over to my bookshelf, I pulled the Diagnostic and

Statistical Manual of Mental Disorders, Fifth Edition off the shelf. I ran my finger down the table of contents before shuffling through the pages.

"Schizophrenia," I narrated, while reviewing the list of diagnostic criteria before calling Lena. I had asked her on a few occasions what she meant when she spoke of hearing from God. When she would say, "God told me," or "God revealed to me." If God was talking to me, how was I supposed to know if it was Him or was I just suffering from auditory hallucinations?

"We are at the prime age of onset, Lena!" I shouted into the phone, having already explained the situation. She was laughing on the other end of the line, assuring me that I was not schizophrenic. I asked her to pray on it, just to be sure.

For the next month or so, the idea of going to church was pressing on me. "The Father's House" by Cory Asbury, for a while now, had been the last song on my playlist to prepare for the sprint that would carry me home. Sprinting the last portion of my run was something I had done for as far back as I remember. I couldn't recall a run that I didn't finish in an all-out sprint. It was so indoctrinated within me as part of the event. I had finished my sprint and was walking my heart rate back down to normal when a verse of that song hit me so clearly.

"Leave your shame at the door, it ain't welcome anymore."

I imagined the beaded sweat that dripped down my arms and legs collecting all my dark secrets and running off me in onyx droplets. I had just received the revelation that shame was the emotion that had plagued me my entire life, that I held a chronic case stretching all the way back to that preschool lawn so many years ago. I didn't know life without shame. And now this song was speaking to a place where I could leave it at the door.

In those days, I harnessed my shame to feed my ego and affirm my identity as an elite companion. Still, I replayed the lyrics over and over again.

"Leave your shame at the door, it ain't welcome anymore."

I couldn't believe that those lyrics were in reference to a church. Then, out of nowhere, I felt an idea spoken to me. *You should give it a try sometime.*

Chapter 21

OLD COLLEGE TRY

2021

I tore through my closet looking for something that did not completely scream "whore." Shuffling between cocktail dresses and athleisure wear, with very little falling in between that spectrum. With the clock winding down, I threw on a long sleeve cranberry dress before snapping a quick picture to send to my mom with the caption. *Is this too short for church?*

I waited a bit to hear back, but if I didn't leave soon, I was going to be late. The elevator doors began to close when a response finally arrived via text that read, *A tad short for church, don't you think?*

I waited in my Jeep until precisely 10:58 in hopes of avoiding any and all people and conversation. I would not be targeted and cornered by these church folk. I made my way into the movie-theater-turned-Sunday-morning-church where the band began to play none other than "The Father's House," to start the set. I had no intention of singing, but it was a nice coincidence.

The service wasn't at all how I had remembered church from when I was younger. The band was surprisingly good, and if there was an out of tune organ in the vicinity, I wasn't hearing it. I was also convinced that everyone in the room led miserable and artificial lives. The only reason I was there was to report back to John and Lena that I went and gave it the old 'college-try,' all to confirm that church was not for me.

Around the second song, an unnerving anxiousness came over me. The type that I had not experienced since college in Dr. S's or Alexis's offices. A rising tightness within my chest and near-distant anxiety that ran up my throat and set fire to the back of my eyes and sinuses.

Fuc! Hold it together!* I talked myself down and quickly searched the room for something to grab my attention.

The campus pastor came onstage to lead communion. It wasn't scripted, and it almost seemed—genuine? I still wasn't buying it. I thought back to the last time I was in a confessional. How I was told a few Hail Marys, Our Fathers, and telling my parents I loved them would absolve me of my sin. I thought of how transactional the suggested assignment actually was. Religion is a transaction, and now, so was my business, and thus, so was I.

I listened to the sermon intently and disagreed with all of it. It went against everything I knew to be true. I was frustrated that I was in a church instead of nursing my hangover at the closest place with a liquor license. I didn't need this. I didn't want this. Screw this. Church then, like most other things to me, was still a sham.

Around that time, a man by the name of Charles flew me out to Kansas City for a 24-hour visit. I didn't like dates that involved an overnight stay because I never slept. It is a different level of trust to be able to fall asleep next to someone. What made this trip different from all others was that

Charles was a pastor, which made this both an opportunity to make five-grand—thanks to the recent raise I gave myself—and again to confirm that religion is a hoax.

There was no shortage of "religious men" in my inbox throughout those years. Men threatening the promise of me burning in hell for all eternity if I did not repent from my sexual immorality. Others referencing whatever ring in Dante's Inferno I would be enslaved in unless I surrendered at the feet of Jesus. It was different from how John and Lena spoke to me. John and Lena made me feel less like an infestation on society and more like a person who just needed shepherding. These men in my inbox just wanted what I felt all men wanted at that time—to control me. To have me submit.

I arrived in Kansas City, and although Charles was a pastor, he wasn't sure how to think of God anymore. A year or so prior to our meeting, he went up to his son's room to wake him for school. Except his son didn't get up, as the Lord had taken him in his sleep. He was seven years old. The devastating loss haunted Charles and had left him depressed, anxious, and with severe feelings of inadequacy, which had led to sexual dysfunction. As a result, he felt he was unable to protect his family, to provide, to be worthy of calling himself a husband, a father, or to lead a congregation.

He sought out women in the escort industry as more of a blurred line that might allow for any sort of trust and emotional intimacy to be culti-vated, which would otherwise be forbidden within the confines of tradi-tional therapy. I didn't agree with it, but I understood his rationale.

Charles barely touched me during that overnight stay, but that didn't prevent me from feeling the dirtiest I had ever felt boarding my plane back to Austin the following afternoon. I didn't want to think about where the $5,000 he had given me had come from. He had called *me*, invited *me*, yet somehow I felt like the bad guy in all of this. Hating him would mean I cared, so I just forwarded any future emails from Charles to spam and continued to despise the hypocrisy that is religion.

The holiday season rolled around, and while the year prior I was washing chocolate sauce out of my hair after having my body turned into a hot fudge sundae for $800, this year I opted for a downtown staycation.

Thanksgiving that year was spent at the Four Seasons laying by the pool with a handful of LSAT workbooks. I had been diligently focused on studying for them for the better part of a month. I watched football in the lobby with an old fashion in hand and checked my inbox every so often for a quick boost of connection.

A man joined me in the lounge and engaged me in conversation, although I pulled open my book at the first indication of a commercial. Unless a man was paying me thousands of dollars to hold my attention, everything short of that was irritating. As the man rose to leave, he approached me and asked me for my number. No part of me was interested, but for some reason, I felt obligated to give it to him. The man exited the lobby and out the same revolving door at the exact same time that John walked in. We had plans to meet for a drink or two and then parted ways for the evening. John returned the following morning just as a cart of room service arrived.

He was holding his coffee cup and looking intently out the double balcony doors when he asked, "What would it take for you to quit?"

I had no answer. No number seemed high enough. I was now operating at $700 an hour and soon planned to implement a two-hour booking minimum. I was making more in a week than I did bartending in a month. Why would I throw in the towel now? It would actually be all kinds of irrational for me to walk away from a job where I was my own boss to go back to nights behind the bar and getting home after midnight covered in beer and lime juice.

Besides, in what world does a career bartender with a now very large gap in her work history ever land a six-figure job? Never again did I want to experience days where depression kept me in bed for two days at a time. My biggest fear was falling back into that dark place I was in back in college or the dangerous recklessness that I dabbled with afterwards. Never again.

"I would walk away if I could lock myself into thirty to forty grand a month for the next two years," I answered. It seemed like a reasonable amount to get me to move on to something different.

A big part of me was hoping he would say he would pay it, and the other part of me wouldn't have given up that lifestyle for the world. I had been discarded my entire life, and now men set my professional photos as their desktop and phone backgrounds. Men I had never met shipped me shoes, and women I had no intention of ever meeting purchased me furniture. I was wanted, and people were expressing to me that I was worthy of investment.

I was still working, spending time with John, and now that church had sparked my curiosity, I kept going back. I had learned to love the separation that the Sunday morning drives out to the hill country placed between me and my life back in Austin.

After service one afternoon, I hopped in my Jeep, started the engine, and then found myself shouting, "Holy fuc*!" when I noticed a man waving at me from outside of my driver's side window. I rolled down the window, and the man chatted me up for a few minutes before asking me for my number.

I had told John on Thanksgiving night that before he had arrived I had given my number to a man I had absolutely zero interest in and how it was eating away at me for whatever reason. So after that day in my Jeep, I was ecstatic to call him and tell him the news.

"A guy asked me for my number, and I said no!" I shouted into the phone.

I didn't understand why it felt like such a pivotal moment or why it gave me such a cathartic feeling. It seemed like each time I said no to a man, I was saying "yes" to a small, undernourished part of me. I realized I didn't need to feed men's egos and shouldn't at the price of my own well-being. It was a slow and unsteady dismantling of my enslaved mindset.

Renée and I had started a new Christmas Eve tradition that year. We met up at one of our favorite restaurants downtown to do dinner and cocktails and to exchange gifts. Renée arrived at the restaurant with two large shopping bags filled with presents. This was in addition to the oversized gifts she already had shipped to my apartment in advance.

"My son wasn't around this year for Christmas, so I shopped for you like my daughter!" she exclaimed. My eyes instantly grew soggy, and I latched them onto the cocktail menu to try and hold it together.

Renée and I filled multiple roles in each other's lives. I was grateful to have a friend, a confidant, and a maternal figure who genuinely cared about me. Someone who understood the life I had chosen to live and could empathize with it. There was a deep, soul-tying trust between us that was without judgment and perfect.

Renée has one son whom she loves with all her heart. Sadly, he had been battling addiction for years. She had sent him to the best rehabilitation programs in the country, but still, her green eyes drew dull when she spoke of having hope that he might hold a job or stay clean for longer than just a few months. We prayed for each other, and I began praying for her son, too. There was zero doubt in my mind that God placed us in each other's lives at a time when, at least, I needed it more than anything.

The day after Christmas, John had asked me to meet him downtown. We rocked back and forth on the Adirondack chairs of the Four Seasons, looking out toward Town Lake. I felt him looking at me, and I did my best not to blush in embarrassment.

"Stop," I said, trying to act serious. Trying not to laugh. John told me he had left his family trip early because he needed to tell me something. He needed me to know that he loved me. And I did know. He had said it with his eyes many months before and really every time he had looked at me since. I wanted the words to feel romantic, but as much as I longed to be loved, I couldn't convince myself that any of this was inherently beautiful. At the same time, I didn't want to know life without John in it. I loved him, too.

It was now a prolonged, purposeful sort of pain we were inflicting on one another. There was no moving forward or back from where we stood. There was only here, as we were, or apart from one another with nothing.

I did not know much, and in fact, I really only knew one thing for certain back then: that God would never want me to end a marriage. At this point in time, in relation to my business, I figured if it wasn't me a man reached out to, it would just be someone else. I was in agreement with myself that all men cheat. Especially the good ones. Especially the noble ones. That it is inevitable. That this was the main reason I saw marriage as a sham.

I once had a woman tell me that a marriage does not fall apart because someone else steps foot on the porch, and that is how I saw myself amidst the organized chaos.

I continued to go to church here and there. Continuing to explore this world of Jesus that seemed to be in direct contradiction with everything I knew. I started to think critically about what was being spoken and preached and was still obsessed with reading my Bible. I traveled with John on most of his business trips. Each time we were both under the impression that it would always be the last.

Back in Austin, we would watch college basketball and shoot pool on Saturdays at the pizzeria at the end of the block, sometimes ordering a pie to go to eat back at my apartment. I enjoyed dark, self-deprecating humor and would often refer to myself as a "hooker" in front of John.

"Stop calling yourself that!" he would say, through a laugh, although I could tell he meant it. He hated it when I referred to myself in such a way.

"I just—I see you, and then I think about your job, and it doesn't make sense," he said.

That's when I was reminded of the man in Illinois with the olive skin and green eyes. And the phrase he spoke to me three times. *What are you doing here?* And the words I heard whispered in search of apple juice at Trader Joe's. *What are you doing here, Kelsey?*

I hadn't understood what it meant until just then in my apartment with John. But I also wasn't planning on explaining or conveying to John that this was just who I've always been. Who I was so fated to be.

"When was the moment you made this agreement about yourself?" John asked. I didn't know what he meant, so he rephrased.

"When was the moment you decided this was who you were?"

I pulled plates from my kitchen shelf, as he opened the pizza box. I couldn't even begin to recall when or where it all started.

"I have genuinely just always felt that way about myself," I responded.

"But what is the memory of the exact moment you decided it?"

I handed the wine and bottle opener to John and gave it some more thought. In seconds, the answer became clear as day.

"I guess it was the first time my mom called me a slut."

Chapter 22

CHEESECAKE PROBLEMS

2021

I allocated most of my time in January to studying for the LSAT. For the three months leading up to the test day, I had cut back on appointments to only a few a week in order to best prepare. I was confident that if God wanted me out of the escort business, He would supernaturally enable me to score a 160, even though I was only scoring between 150-158 on my practice exams.

The test began, and I just couldn't focus. I scrambled as time wound down to bubble in random answers. I totally choked. Hunched over in my chair, I thought about the cumulative hours I spent studying, which could have been hours spent making money. Mostly, I thought about how, once again, God hadn't shown up when I needed Him most.

I headed to the lobby and ordered a Monkey 47 gin martini with a twist. The lounge server politely noted that the martini would cost $32.

"F*ck it! Bring me two! I just failed the LSAT!" I replied.

I checked my work email to lift my spirits. Running back to a world filled with individuals that embraced and adored me while seated in another that didn't seem to want to grant me membership or offer me admission.

I wasn't sure what to do with the rest of the evening, let alone the rest of my life. I wanted to hate God, but at that moment, all I could think to do was to read my Bible. So, for the first time in a public setting, after a botched exam that I had hoped would change the course of my life, I opened to the book of Matthew. I was reminded of a time at The Tavern when a younger woman sat down at the bar top and opened a Bible of her own. How I had rolled my eyes at the sight of it before handing her a menu.

I sipped on my hotel-surcharged glass of alcohol and searched for inspiration within the Gospels. "I want to believe," I thought.

The X-Files flying saucer poster came to mind. But how could I when I thrived in sin and floundered in attempts to move beyond it?

At church was the only place I was worried about having to falsify a career. I didn't know how to not lie to every person who asked me what I did for a living. It is a pretty standard second or third question asked, regardless of setting or circumstance, after exchanging names. After a service, I decided to draw a line in the sand. I would either dive into this "church thing" or I would have to burn every bridge on the way out. I had never been one to give anything less than my all to anything and everything I was doing, and church would be no different.

I attended an information session after one of the services to learn more about the church's vision, small groups, and volunteer work. I was so curious about Jesus, and while I hoped it would be a low-key information session, the woman who sat down next to me asked me my name and then what I did for a living. Enough was enough. *I'm a fraud. They all know I'm a whore.* Ran through my mind. What was I doing here? How could I leave my shame at the door if I could not completely disassociate from my job when I got here?

If there was a self-destruct button, I would have pressed it right then and there. Instead, I decided to do the next best thing. I walked up to the campus pastor and introduced myself before saying, "Listen, I need to tell you something, I am a prostitute."

"Hey, Kelsey! I am just happy you are here, joining us on a Sunday morning! How long have you been coming to Drip?"

"Did you not hear what I said I am?" I asked.

I wished he would just get on with it. Tell me what I wanted to hear so I can go have a boozy brunch already and never have to step foot back in this sad excuse for a church again.

"Kelsey," he began, "Whatever your sin, that is between you and God. I am just here to help you on your walk with Jesus. How is that going by the way? How long have you been walking with the Lord?"

Six of the seven stages of grief seemed to hit me all at once. What he said didn't make any sense. I wanted to hate him and this place, but instead I was mortified. I tapped into the part of me that was pleasant and agreeable, before saying goodbye and exiting the building.

I gripped my Jeep's steering wheel that Sunday afternoon in the Belterra Village. I replayed the conversation over and over again. I didn't understand why he had said I was welcome there. I was twenty-nine years old when the thought crossed my mind, *"Maybe I am not completely worthless."* And if I had been wrong about that all this time, what else could I be wrong about?

Back in Austin, I was still seeing clients, though not in my apartment. Not since the day I pulled the DSM-5 from my bookshelf. I hosted William, a nerdy guy in his mid-thirties with sand colored hair at a separate location.

That night was our second date, and we spent the first of two hours sipping wine, catching up, and taking bites from the three types of cheesecake he had brought to accompany my envelope. It was the first night I was conflicted over where I was, what I was doing, while also trying not to think about God.

The conversation soon thereafter moved from the couch to the bedroom where William's demeanor switched quickly from nervous tech nerd, to forceful, assertive, and demeaning. He began hitting parts of me without my permission and calling me degrading names. I asked him on two occasions to stop. The third time he hit me so hard it stunned me with pain. This date was over.

That's when he grabbed a fistful of my hair and pushed me face down into the stack of pillows. Harder hits. Louder name-calling.

I reminded myself to fall in love with the pain and to also leave my body. Things like this did not happen often. So on the rare occasion they did, I considered them a bad apple, an outlier.

I returned home later that evening and dropped everything at my front door. I stripped my clothes and underwear off in the hallway before placing them into the trashcan under the bathroom sink. I was good about not keeping anything that might serve as a reminder of the bad times.

My body was covered in red welts, and handprints were visible on my hips, the sides of my rib cage, and backside. I ran the shower and plugged the base of the tub so the water would pool at the bottom. I focused on the sound of what I imagined to be similar to a monsoon in the rainforest.

I stepped into the tub and envisioned the contact of my toes with the water resembling an oil spill in open water. I hugged my knees into my chest, then laid back, closed my eyes, and prayed. Prayed that the marks on my body didn't bruise. I had to work the next day.

Cheesecake Problems

Even though I was told I was still welcome at church, I was too ashamed to go back any time soon, and even though I had a poor experience with William, and, for a while, had taste aversion when presented with cheesecake, I threw myself into my work.

Around that time, I began meeting with a man named Andres. Andres and I would meet one to two times per month where we would meet for strictly dinner and conversation and nothing beyond that. I had a handful of clients like this. Those just starved for human connection, conversation, validation.

Andres was a businessman who had moved from Madrid to Austin with his family a few years prior. As he tells it, his wife hated America and was always flying back to Spain for weeks at a time. Andres was aware his wife had a boyfriend back in Spain but hoped that she would grow to like America and be open to exploring and getting to know Austin eventually. However, it had been two years since their move, and he said that she had no interest in and was closed-off to accepting Austin, or America, as her home. Meanwhile, Andres could not fathom dragging their two young boys through a divorce.

Andres hired me as a dining companion so he had someone to try new restaurants with that was not a buddy or co-worker. Being the sole provider for his family, our time together—as he would say—was the three hours he "selfishly" gave himself a month.

"I wish I could take my wife here," Andres said, holding a spicy Szechuan cucumber in his chopsticks. We were dining on the west side of town at a new dim sum restaurant. "A few of my coworkers have recommended this place to me, and I was hoping this might be a place that piqued her interest."

"Instead, I am pretty sure she is packing to meet her boyfriend in Portugal. She doesn't even try to hide it from me anymore." His voice was laced with brokenheartedness.

Andres told me he worked seventy hours a week and on the weekends was traveling with his sons to their soccer tournaments. Ones that his wife did or did not attend.

"That doesn't sound like there is a lot of time left over for the two of you to share," I said.

"She just won't even give Texas a chance," he responded. "She doesn't like the food or music here."

After about five months of dinner dates, Andres had just placed our sake orders at a new omakase restaurant when he told me the news.

"We are officially going through with the divorce," he said. His eyes were locked onto the tiny dish that held freshly sliced ginger.

"I told her I would give her half my net worth if she didn't contest custody of the boys. She agreed."

I had found that in these situations, and I found myself in them a lot, there is never an appropriate response outside of giving yourself fully to the moment. To lean into the stillness, to open up the part of your heart you would otherwise shield. Maybe I never "needed" to be this person, as much as I could not help but care. Andres told me that his wife was moving back to Spain at the end of the year. He asked me what kind of mother takes a payout over fighting for their kids. Then our sake arrived.

Chapter 23

PARLOR TRICKS

2021

That winter, Lena came to visit me in Austin, and we went on to have our first fight. Lena was well aware of my lifestyle and what I was doing to support myself, but on the third day of her visit, a shouting match ensued inside my tiny studio.

"God is not going to bless you if you are living a life of sin!" Lena shouted.

"You've had no problem accepting my donations to your missions with my dirty money, though. Did you?!!" I shouted back. I didn't expect her to understand that this was the only thing I had ever seen even remote success in.

If I was meant to choose right then and there between the life I had created for myself and gambling on a God in hopes of something more, it was a no-brainer. I wasn't ready to give up my life of luxury on chance. Never again would I build my life upon the false promises of men. And I viewed God as the sum of every man who had hurt me.

I dropped Lena off at the airport later that evening, and outside of the car she pulled me in for a hug. She told me that she loved me, that I was her best friend, and then pulled away to wipe the runny mascara from underneath her eyes. We did not speak for months after that, and in that time, I threw myself into my work. I flew to Fort Lauderdale for twenty-four hours and was able to book three dates for two hours each, only to fly back to Austin, rest for a day, and then accept a 24-hour reservation for the following afternoon.

In Florida, I had already seen my first two clients and was preparing to see my last of the day, who was scheduled to arrive around four that evening. I had hoped to catch up in the living area of the suite, but upon my client entering, he went to the bathroom to wash his hands and then made straight for the bedroom. I had seen this client before, but unlike the last time, after only five minutes of chit-chat he fervently threw himself on top of me. The clock read 4:19 after it was all said and done.

I was annoyed that I was not in control of the timeline. At the same time, I was so emotionally drained that I wasn't fighting it nor standing my ground. Giving my body over in these circumstances always seemed like the better alternative than remaining anchored in the present moment and forced to engage in conversation. By the end of the two hours, he had his way with me two more times.

I couldn't look myself in the eye for a while following that trip. I was a sullen corpse, cemented to the cold earth. I left Florida after twenty-four hours with heavy pockets, but that last guy certainly got his money's worth.

It was a good two months before I had the guts to drive out to Dripping Springs again after confessing my job to my pastor. I was sitting in the far back corner of the cinema when Connie, the head of the women's ministry, approached me and asked me out for coffee for the following week. I agreed to have coffee; we exchanged numbers, and I prayed that she would not follow up with me about it.

The following Wednesday, Connie and I were seated inside a coffee house where she was asking me to tell her "my story." I already needed a drink. Not only was Connie the head of women's ministry, but Connie is supremely smart. Marriage, family, therapist, high-on-reading-emotional-intelligence type of smart. She was not falling for any of my bait and switches or receiving any of my deflections or attempts to shift the conversation. She was focused, intentional, and had an academic way about her that kept her on the subject and topic at hand.

Even with my guard up, however, she was enjoyable to talk to, and there was a warmth about her that rippled and radiated. A heartfelt softness, like salt-water taffy left in the car during summertime. She was completely fascinating. So much so that the second time we got together over lunch, I didn't even mind that she wasn't paying me two grand to do so.

"We have a leadership meeting in two weeks, and I want you to come!" Connie said as her petite frame cut into a plate of steak and eggs.

I did that thing again where I laughed, thinking she was kidding, before realizing she wasn't. A group of married church women in a remote chapel in the middle of nowhere where we will do team-building activities? Hard pass. I told her I had plans that day but thanked her for inviting me, all while resisting the urge to order a second glass of Sancerre.

Two weeks later, I found myself driving through the winding backwoods of Dripping Springs. When I finally arrived outside of the tiny chapel, I asked myself, "What on earth am I doing here?"

Hope Chapel is nestled between rolling hills in the center of a clearing. Herds of deer and other wildlife roam the land around the chapel, and that day as the spring rains subsided, a fog lingered and settled within the valleys in the distance. The chapel is located on a ranch owned by a woman named Marcy. A woman with the type of captivating eyes you find yourself staring at for a few seconds too long. Marcy had short, sleek shoulder length gray hair and a smile that made me feel authentically welcome on her property.

The meeting consisted of introductions, announcements, and prayer followed by a time of worship. I did not know any of the lyrics of the songs or why I was there, but I closed my eyes wondering if, by some means, whether mentally or spiritually, I might be able to make myself disappear. I didn't want community; I wanted to vanish. I was filled with shame and conviction.

Since that day I heard the Lord's voice in my apartment month's earlier, I had wanted Him to see me. I searched for Him during the day and sought Him out at night. Outside of my "working" hours that is. Slowly and unknowingly, I was re-establishing within me a mind-body connection that I had never allowed myself to fully experience, cultivate, or manifest. The more I sought Him out, the greater my awareness became and the quicker my body seemed to react. I craved church on Sundays because it was the only place I allowed myself to feel and open myself up to experiencing anything other than autopilot.

For over a year I could not go through worship without crying, and on a few occasions just bawling my eyes out. I acknowledged there was a major repair to be done in me, but I saw it as exposure to the sum of my brokenness. I started to see that maybe my life hadn't been all that normal after all. That all this time I hadn't known the truth.

At Marcy's Chapel that day, I allowed myself to tear up in silence as I used the back of my long sleeve to wipe the tears from my eyes and blunt the sniffles from my nose. In this room filled with people, I had never felt more alone. I decided since I was there, I might as well try to sincerely apologize to God for every mistake and poor decision. For the bookings already marked in my calendar and the requests in my inbox I planned to respond back to when I got home. For the job I didn't want to quit because I was convinced it was what made me feel wanted, what gave my life any meaning. I just surrendered to it all. I didn't care about optics or anyone else there. I broke down.

I buried myself alive in the form of the many sins that ran through my mind. Many so bad I resisted all promptings to fully remember them.

I was brought to my knees and overwhelmed with guilt, shame, fear, and sorrow. Then, He touched me. My body trembled and shook as my mind stood still and attempted to decipher, translate, and interpret whatever it was I was experiencing. There is not a word in the English language that encapsulates the sum and extent of the emotions I felt that day, all at once. It was forgiveness; it was compassion; it was jealousy for me and anger for the hurt inflicted upon me. It was frustration and then sorrow for the decisions I continued to make, and it was hopeful, inviting, and at the same time a complete celebration. It was my first encounter with love.

A spiritual hot rain poured over me in the form of "don't be discouraged," "I have a plan for you," and "I have been waiting for you to want to know me," simultaneously and void of spoken words.

Two women I did not know came to my side and held me. It somehow seemed safe. The April rain broke and streamed down outside the chapel while I attempted to pull myself together. Of all the times I had taken my clothes off for men, I had never felt more naked than that day when I was fully dressed, surrounded by women, after completely losing it on the hardwood floor of a backwoods chapel.

A woman with short dark hair, cat-eyed glasses, and a flawless tan began moving about the room. She began praying with the women I was later standing with in a circle in the center of the chapel. The woman prayed and offered words in the form of gifts of hope and encouragement. I didn't know what to believe anymore. I couldn't unhear what I had heard in my apartment or unfeel what I had just felt. Yet, Alison, the woman with the flawless tan, was now performing what seemed like some sort of parlor trick. Her voice drew nearer to me, and I prayed that she would not touch me.

Please don't touch me. Please don't touch me, I thought, doing my best to abandon all memories I held in attempts to scramble and replace them all with good and acceptable ones. None came to mind, so I decided to make up a memory, just in case.

I got it! A cornfield! I will just envision a cornfield if she touches me. Then I thought about it—that is the dumbest idea imaginable. But it was too late! Alison had her hand on my shoulders. If she was the Dripping Springs Medium, this entire chapel was about to know what I did for a living.

"You have broken paths behind you, but the path ahead of you is straight!" It was uplifting. I was probably getting all worked up for nothing. I'm pretty sure I read the same thing on a fortune cookie a few weeks prior. Then the energy around her shifted.

"That's strange," Alison began.

*Oh fu*k, Oh fu*k!* I thought.

"I see ... a cornfield? Does that mean anything to you?"

I left that chapel that day with a few more experiences that I could not unexperience. A few more encounters with God that I would just continue to push aside.

On a separate rainy afternoon, Connie invited me over for tea as the rain pitter-pattered down on the roof and the patio outside her second-story office. The room was cozy and delicate with sandy beach tones, textured wall accents, and a bookcase filled with spiritual and psychological texts. I had no intention of spilling my life's traumas out on Connie that afternoon like Kevin's famous chili from that episode of *The Office*. It just sort of happened that way. I needed to confess. I needed to sabotage whatever our relationship was becoming. I liked her, and it was inevitable that sooner or later I would disappoint her.

Connie then said something that shattered my world that day.

"It's not my job to judge you; it's my job to love you. To help bring you closer to Jesus."

When Connie said those words, I believed her. Part of my mind shifted and came into agreement with myself that she was speaking the truth. I saw that she meant those words that had just grabbed hold of my heart and forged a new path in my way of thinking.

The rain had stopped, and steam rose from the damp pavement as I made my way back to downtown Austin. I was starting to think that, maybe, I had just always slept with people so they never had a chance to truly see me naked.

I told Marcy and Alison what I did for work shortly thereafter. They each offered to help network, to make introductions, and help me find a job. But unless it was a six-figure situation, I showed little interest. The idea of downgrading my pay and being locked to a desk not only sounded much worse than my life of sin, it completely terrified me.

The highs always seemed to be followed up by the lowest of lows. Later that week I had a date with a man in his late thirties who invited me to his quaint neighborhood in North Austin. His screening information checked out just fine, as he was a decorated academic in Austin. He welcomed me into his home that was void of any furniture aside from two lawn chairs placed in what would normally have been a living room.

Mangy cats roamed around the kitchen counters, reaching their paws and mouths into a left open box of cereal and a half-eaten sandwich next to it. The place reeked of cat litter and rancid chicken noodle soup.

FOLLY

He had asked me to join him in the lawn chairs to discuss a proposition he had for me. He told me he had recently liquidated all his assets and that fall he would be moving to a commune in Vermont. The real reason for my invitation there? He was looking to knock someone up before he committed to a year of celibacy.

I removed five bills out of the envelope he had given me and laid the rest of it on the arm of the lawn chair. A flood of copy-cat crimes flashed before my eyes, and I prayed to Jesus that on my way out the door, no one would pop out of a side room and hit my mouth with a chloroformed towel. New policy: no home visits.

Chapter 24

RUTHLESS PRAGMATISM

2021

Lena and I had been eating açaí bowls sprinkled with strawberries, shredded coconut, and wild honey in a Boulder cafe months before that fight in my apartment. It was there that she confided in me that she had prayed for God to reveal a book in the Bible to share with me. Lena had never read the book of Ruth before God had told her to share it with me, and neither had I, for that matter. But since that day in Boulder, I must have read the story of Ruth one hundred times. Sifting through it like flour to better understand whatever symbolism it held and how on earth it might relate to me back then. The only parallel I could draw from the book of Ruth in 2021 was that she and I both had an affinity for older men.

Back in Austin, I was folding blankets and tidying up my apartment as I rattled off the master list of all the things in my life I was now starting to view as sort of sinful. Porn was one of those habits that I never much viewed as an addiction. It had always just been something I needed to watch in order to both get out of bed in the mornings and to fall asleep at night. It was part of my routine just like brushing my teeth or drinking water.

One morning while brushing my teeth, I removed my toothbrush, my mouth filled with paste, and looked up at the ceiling and yelled, "Well, God, if you didn't want me addicted to porn, you shouldn't have made me this way!"

I saw a client later that evening, and by the time I was home and showered, I was exhausted and fell straight asleep. The next morning, I was just ready to get out of bed, so I went straight for my French press and then took a walk around the lake. After a couple of weeks, I realized that I hadn't watched porn in a while, that my disinterest in it started around the time I had shouted out to God that morning brushing my teeth. And I haven't watched it since.

I spoke to God all day long. "God, I am a hot mess! Good luck filling all these holes and voids in my life. I am like a walking slice of Swiss cheese over here. You have your work cut out for you!"

I began praying with Connie, Alison, and Marcy more and more. And by that, I mean I held their hands at church, or when we grabbed coffee, they prayed, and I listened and usually just cried. Alison seemed to always be speaking radical and farfetched things over my life. She often repeated a job title that came up during prayer. A job that involves public speaking, and not hiding in the shadows. While I appreciated the sentiment, if she actually knew me, I felt she wouldn't say such things. Things she said were in direct contradiction to who I was and as such, what I thought I was capable of doing.

"He has a job for you, He has a home for you, a purpose for you," Alison said before pausing mid-prayer and starting to laugh. "He says there will be no Swiss cheese!"

John and I never stopped speaking or spending time together. We were snacking on takeout sushi and seaweed salad on my balcony one afternoon as we took in the views of the sleepy Texas sun.

"God told me that one day you are going to write a book about your transformation out and away from this life," he said.

I looked at him, concerned, before moving his glass of wine a bit further out of reach. "Now you're talking crazy," I said.

It was a nice thought though.

Growing up I had wanted to be a writer and be just like my grandmother, who was always reading a new book or working on a crossword puzzle. Our house was unusually silent, but when she visited, she parted the noiselessness down the middle with her melody of hums that often transformed into song—the type of songs they play at jazz clubs and Italian restaurants, that make you feel as though you stepped into a 1940's Hollywood film, like *Casablanca*, *The Big Sleep*, or anything starring Humphrey Bogart.

She was always wearing an expression of complete and total tranquility and carrying with her small notepads, decorated with sketched images of butterflies and wildflowers, where she would write out for me in her beautiful calligraphy handwriting, small, simple words like "rice," "apple," or "tree" in Aramaic. Slowly teaching me words and telling me stories of my great-grandparents and their village in Assyria, modern day Iraq. She would sometimes leave books behind, and I would flip through their tea-stained pages and mirror my grandmother's mannerisms. She spent time staring at me in awe and wonder, which at a young age, I found odd and didn't understand, since the incidents were so isolated and only came from her.

It wasn't until John, and what I now recognized as a loving gaze, brought the memory of her back to life.

I reached for another piece of nigiri and told John that it was a nice thought, but I was the farthest thing from closing up shop and telling the world I was a slut. There was a zero percent chance any skeletons would be breaking out of my padlocked closets.

In a very short amount of time, I had learned a great deal about myself. The biggest awakening for me was the discovery of how deeply rooted and concealed my self-hatred was. I began to take both note and action of everything I said to myself on a daily basis.

"I'm fat. I'm ugly. I'm not worth that much. I'm not attractive. I'm stupid. I need to lose ten pounds."

So began the process of capturing those thoughts and refuting them while trying to prove to myself they were not true.

I received my LSAT scores back, and although describing them as *deplorable* would be too generous, I still planned on applying to law schools. This might just be the miracle in my life God was waiting to give me. He would place me in favor with whatever admission office of the law school I was meant to attend, warming the hearts and minds of all those in review to be blown away by my personal statement. UT Law, here I come!

I continued on my walk and checked in on emails and inquiries I had missed while sleeping. How most people check their social media, in those days, I checked my work email. It was the clearest route to instant gratification and the quickest way to achieve a hard, full hit of dopamine.

I perused my submission forms from my website. That morning in particular I had an unusual amount of odd requests. As my rates continued to increase, the non-serious and outlandish inquiries decreased. If an email contained any sort of acronym, it was now ignored. However, one of the emails that morning was from a man who wanted to hire me as a "surprise" for his girlfriend the following week for their anniversary. Another, from a woman who wanted to play out her female fantasy in her home while her husband was away on business.

I forwarded them to spam and continued my walk, appalled and unnerved by those last two inquiries. Do people have no decency?—As if I were a pillar of righteousness.

A mile or so later, I was stepping onto the boardwalk when I was reminded of Anthony from back in college and that peanut covered bar floor in New York. I tried to never think about him or that time in my life. And when I did, it only acted as a reminder of how ignorant and naive I once was and would never be again. Anthony could not have paid me more than ten grand in the year or so we had seen each other. A dollar amount I now made in less than a week. It sickened me to think about all the pain he put me through. All for next to nothing.

I focused on my audiobook to take my mind away from him. The atrium-style ceilings and white walls of that Ritz-Carlton restaurant soon flashed before my mind's eye. The scorpion bowl at the Irish bar, the blisters from my wedges. I tossed back the rest of my latte before slamming the cup down into the closest trash can and rewinding my audiobook to playback what I missed.

That's when it hit me.

He hired her. Anthony had hired the girl at the hotel bar with the braces and those stupid Old Navy flip flops. After a decade, a mystery I did not know needed solving, now had been solved.

Everything suddenly made so much sense. Booking the suite, the three glasses with the brut already on ice, all the shots, the racing back to the hotel bar, letting that girl stay in our suite, etcetera.

I leaned over the boardwalk railing thinking I might be sick as a dizzying disorientation spread over me. The rotting and musty smell of the algae that sat atop the lake's surface overwhelmed my senses. I was seeking truth, and little by little, it was being revealed to me. I wondered if it was too late to rescind that request.

Chapter 25

THE PARABLE OF THE BEE

2021

It was in the gym with my trainer, Sean, where I started to notice the shift and renewal of my mind. Where building physical endurance rippled over into other areas of my life. After a year or so of workouts with Sean, my f-bombs were close to non-existent. Working out was once a chore but now something I celebrated as being able to do.

In college, my thoughts were consumed with failure, with inadequacy, with death. My focus was on surviving the next drill, sprint, or time with Anthony. Now I fought to supersede the negative and disparaging thoughts of my younger self. Here, my mind told me: *"I'm strong. I can."* Over and over again.

If I had convinced myself to fall in love with other types of pain, I didn't see why I couldn't fall in love with the pain that would strengthen my willpower and sculpt my body, all with the ultimate goal of allowing me to charge more for it as a result.

That gym and my church inside that cinema had become two separate sanctuaries where I embraced staying mindful and within my body—a body I used to hate and try to detach from that I was now slowly growing to like. Tuesday and Thursday mornings with Sean had gone from the time I dreaded to the highlight of my week. Outside of Sundays, he was really the only person I had an ongoing professional, yet comfortable, relationship with.

He was always saying cute things to me like, "Three more sets," after already having done three, "Lets go ahead and add another plate" or "How about a 1,000 meter row for time as a cool down?"

At the same time and what felt like for the first time, I had someone rooting for me, fighting for me, challenging me, and teaching me. It was in that gym with Sean that I began to get my fight back.

"Do you seriously think I am capable of that!?"

"What makes you think I can do that?!"

"There is no way I can lift that!"

Were lines often tossed in Sean's direction.

Sean always answered with a positive and cheeky remark along the lines of,

"Well, I sort of do this for a living!" "I have done this once or twice," and "I happen to be aware that you are stronger than you think!"

It was the relationship that reshaped my belief I had attached to all men—that they were the worst. That they were all the same.

Sean, aside from making me do all the heavy lifting, was one of the most respectful men I had ever met. I felt blessed that God had put such great people in my life since being in Austin, and I couldn't for the life of me understand why.

The Parable of the Bee

One morning, during my last set of squats, the barbell was resting on the base of my neck as usual, but this time stress took hold of me, as I feared my back might buckle from the weight and my own fatigue. It was a second before it did that Sean lifted the barbell up, off and away from my shoulders.

"Were you waiting for it to crush me?!" I asked.

"A little struggle is good," he began. "But I was right here, standing by and ready to take it from you before anything happened."

God spoke to me a lot through Sean. I learned bits and pieces of God's character from spending time with him in that gym. The lines stuck with me throughout the day and slowly reshaped the notion that God was not against me.

In addition to my workouts with Sean, I had a boxing coach, Alex, who I trained with once a week. I fell in love with boxing because for thirty seconds, I threw every unidentifiable pent-up emotion into the bag. I would stay in my body and continue to catch and release the defeating thoughts that told me I was weak, that I was worthless. That I would always be unremarkable and unimpressive.

"No mercy!" Alex would shout, as I threw punches.

"Never quit! Never surrender! I'm going to turn you into a fighter!"

The clock would beep, indicating it was time for me to run a set of stairs. As I took off, Alex, in his deep and burly voice, would say, "I'm proud of you!"

Four-ish words that I allowed to nestle themselves within my inner ear. That I played over and over as I ran up and down those concrete steps or jumped rope, as I imagined one day my Father in Heaven might say the same words to me. I imagined that one day, I could look in the mirror and say them whole, even half-heartedly to myself.

John had invited me to travel with him to Atlanta for work. I had been to Atlanta before on "business," so he asked where I wanted to stay, initially suggesting the Ritz-Carlton.

"Yuck! I hate the Ritz-Carlton," I replied.

He asked me why.

"I just have never really liked them," I replied. I suggested two other hotels as a replacement. Then I was honest with myself as to why, for as long as I could remember, I had a distaste for the brand. Again, I flashed back to Anthony and the girl with the Old Navy flip-flops, and waiting in the hotel lobby in my drunk and disheveled state for him to come and get me. I put away the memory and called John back.

"I changed my mind. Let's do the Ritz."

Anthony was not going to have any power over me. He was not going to ruin a nice hotel experience for me, just like I wasn't going to let the memory of William ruin any type of dessert for me. So started the long list of self-imposed exposure therapies, which first began with eating cheesecake at the Ritz-Carlton.

It was the perfect day in Atlanta. I was sitting outside with John at a midtown Parisian cafe as the town's grounds crew planted fresh flowers in dark soil up and down Peachtree Avenue. Plates of Benedicts, and pastries and trays of cappuccinos passed by, and the atmosphere around us was light, and nothing seemed to be in excess. A rare moment where I was not worried or concerned about money, my weight, or my future. That moment was perfect.

Then John had to go and ask me about my family. What they thought I did for a living, how often I talked to them.

"They just have never known me," I said. "The version they have of me in their heads is far better than the truth or how they would perceive my reality."

The Parable of the Bee

They wouldn't see all this job had done for me. They would see a girl who was kicked off her college team, arrested for a DUI, and even with a master's degree had chosen a career mixing poisons, remaining single, and selling her body.

As my aunt would say, "You can put lipstick on a pig, and it's still a pig."

I could still hear my dad's voice tossing the line, "Why buy the cow when you can get the milk for free?" in my direction. A phrase I never really understood until I started escorting.

I was then reminded of an afternoon in my parent's basement when I was six or so. My mother had gathered my siblings and me at the foot of the stairs, instructing us to run up the stairs and greet our dad with hugs and shower him with "I love yous" when he arrived home from work, that if we didn't, he was going to leave us.

My mom's request that day seemed like the perfect opportunity to test out my acting skills. A scene from *Full House* pranced through my mind that I would try to emulate. The side door of our house hinged open, and my mom ushered us up the stairs. My siblings' and my arms wrapped around our dad like in the movies. Only his face revealed an expression of frustration and annoyance. It was the day I realized the concept of family was a farce. That everything in this world was just acting.

The height of summer was quickly approaching, and with it the June rains of Texas began to subside. Late one morning at my apartment, I slid open the sliding glass doors to fill the room with crosswinds. Worship music played in the background as I threw frozen fruit, protein powder, and almond milk into my Nutribullet as I admired the three floral arrangements I had placed around the room. They usually came with notes that read "You're amazing," "I love the space we share together," and "Just because it's

Tuesday and you're still stunning." I couldn't believe it took me that long to discover escorting, to finally capitalize on who I was.

I showered and returned to the living room to find two bees hanging out on the wrong side of the window. I was not in the habit of leaving my patio doors open, but rarely, if ever, did anything crawl or fly in. I grabbed my Swiffer from the closet in an attempt to corral the two bees onto it so I could usher them toward the open door and back outside.

The first bee climbed onto the Swiffer rather quickly, and I promptly heaved him out the open patio door. The second bee, however, was testing my patience. In all my attempts, he continued to move further in the opposite direction and away from the open door.

In frustration, I shouted at the bee, saying, "Don't you see that I am trying to help you? I know it's scary and it doesn't make sense, but I see the bigger picture! I am trying to save you!"

That's when I heard God so clearly say, *"How do you think I feel?"*

Following a women's leadership meeting for my church out in Dripping Springs one weekday night, I hopped back into my Jeep and made my way home. Twenty minutes into the ride, out of nowhere I grew a hankering for ice cream. I dismissed the thought and found it weird. I wasn't really an 'ice cream' person.

That's when I saw a Sonic about 200 yards up on the right. Lately, I had been allowing myself to indulge in my cravings while practicing intuitive eating. I had found that if I did not deny myself certain foods, it prevented me from binging and ultimately purging later on. I pulled into one of the mini carports and ordered an ice cream concoction with Oreos and cookie dough. I took a few bites before merging back onto the main road.

A few miles up I saw smoke and a car parked horizontally in the middle of the road. A man outside of it was waving his hands in the air. Shouting at me to turn around. That's when I saw the cause of the smoke shortly ahead in the distance: a car that was completely flipped over and smoking. I couldn't help but feel that the car was meant to be mine.

I looked at the cup of ice cream in my center cup holder and decided that maybe I could begin to trust my gut instincts. That, maybe, the Holy Spirit had been revealing more to me than I was fully aware of.

I continued to live my double life, and on occasion, Renée would meet me at church. We would pray that we both had fruitful weeks and generous clients. We would pray for her son and for us both to stay safe in our work. Over time, those prayers evolved. We prayed for opportunities to move beyond sex work and break free from our dependence on alcohol. It was an evolving friendship, and I saw God's hand on my friend. I saw God using us to help one another, to collectively make our way back to Him.

Chapter 26

UNDER THE FIG TREE

2021

J had made a reservation at a chic, contemporary Mexican restaurant downtown where I had plans to meet "The Trinity" for dinner. That is the term John coined up when he was referring to Alison, Connie, and Marcy as a collective. When I told the three of them this, they all argued over who could be the Holy Spirit. Apparently, He was the coolest.

I arrived early so I could have a cocktail, settle in, and catch up on unanswered emails before logging off for the night. Two of the three members of *the Trinity* didn't drink, so I typically had one or two before or after our dinners. The fact that they didn't drink didn't bother me; I just had to be more strategic about my drinking—which actually made it all the more fun.

The Trinity arrived, and we were seated in the dining room, and like always, our meals lasted just shy of four hours. The noise around us blotted out, as if we had been seated in our own private dining room that just happened to be in the middle of the restaurant. At that table, I dined with three leaders of my church, all of whom still wanted to eat with me knowing how I paid for my outfit and how I was going to pay for dinner. I was in disbelief how much I got along with them, enjoyed spending time with them, and had things in common with each of them.

These women did not look at me and see my sin. They each spoke from experience, motivating me to lean into Jesus while offering encouragement and sharing personal stories, as well as stories from the Bible. They were each so much more interested in having me develop a personal relationship with Jesus than pushing to get me away from my sins and spur me to make a drastic lifestyle change. They trusted that God's timing was perfect, that His love is unconditional, and that we all have sin in our life. All of it was so new, yet so overwhelmingly beautiful. It was the point of my career that I was in love with everything, that life seemed perfect. That I was under the impression I could exist in both worlds without shame.

Marcy and I were bookworms and were always exchanging titles with one another for our next read. We shared common interests in things like memoirs, self-development, business, biography, leadership, spirituality, and anything that made reference to the Holy Spirit.

God told me to give you this book, Marcy texted me one afternoon. She sent me a screenshot of the cover of a book titled *Open Blind Eyes,* by Rachel Timothy, and said she would bring me a copy to church on Sunday. Instead, I just added it to my Amazon cart, and I cracked it open a couple of days later when it arrived.

Open Blind Eyes is a memoir of a woman who grew up in a small town in Illinois, only a few towns away from where Marcy had grown up. The author discusses her upbringing and how, at the age of nine, she began being trafficked.

I must have read that book straight for two hours. Right up until it was time to shower and get ready for my date that evening. The next afternoon, I took the day to relax around my apartment and do absolutely nothing. My money from the week was lobbed into one giant pile on my coffee table. I would glance over at it every so often to remind myself I was someone now.

It was also in this season that I began to ask God the hard questions and to pray for the answers to them. Questions like: Why had I hated myself my entire life? Why, for as far back as I can remember, I always thought I was fat?

That second afternoon of reading, I decided to stir myself a gin martini and read some more. About ten minutes into reading, a slight nausea came over me. I removed the martini from the scene and swapped it out for a glass of water before returning to both the book and my couch.

The story itself details the moments that led to the author's trafficking, by her teacher and coach, well into her young-adult years. I continued reading before feeling a churning in my stomach, which led me to throw the book to the floor and rip the blanket off me that I had been swaddled under. I ran to the bathroom, holding my hair back as I lost my martini and a now-deconstructed green olive in the base of the toilet. I hadn't eaten anything weird that day, so I chalked it up to be the painful reality of the book. Tears streamed down my face periodically throughout reading it as I mourned for the little girl and the abuse she suffered.

I had planned myself a quick three-day vacation in Maine the following week where I intended to do nothing but read, write, spend time with Jesus, relax on the beach and eat oysters and clam chowder—and not necessarily in that order.

I decided to take a mental break from the book and start packing. I pulled a few bathing suits, pairs of running shorts, and a couple of sweaters for the chilly coastal nights from my closet. That's when certain memories of Vinny and Nico came to mind. I've expressed how I wanted nothing to do with the girl I was in those days—a girl I no longer identified nor associated myself with. Still, those cars covered in tarp and that nightclub garage came forth, as did chatting with Officer Bennet at the front of the club.

I brushed off packing and went to answer some emails and schedule some bookings for when I was back from Maine. My phone made the sound of coins being showered into a piggy bank and then a ding to indicate I had just received two deposits for future dates. Two dates I would now mark in my calendar. I later returned to the book and my couch. Again, I was hit by an onset of what felt like seasickness. A few minutes later, I had returned to the bathroom and was holding back my hair in an attempt to prevent it from falling into the toilet. I flushed the contents of my stomach, but then continued to stare into the pooled water that rested at the base of the bowl, as if it held answers.

I did not understand why these memories were resurfacing after nearly a decade of not thinking about them. But I was still nauseous and did not have the mental stamina to keep pushing thoughts of the brothers and that nightclub to the wayside. Another series of memories then gently knocked at the forefront of my mind. I sat down on the bathroom floor and leaned back against the wall.

It was as though God just engaged me in casual conversation or a tender interview. Like gingerly leading a horse to water.

What was your relationship with Vinny and Nico?

Well, I dated Vinny, and then Nico was his brother. We were all friends.

Where did he take you out on dates? What restaurants?

I thought about it. I guess we never actually went on traditional "dates." But we did spend a lot of time together.

Where?

We really only ever spent time together at my place, the club, or driving from one to the other.

Anywhere else?

I thought of the club's garage. I remembered him in my room at the townhouse and—oh! That night we all went out for breakfast with the staff.

Who was there?

The staff. They shut down the bar early, and the bouncers and bartenders all met us there, the brothers, me and Officer Bennet.

Then what?

Then what? Then nothing. Everyone showed up, and we ate breakfast.

I raised myself up from the bathroom floor, splashed water on my face, and gargled some mouthwash. I threw up enough to know that brushing your teeth immediately after vomiting could ruin your enamel. So, I'd have to wait a few.

I collapsed on my couch and stared up at the ceiling.

What happened after you left the booth?

I didn't want to think about this. I listened to the rain outside, smacking itself against my patio furniture and the cement ledge. It reminded me of the drive home that night all those years ago. I recalled the shouts and the cries and how they felt in the back of my throat when I threw them as I tried to catch my breath at the same time.

What happened before that?

Nothing. We were in the booth, and then I went to the bathroom and washed my hands. Then we left, and I was shouting random dramatic things.

Like what?

I placed myself back in that front seat of Vinny's car. "Why would you let him do that to me? I thought you cared about me!"

Then I was back in that bathroom, pulling the brown paper towels from the dispenser on the wall before Officer Bennet walked in. "Excuse me, Officer," I said in a sweet and sarcastic voice, "The men's room is across the hall."

I threw out the paper towel and reached for the door handle. Only my hand didn't make it there. Officer Bennet caught me by the wrist before I ever did … and then we probably just hooked up.

Why was I thinking about all of this? Lacrosse, Anthony—I had locked it all up and had thrown away the key. Yet, after some thought, parts of that night didn't make much sense. Why was I crying on the drive home? Like, embarrassing, ugly cry, crying.

Then the memory was released. How it felt hitting the wall, the heat of his breath and the words he spoke into my ear.

In 2022, I started taking flight lessons. When I was younger, I had dreamed of being a pilot, so for about a year by direction of my flight instructor, we began taking a Cessna Skyhawk 3,500 feet up and where he began teaching me all the basics.

One of the first things I was taught was power-on and power-off stalls. A power-on stall occurs when the aircraft wing stops producing lift due to an excessive angle of attack. The decrease in lift will cause the airplane to start to sink. A power-on stall is practiced to simulate a potential stall during takeoff. It was one of two maneuvers I practiced during my flight lessons that never ceased to spur my motion sickness.

I mention this because when preparing for the plane to be thrown into a stall, you are to pull back on the yoke, while maintaining coordination with the right rudder. The right rudder counteracts the plane's tendency to twist or "yaw." One of the main objectives of this maneuver is to keep the wings level and to stay coordinated with the right rudder in order to prevent any potential spin or downward corkscrew spiral of the aircraft.

That day in my apartment, there didn't seem to be enough right rudder to prevent me from being launched into a downward spiral. After I connected all the dots and realized we all weren't just "having a good time." After I could see the truth of what happened following that night in the diner bathroom. They were trafficking me, and I had no clue.

I canceled my trip to Maine and spent the next day in bed crying off most of my eyelash extensions and staring out my window into the bright and lively city that I now called home, in complete awe of my stupidity and blindness.

Everything came flooding back: the follow-up visit from Officer Bennet that broke me, the instructions to leave a rock in the door, the pictures they would each take of me at the end, providing proof of purchase, and the two occasions they brought me back to that nightclub garage to teach me a lesson.

But mostly, I remember the jovial and gregarious person I was. The distorted perception I had in my mind that I was just somehow dating all of them. How all of it just seemed normal because of Officer Bennett's title and how much they all seemed to like me.

This entire time in Austin I thought I had been the one calling the shots. Setting my own calendar and rates and expecting a level of etiquette. Now, all of a sudden, I didn't know what was overcompensation, lies, self-deception. I also refused to acknowledge that I was a victim. Admitting I was a victim would mean I was not in control. I hated Marcy. I hated her for giving me that stupid book. I hated that it led me to the truth.

I met John the following week. We were enjoying our post-meal coffees as we often did, and he was looking at me the same way he always had—with a mix of deep love and inevitable sorrow. I usually loved the way he looked at me, but that day, I wasn't a fan.

I asked him point blank, "Have you ever thought about how many people I have slept with?"

John always had the perfect response to everything and was always and forever delicate in answering.

"No, I guess I haven't."

"You're joking. I screw people for a living, and you have never thought of my count," I snapped back.

"No. I haven't."

I wanted to hate him for not being the adult here, for not being the stronger of the two of us, and for not ending whatever it was that we were already doing. I didn't understand how I could be both people: the girl who allowed her high school teacher to give her pints of vodka and drive her to a by-the-hour motel for free and also be thinking I was an elite companion.

It had been a year since I first met John, and we had gone on countless trips together to a handful of cities. Nights were spent at intimate restaurants in a cocoon of silence as we exchanged loving looks from across the table and held hands underneath it, our free hand gripping a straggling wine glass or coffee cup on top of it for optics.

The love I had experienced had always been coupled with sex. But somehow, holding John's hand in the back of an Uber or on a flight with his sport jacket draped over our arms seemed to be the most intimate thing I had ever known. Nothing made sense.

We went back to my apartment and hid ourselves under the covers. The sun dawned, coating everything outside of the long shadows cast in the apartment in a shade of warm peach. I climbed on top of him, kissing him passionately, until he tersely asked me to stop. But I didn't. I didn't believe he meant it. He asked me a second and third time, until finally I pulled away from him shouting, "Why won't you have sex with me!?"

As I burst out into tears and locked myself in the bathroom. I saw my life as some twisted dark comedy, and I wondered, if God was in control, why He was allowing any of this to happen. Of all the single and available men I saw, it was the married Christian guy who bought me a Bible and basically packed my lunch for the first day of church that drove me up a wall.

I didn't understand how John didn't see that it was all the same. That taking me on trips and convoluting my messed-up mind any more than it already was was doing neither of us any good. How the emotional affair we were having wasn't any "less bad" since we were not being physical. I hated all the men in my life for not being adults, but I hated myself more for having allowed it all to happen.

Exiting the bathroom, I meandered to the kitchen to pull two glasses from the cabinet. I filled them both from the tap on my refrigerator and set them down on the counter.

Then I asked him, "Have I ever told you about how I used to drive to Rhode Island in college?"

Chapter 27

IN THE LIGHT WE SEE THE DUST

2021

*J*never planned to tell John about Rhode Island or what I would allow Tory to do to me in that dingy motel with the maroon patterned quilt. It just sort of spilled out of me, like all those crumpled up hundreds and business cards from his pocket had that first day we met. I had taken appointments after that day of discovery in my apartment, but after my mental breakdown with John, it only seemed appropriate to "step out in faith" like Lena and the ladies of *The Trinity* had suggested I do. So that's what I did.

Later on, John and I toasted to my retirement at a Rainey Street bar. A retirement that I had not seen coming, especially because I had just recently raised my rates to $800 an hour and had also implemented a two-hour booking minimum.

"God told me this is your retirement present," he said, as he motioned for me to open my handbag so he could drop $10,000 cash into it.

It was now nearly two years to the date since I had moved to Austin and, once again, I found myself shopping for a job in July while also waiting to hear back from the fourteen law schools I had applied to.

I lasted about three weeks without escorting before I missed the money and the attention. I scrolled through my email for a lengthier date option to make the backslide worth it, stumbling upon an overnight invitation that, at the time, I had priced at $7,500. Boom—done.

After some thought, it only made sense to book out the remainder of that week. Or what was the point in even sinning again? Then, a few of the inquiries spilled over into the following week, so it only made sense to capitalize and fill up my calendar for the month. I wanted to meet my financial goals one last time.

I was soaking up the summer sun at the pool at the W hotel when I decided to phone John.

"I'm unhireable!" I grumbled. He assured me I wasn't. Still, I had a very large gap in work history and a supremely underwhelming resumé.

I felt clean for one hour at church on Sundays while the rest of my life eventually went back to business as usual. I raised my rates to $1,000 an hour predicting I would receive less inquiries, and, as a result, would be tempted less often.

The first time I increased my hourly rate to $1,000, I was met with crickets in reference to serious inquiries. Plenty of men, however, voiced their opinion on the matter: that I was charging absurd prices, that I used to charge half that, that they planned on booking me but would now go elsewhere. What was once roughly fifty serious inquiries a week was now, all of a sudden, hovering closer to ten. At least now I knew I was not a $1,000 an hour girl.

I bumped my rate back down to $800 an hour and business was steady again. Somehow, nothing about that felt like a win.

Weeks earlier, I had proudly announced to *The Trinity* that I had walked away from my life of escorting, and just like that, I was back in it. I was ashamed and didn't want to face them at church, so I just stopped going altogether. I prayed; I had a relationship with God; I was set.

I flew to a handful of cities during this time, where I would see two to three people a day for anywhere from two to four hours. I would spend two days in a city and go back home to Austin. I was making so much money, but knowing that God saw everything I was doing made me want to isolate myself even more and place greater distance between Him and me, between me and everyone.

One evening, I was submerged in a clawfoot tub that looked out over the Chicago River. I was surrounded by a sea of bubbles and white marble and couldn't help but feel this would be a beautiful way for me to die.

I craved the presence of Jesus and, most times, felt ashamed for seeking Him out. Spending more and more time in His light brought that much more exposure and awareness to the truth behind everything I was doing in the dark. Little by little, God was removing the scales from my eyes and revealing to me ugly truths. That night, I thought of all the ways I could kill myself in that bathroom, and at one point I just started blasting *The Goodness of God* from my phone to try and counteract the thoughts of suicide.

It was then I realized that I didn't want to do this anymore, but I also had no idea how to stop. Life was easier when I didn't know the heart of God and when I was convinced I was alone. Convinced that if I continued to disobey, He would sooner or later abandon me and move onto the next hooker with a heart of gold.

I was on the brink of getting caught up and lost in this world forever. The world where I could justify that I was a small business owner, that Jesus loves prostitutes, and that there is no condemnation in Christ. I didn't know how to detach from this job, but I was also fully aware that it was slowly killing me.

I flew back to Texas and raised my rates to $1,000 an hour and made a promise to myself that I would never drop them back down. Then the impossible happened. I began getting *more* bookings than ever before. More money, more attention, more rewards.

Being an escort at that time and during that stage in my faith was like eating an entire pizza. Was it bad for me? Yes. But was I going to continue to do it when men were paying me tens of thousands of dollars? Also, yes.

Connie reminded me that, like how God had once parted the Red Sea, sometimes He will deliver us out of a situation. Other times, He will look for you to put down and walk away from whatever it is He has called you out of, so He can lead you out.

"He leaves nothing unfinished," Connie said, scrubbing a coffee pot. I was on drying duty that Sunday morning. I didn't understand the patience she had with me, how someone like me was deserving of a friend, a mentor, and a role model like her. How my own sin didn't make her want to be my friend any less. She still sought opportunities to minister to me, to listen to me, and to love me.

I used to joke with Connie, telling her that if I had met her when I was younger, I would probably be on track to be president by 35.

Connie just shook her head side to side wearing that beautiful smile of hers.

"Don't worry. He has you right where He wants you."

Chapter 28

ALEXANDER HAMILTON

2021

I used to think all men were stupid, especially the ones who shelled out $10,000 when I raised the rates of my overnight stays. I figured that these men must have the saddest, most pathetic lives to want to spend that amount of money on someone like *me*. What was even more pathetic was that I used to provide the same service unsafely and for free.

I was never sure if God was blessing me with these big paydays or the devil was tempting me, as business had never been better. Does not every good gift come from God's hand?

I began having nightmares around this time that caused me to toss and turn in the night and wrestle with God. I would wake in the night and lunge for my Bible in attempts to speak the name of Jesus, only to then find myself paralyzed and unable to release the words. I used to never drink before seeing clients, but soon it was the only way I could mute my conscience and silence the part of me that now fully agreed that what I was doing was wrong.

During the day, I played worship music and was in an ongoing conversation with God. Then when it came time to get ready for a date, I would turn on Rage Against the Machine radio and pop a bottle of champagne in an attempt to push God out of my mind. When my dates ended early enough, sometimes I would jaunt around downtown and get drunk. This would of course lead to late-night binges, purging, and reckless spending.

For about three straight months, I continued to say that the next month would be my last. That "next month" I would call it quits and finally walk away from the biz. I had saved roughly $150,000 as a nest egg, but I feared I would never see money like this again, that I would never be admired the way I was at that time by my clients.

When I finally did step away for a second attempt at retirement, I lasted, again, three weeks before an established client reached out to reserve me for a week in San Francisco. A package I had priced at $30,000, not including five-star lodging, roundtrip first class airfare, and a small travel fee. I told myself this would be one last pay day, and I would again call it quits.

Mr. San Fran planned an amazing week of dates and activities while I was in town. We strolled Mir Woods, went on drives along the coastline and out to wine country. We spent time at the spa and dined in the best restaurants the Bay Area had to offer. I had never had anyone be so intentional and go to such lengths to plan such a creative itinerary.

I once told a client that my biggest fear was to live a mediocre life. We were in his truck sipping Negronis from red solo cups and looking out onto a scenic overpass. And while God was slowly imparting upon me that I had confused mediocrity with a sincere lack of true love, I was still addicted to being desired. This job was still a bad habit, and I feared once I left it, these experiences might never come around again.

Alexander Hamilton

On the third day, Mr. San Fran picked me up from my hotel, and we drove to the bay and boarded a small sailboat with a cooler of snacks and a bottle of wine in hand. It took exactly ten minutes after we set sail for me to be folded over the side of the boat, losing my breakfast into the bay. What a time to find out I get seasick.

I wanted nothing after that excursion other than to head back to my hotel—alone. But I had been paid for a week's worth of whatever, so I convinced my date I was good to go. I could not quit this close to the finish line, especially as Mr. San Fran had expressed interest in my monthly reservation package priced at $60,000 *(plus taxes and fees of course)* for the following month, and I could not think of a better way to conclude my stint as a companion than with that payout.

The thing was, I liked Mr. San Fran. We had fun, and he was an absolute gentleman, but the idea of allowing someone access to my body was now causing me severe distress. I was no longer drinking to outrun my past; I was drinking to derail myself from forming future memories. But leaving without putting out that day was not an option. I needed to make sure Mr. San Fran was getting the most out of his $30,000 investment because next month I wanted an investment of $60,000.

On our fifth night together Mr. San Fran and I hit a couple of cocktail bars before settling into the claret velour seats of the Orpheum Theatre as a rap battle between Thomas Jefferson and Alexander Hamilton unfolded. I crunched some numbers to see if the collective hours we had spent together that week already equated to $30,000 worth of "time spent."

It didn't matter though. If I wanted to lock him into purchasing my monthly package, I needed to comply tonight. The guy was in love with me. All I needed to do was stay the course and play the part, and I was guaranteed sixty grand in a couple of weeks. *$60,000. $60,000. $60,000.*

The hotel was only a few blocks away, so we decided to walk as we discussed the highlights of the show. I found myself at a place of convergence, torn between "What's one more?" and the verse in my devotional that morning that was eating away at me: Hebrews 10:26.

"Dear friends, if we deliberately continue sinning after we have received knowledge of the truth, there is no longer any sacrifice that will cover these sins."

All I could think was that I was spitting in the face of Jesus, as I continued to plot sins against my own body and to deny the truth that had been imprinted on my heart. Jesus who had died for me. Jesus who had opened my eyes and revealed to me so much truth. Jesus who had given me not just one person to care about me, but many. Then, so clearly the question came to me like a whisper, *"Why do you feel enslaved to this man?"*

I didn't know the answer to the question, but I found myself thanking Mr. San Fran for a lovely evening, before telling him I was tired and calling it a night.

I had a dream that night that I was in Hell. I was thrown into a deep pit of bodies filled with other sinners, as those all around me, above, and beneath me, clawed, pulled, tugged, and trampled on one another so as to not sink to the bottom. The further those sunk into the pit, flesh was ripped away, and limbs were torn from them. I awoke shaking in anguish and crying in fear. My skin still felt hot to the touch, and my body felt like it had taken a beating.

All I could think of doing was text John. To ask him to pray me out of a challenging situation. I stared at the vase full of red roses and the bottle of nearly finished champagne that Mr. San Fran had welcomed me with. A year ago, I would have been over the moon to have met the man I was here with, yet as I sat at the foot of my bed, praying to God, all I could think was that

I never wanted to do this ever again. That I wanted to go home. That there was not a dollar amount high enough that could justify sharing my body or giving the other precious and intimate parts of myself, my new heart and renewed mind, to another. Not like this.

Chapter 29

LITTLE SLICE OF HEAVEN

2021

I hadn't worked in two weeks since returning home from San Francisco, but in that time, I had been having nightmares of Morocco in which I was handcuffed to a bed as drugs were injected into my arm and as men would take turns climbing on top of me. I would wake up screaming and clawing at my arm in attempts to remove a needle that had never been there in the first place.

It was another morning and another walk around Town Lake as I thought back on that trip to Morocco so many years ago. I was reminded of the handsome man I had met with the green eyes and five o'clock shadow on my last day in Marrakesh. Reminded of the lunch he had invited me to his house for and—then the dots were connected. It was all crystal clear. The girl in the bed, the two young boys with the knives in their belts coming into the room to watch me and the woman with the milky-white eye that threw the fear of something or other into me.

I should never have made it back to America. I should have been sold that day in the eye of the Kasbah. After four years, it finally occurred to me that we were never waiting for his mother to return from the market.

I wasn't sure how many memories from my past I needed God to resurface to show me that He had always been saving my life, that even when I spited Him, He was still deploying His occasional angels.

I was still trying to walk away from companionship for good, but after I received the final law school rejection letter, officially marking me as 0-14, I decided I needed a boost of self-esteem.

Roy was a neurosurgeon who usually booked me for four hours. That day, we met at an Italian restaurant before heading to our hotel. It was there that Roy opened up to me about why he had initially sought out my companionship.

"I need a break from all of the death around me," was his answer, as if speaking it made it less real. His kids were grown, but he came home each day to a wife who was chronically ill and had been bedridden for nearly a decade. As of late, he was now watching their two family dogs embark on their final days.

I'm unsure if Roy was aware that he spoke the same line each time our date came to a close and he headed for the door.

"Well, this was just a little slice of Heaven!"

I was positive, however, that this was nothing like Heaven. And in the event I was wrong, and it was, I had no interest in going.

About this time, I began giving myself ten minutes when I arrived home from dates. Ten minutes from when my heels were kicked off, my bag was set down on the side table, my clothes stripped off, and the shower started. For ten minutes, I would sit at the base of the tub and hug my knees into my chest. I would allow myself to feel all the things: alone, stranded, abandoned, dirty. I would cry out to God each time, from an ashamed, apologetic, yet still hopeful heart.

Then, I would stand, lather up my loofah and start to scrub every inch of my body clean. It was time to now compartmentalize because I was powerful. Because I was independent and a business owner. Because I was making more money than I ever dreamed of and because I was sought after and sometimes loved. Because I was the smartest girl in the world.

My plan was to be done with this life come the New Year. So, I got a jump start by closing up shop after Thanksgiving. I figured if I slipped up, I would still have time to recover. The new year rolled around, and I was still in search of a job and certain that I would not go back to bartending or escorting. Yet with each job application ending in silence or polite decline, twenty emails filled with flattery and another opportunity to make a few grand arrived in my inbox.

I watched the fireworks stream and flare over Town Lake. It was now 2022, a new year, a new apartment, and an upgraded view.

Sometime later, I sat down cross-legged at the foot of my bed and began grieving that part of my life and praying that I would last another day and not go back to escorting. I would pray to make it through the day without scheduling or taking a booking.

It was during this time the cherry tree on the side of my parent's yard began to stir in my mind, and the memory of the old man next door, which I had entirely forgotten about but always sort of remembered, resurfaced. I went back as far as I could remember in attempts to make peace with every person and memory, to break every soul tie attached to me and rid myself of these unresolved traumas.

By the time the thought of Anthony came around, I was trembling, and tears were already running down my face. The pool at the casino; the shattered glass on the bathroom tile; each time he wrapped his hands around my neck; what it felt like to drown with a wet towel over my face. I relived the stomach aches, the headaches, the hits, bruises, and bite marks that he would tell me to wear with pride and honor.

I relived the times I would wake up to things being done to my body and each time he abandoned me without money or transportation.

That night I cried thirty years' worth of tears. Thirty years of cauterized derangement.

I lasted another month before taking a date. By now my own wishy-washiness with separating from this lifestyle acted as an additional source of shame.

In 2022, when the prices of gas, cattle, and interest rates were all on the rise, I was, by all counts, working in one of the safest industries there was with respect to job security. The sex industry and the pizza industry still held true as staples in the economy. Although, living in Texas, maybe I would swap pizza for tacos.

"I got pretty excited when Natalie shot me a text back last week," Parker said. Parker was a lean man with gray eyes, golden hair, and hailed from old oil and cattle money. I exceptionally enjoyed it when Parker handed me white envelopes, as they were typically weightier than most, often including a Krugerrand or some type of gold bullion that he would use to put towards a future date.

"I think I speak on behalf of all men when I say, I am glad retirement didn't suit you." Parker raised his glass filled with Blanton's bourbon and toasted to my wits, beauty, resourcefulness, and the most flattering part— my intelligence. I raised my glass to meet his. I missed both the company and conversation that the job provided me. I was starved for connection, but at the same time wanted no one to come close.

Later that month, dinner started with sake and progressed to Toro Tartare topped with caviar, a selection of sashimi, raw oysters, and shishito peppers in Dallas with a client named Tom. He had flown me there from Austin for an overnight visit. I had already sinned meeting Parker, so I figured, what's one more? Also, it would be stupid for me to turn down ten grand.

I had been seeing Tom, a partner at a Dallas law firm, for over a year now. Given his profession, he often sought updates on my law school journey. I told him that law school wasn't in the cards right now, but that I was grateful it hadn't worked out since my career goals had shifted.

Tom had attended The University of Texas School of Law in Austin and had offered to lend a helping hand by phoning a few of his contacts to aid in the admissions process. It was a Pandora's box that I never wanted to open: clients knowing my real identity. Anyone holding that leverage over me seemed a million times more threatening than any rejection I might face in the world of law schools or above-ground America. I was a fan of clean-breaks and sharing my identity would rule that out as an option. It was a boundary. Plus, I had learned my lesson the hard way with Wayne.

Since law school was ruled out, Tom now offered to assist with the job search. I was not secretive with my clients about my desire to have a career, to move beyond this line of work, even after the whole 'law school thing' didn't pan out. About three quarters of my clients admired the ambition, and the other twenty-five percent were okay with it—as long as I still made time to see them, like I was seeking their permission to do it or something.

"That would, of course, require my eyes on your resumé," Tom said, as he ordered us another round of sake.

Tom was sincere in addition to being a helpless romantic. He viewed me as part damsel in distress, part confident businesswoman, and also as his high school crush with whom, as he tells it, he never had a fighting chance. I thanked Tom again for the generous offer to help me source a job, but again, I would have to think it over.

Back in the room, we poured a glass of the champagne we hadn't finished earlier. I had arrived at the suite at The Mansion to a large bouquet of twenty-four roses in a large vase, in addition to a large domed glass cake plate filled with white, dark, and milk chocolate-covered strawberries, a bottle of Dom Perignon on ice, and a small blue Tiffany's box.

Tom began to rub my shoulders, which was something I did not normally allow, but ten grand and our history allowed for some compromise. My eyes locked onto the now empty Tiffany's box that had earlier contained the earrings I had since put on. Just like that box, this entire experience seemed meaningless and empty. I felt so alive in the presence of Jesus and so dead in this room. Tom continued to rub my upper back, neck, and shoulders before, in an attempt to be seductive, he whispered the one word I never wanted to hear him say into my ear. "Kelsey."

Chapter 30

ASANTE SANA

Swahili for, "Thank you very much."

2022

Jcontinued to attend the downtown location of my church and steer clear of Dripping Springs. After another failed attempt at retirement, I was still too ashamed to face *the Trinity.* Connie reached out to me after some time went by asking to get together over dinner, mentioning that she hadn't seen me at church in a while. I told her some excuse about the convenience of the downtown location and doing my best to lessen my carbon footprint, before sharing a bit of the sincere truth. I had no idea how to stop going back to "the job."

"This to me now sounds like an addiction," Connie said. Holding a packet of Sweet N' Low she was prepared to shake, rip open, and pour into her hot tea. And I knew she was right. My conviction and anxiety were now so intense that I was getting ill while getting ready for dates. I wanted to keep drinking to disassociate, which was a domino effect and the gateway for all other forms of self-sabotage.

225

I used to see my "dates" as cloaked in the luxury of nice restaurants, money, presents, and conversation, but now I saw past that veil. I saw it for what was *implied* I was supposed to do. What I didn't know was how not to place myself in those settings and environments.

I was consumed by guilt and fueled by fear—fear that God would bring my bank account down to zero and that I would have to go back to bartending. That I would become a different sort of slave to money and fall back into depression. I feared God would punish me the minute I walked away from sex work.

Connie was not looking for an excuse or rationale as to why she hadn't seen me as of late. She was not there to teach or preach or set my mind right about anything or everything under the sun. She was just happy I was still going to church. Connie is wonderful like that. She reassured me that Jesus would continue to meet me exactly where I was. If everyone could be so blessed as to have a friend like Connie.

I was praying heavily to God during this time, crying out to Him, worshiping Him, praying that He would put a job in my path so that I could walk away from the addiction I couldn't outrun: the addiction of attention and money. Since I didn't know how to turn those things away, I prayed to God and asked Him to send me men with pure hearts.

My rate was still set at $1,000 an hour, only now I had a three-hour booking minimum. That March, I did meet men with the purest of hearts. I also brought in a new record high of $71,000.

Henry was one of the men I met during that month. I loved Henry. He was brilliant and worldly, humble and driven, and guarded in a way I recognized. Henry was also a widower. Our three-hour scheduled date somehow turned into a 24-hour encounter. I had a client flying me out to Atlanta the following day and ended up canceling the trip. I was having too much fun with Henry in Austin. Our time together unraveled organically, and hours felt like minutes.

We only saw each other a few times in total, and during that time, Henry had been dating someone. The plan discussed on our third date was that he needed to end "that" before he could start "this." It was like in the movies where one of the main characters goes to cut ties with some part of their life, telling the love interest they would "be right back." Only, once they are back into their old life, the familiarity brings with it old comforts, and those plans fade into the background.

I often asked myself if things would have worked out differently with Henry if we hadn't met in the underground world in which we had, if I wasn't a professional girlfriend, and if he wasn't so heavily convinced I was just after the money. I didn't blame him. How could a man not think that everything I said or did was staged? How could he ever know for sure if my affection was genuine and my interest in him sincere?

I didn't see Henry again for nearly eight months after that third date. I was retired when we connected outside of Austin shortly thereafter. Over dinner one night, I asked Henry what the truth was, and why he said he would see me in a couple weeks and then here we were eight months later, with not much to be said in between.

His answer: "I lost the love of my life, and now I settle for what's fleeting and available."

His agony shone through the deepest parts of his eyes, and his heart was conveyed in his words.

If there ever was a time I saw all of someone and it was both heartbreaking and beautiful, it was then.

The Bible tells us to guard your heart above all else, for it determines the course of your life (Proverbs 4:23, NLT). Other versions read: "For everything you do flows from it" (NIV). And "For from it flows the spring of life" (ESV).

Henry and I were so different but so similar. We each sought a space where we could be our true selves in real time, without the fear of judgment or obligation of commitment; a space dedicated to intimacy, rooted in vulnerability and set upon the cornerstone of emotional validation. It is the artificial harmony that falsely mirrors coming into a relationship with Jesus—one that you can walk away from at any time.

The hug I shared with Henry outside of that Greenwich Village restaurant was again one of the most intimate things I had shared with anyone up until that point. At least now there was closure.

SPRING 2022

It was still that same record-breaking March when I was flown to Atlanta for that rescheduled 24-hour date, only to arrive back in Austin at baggage claim with a bottle of Nicholas Feuillatte in my bloodstream. It was at my carousel that I ran into no one other than the good-looking guy who lived in my apartment building. I had met him a few months back at a neighborhood bar where he had been drinking with a few other people. His name was Logan, and his flight from Raleigh had been assigned to my same carousel.

We chatted for a few minutes before parting ways, and he made his way over to a girl texting against the far wall. They picked up their bags and walked out the terminal together. I assumed it was his girlfriend and that he had just kept her waiting so we could talk. I thought I must have *Professional Whore* written across my forehead or somewhere on my luggage tag.

After about eight months of silence following my fight with Lena in Austin, we were speaking again. Remember? The one where she said God wouldn't bless me until I stopped sinning? During those eight month Lena had been over in Zanzibar spreading the Gospel. One afternoon, in Stonetown, Lena and two of her fellow missionaries found themselves in a parking lot where, as Lena tells it, God told her to buy one of the women prostituting themselves for the evening.

"Kelsey," she said with endearment, "if we never got into that argument, I would have never known how to approach the subject with such empathy."

Lena was obedient to the instruction and approached a few of the women. A few of them laughed in her face, but there was one woman who agreed to the offer: she would get paid to learn a little bit about Jesus. Lena, the local woman, and her fellow missionaries went back to the woman's apartment where they began sharing with her the Gospel. The woman soon broke down in tears, claiming that she had been praying for rescue, for a sign, for help. That woman gave her life to Jesus right then and there. Never again did she go back to that parking lot. Never again did she sell her body.

I went to visit Lena later that spring in Zanzibar, and by the time I had, over forty women had been impacted through her ministry.

I was in awe of the bravery of these women and ashamed that I lacked it. Lena relayed that many of these women sold themselves for the equivalent of five dollars just to put food on the table for their families. Many were often victims of gang rapes, beatings, and more. And now many of these women who were curious about Jesus were starting up Bible studies and getting baptized in the Indian Ocean.

Dragging my suitcase through the muddied airport parking lot of Stonetown, I waited patiently for Lena to arrive. That's when a blonde dressed in a pink and decorative kanzu and dangling wooden earrings emerged from a large white taxi van.

"Jombo!" Lena said, making her way toward me wearing the most sincere of smiles and embracing me in one of her famous hugs.

She was still rocking a pair of large black sunglasses that I presumed would forever be her trademark.

"Karibu, my friend!" she said with her arms wrapped around me. (Which means "welcome" in Swahili.)

In the weeks leading up to my arrival, there was a one hundred percent chance of torrential downpours and thunderstorms for two straight weeks. My first morning in Zanzibar, however, we awoke to clear skies and enjoyed four days of uninterrupted sunshine together. Only God.

Strolling down the beach one afternoon, we stopped in a restaurant and ordered a couple of shredded coconut and mandarin salads. We ate them outside on a picnic table with our feet immersed in the sand. A local girl, maybe twenty, sat with a man fifty years her senior to my right, and on my left, a drugged-out man smoking a cigar tossed back shots of whisky. He had each arm wrapped around the shoulders of two young local boys that couldn't have been older than eight. He was shirtless and puffed circles of cigar smoke into the ocean air as the two boys looked to him for permission to eat from the small plate of french fries set before them. I thought I was going to be sick.

"It is just so common," Lena began. "I have to accept that I cannot save them all."

It was our last day together before I flew back to Austin, and we spent that time poolside, past the veranda of the Park Hyatt as we were served tropical mocktails with flavors like passionfruit, mango, and lime, and noshed on guacamole. We looked out past the infinity pool and onto the pale turquoise waters of the Dhow Harbor that broke out into the ultramarine waters of the Indian Ocean. We talked about Jesus and the journey that was us arriving at that moment surrounded by the historic Zanzibari whitewashed walls and coral rooftops and brought together under the coastal East African sun.

If someone would have told me five years ago that Lena would one day be a missionary in Africa, with the sole mission of bringing addicts and prostitutes to Jesus, I would have laughed in their face. However, if someone had told me that one day I would be an escort in Texas ... Meh—I'd say it wasn't terribly farfetched.

Down at the other end of the pool, two heavier-set British men were kicked back in lounge chairs next to a local woman in her early thirties. The woman's daughter, who I would have guessed was about ten, splashed around in the pool, shouting for her mother's attention.

We prayed for the woman and especially for her daughter. We prayed that she was and would be removed from it all and that no hurt would come to her. One of the men yelled at her incessantly, threatening her with a spanking if she did not quiet down. The other man then snapped at the server to bring them another bucket of beer.

The young woman was silent and expressionless as she stared out onto the ocean. Occasionally directing her attention and giving a small smile to one of the men who just carried on the conversation with himself.

All I wanted to do at that moment was to shout to her from a heart of desperation, "You are amazing! You are beautiful, and I know you are smart! There are people that love you! You can do anything you want to do in life! You don't have to do this!"

It was at that moment, so quietly in my spirit, I heard God say, *"Don't you think I feel the same way about you?"*

A wave of clarity rushed over me like the warm salty waters washing up on the Zanzibari white sands. A part of God's character that I never fully understood had been revealed. God didn't want to punish me anymore than I wanted to punish the girl at the other end of the pool. I was overwhelmed with compassion and anxiety-induced jealousy for the girl. I finally understood what is meant by "God is jealous for us."

I couldn't understand why it was so easy for me to see this woman in front of me as pure and blameless, yet I still deep down held the belief I was filthy and unqualified to receive forgiveness.

After that trip and witnessing the heartbreaking prostitution, I knew this time it would stick. When I returned to Austin I would be done with companionship. I would stand firm in faith.

Chapter 31

UNSUSTAINABLE DIET

2022

"Does your appearance and upbringing affect the way you trust people?" was the first thing Logan, the guy from the baggage claim, asked me once we sat down at my apartment bar.

Woah. What a thought-provoking question. My focus bounced around, like a pin-ball machine between my two identities. I asked myself how a 'normal' woman might respond before giving some generic answer and tossing the ball back in his court.

Logan spoke directly about his relationship with his mother and how he never felt good enough. He spoke of his last long-term relationship he was in and how that surmounted to engagement and ended the year before. I was blown away by his sincerity and was touched by his vulnerability.

The following day, we worked out together at Zilker park and grabbed sushi after sunset. There was a warmth about him and a pain behind his eyes that disarmed me, while at the same time left me intrigued.

I had taken a few more substantial paying dates when I had returned from Zanzibar, but after only a few hangouts with Logan, I had decided it was, yet again, time to leave the business. Only this time for good. I refused to allow the truth of my past to create lies in my future. It was either escort and forever single or the possibility of something else if I let it go.

That Friday afternoon, Logan asked if I wanted to head to his lake house for the weekend. I immediately canceled my Friday night "date," returned the guy's deposit, and quickly threw a bag together for the weekend.

All the things that had always been off-limits when I was escorting I was now open to. We would lay on the couch together and watch movies, and he would call me by my real name.

We worked out together in the mornings, spent the evenings cooking fish on the grill and watching standup. I couldn't remember the last time I did all this. I couldn't remember the last time I was in a remote place with a person and didn't feel trapped, the last time I wasn't concerned about when I was allowed to leave or how many more hours I had to stick around.

We arrived back in Austin Sunday afternoon, and that week I returned roughly $8,000 in deposits for future dates. It had been nearly a year since the first time I had tried to walk away, and I had lost track of how many times I had attempted.

Logan and I started spending more time together. The conversation always drifted wayward when he would ask me, "So what is it you do again?"

I always had a vague and uninteresting answer before changing the subject. I was insecure about my past, but I was also not completely comfortable sharing my faith with others either. The first time I invited Logan to church with me he politely declined, but the second time he replied with, "I have plans tomorrow. But I think it's cute you're in a cult!"

I assured him I wasn't in a cult and even explained how three years earlier I felt the same way toward Lena and the way she spoke of her church. I understood where he was coming from, so it wasn't a dealbreaker for me.

I had planned my mother a surprise birthday party in Connecticut, so I flew back for a couple of days. I hadn't prepared a speech, and being a family of very few words, I took the initiative, corralled a few thoughts, and took hold of the mic. I thought about what little I knew about my mother and how, by my age, she already had three kids, a husband, and a full-time job. I remembered the first time I saw her cry was in 1997, over the death of Princess Diana, who was a main source of hope and inspiration for my mother.

I was also reminded of winter and the late mornings and early afternoons when she would shovel snow off a section of the high school track as I performed plyometrics and warmed up in the cleared parking lot. She would be holding a stopwatch and jogging in place as she timed me on my sprints, pushed me, and encouraged and challenged me.

I raised a glass to my mother that day for all she had done, for her selflessness, and for always pushing me because she wanted to provide a life for me and my siblings that she never had access to. Also, for giving so much of herself to everyone all the time. During the party, a couple of our former neighbors told me about how when my sister and I were born, my mother would strap one baby on her back and another on her front as she mowed the lawn.

"Your mom had things to do, and she was not going to let anyone stop her!" And it was true.

I usually stayed at a hotel when I went back to visit, but that trip I decided to stay at their house. The next morning I grabbed some coffee and joined my parents in the kitchen, where my mom scrolled through her phone and my dad read the paper. I lived almost 2,000 miles away, and they hadn't seen me in over a year, but that kitchen table was still silent. After all this time I was still invisible. I left my first-class tags on my luggage and toted around expensive jewelry and handbags in hopes that they would notice, and it would spark a conversation. But just like the holes in all the clothes I used to shoplift, it went either unnoticed or unacknowledged.

I boarded my plane back to Austin with no plans of ever returning to Connecticut. I left and came back fitter, smarter, stronger, and better. I had invested so much in myself, but there I continued to be reminded I held no value.

A few nights later, I met Logan at a dive bar by our apartment. He ordered a chicken sandwich, and it came up in conversation that I was a pescatarian. Logan ordered another round and then made a comment that my protein levels were not where they should be. No one cares about your protein intake until you tell them you don't eat meat, and then all of a sudden, your health is in jeopardy.

Logan, along with the man next to him, began ragging on the deficiencies in my "unsustainable" diet. I grew quiet and poked at the lime in my glass with my tiny bar straw. That feeling took hold of me—the one that made me shut down and retreat back into my shell, out of the light and harm's way, relinquishing any and all desire to stand up for myself. I was thrown back into submission, subservience, and mindless obedience.

That's when Logan reached for my hand under the bar and looked at me with affectionate eyes.

"What else do you want me to teach you about?" he asked with a smile.

He held onto my hand before moving it to just above my knee. I didn't understand why all of it felt so familiar.

"I'm going to head back. I'm not feeling great," I said, standing, before scooting back in my bar chair. A look of extreme offense came over Logan's face.

"What's your problem? Why are you being so sensitive?"

Was I just being too sensitive? I wasn't sure but apologized and headed back to my apartment anyway. I wanted to be alone. I didn't understand why all of this struck a raw nerve within me, but for the next few days, memories of Anthony began to resurface. So I did my best to drink him away.

Chapter 32

THE BATTLE OF THE WITS

2022

Logan forgave me when I asked for forgiveness. I wasn't sure how I had done anything wrong, but I figured I had probably been overly sensitive to the topic of meat and macros at the bar.

A few blocks from my apartment was the downtown branch of my church, where I had been attending for the past few months. Walking to church and back I would pass a steakhouse and recall all the times I had dined there with clients. Now, I was heavily considering walking in to ask for an application. When I eventually did, I was told they were not hiring. The bold and confident part of me came out then. Attributions I still associated with "Natalie." I asked the manager for ten minutes of his time to get him to change his mind. Two weeks later, I showed up for my first day of training.

At first, Logan found it odd that when we had met, I was an entrepreneur and business owner, and now, two months later, I was working part-time at a restaurant downtown. He and I both. I relayed how my business was heading in a direction that no longer aligned with my current values, that it was time to step away from it, and that bartending was just something to do in the interim while I figured out my next move.

I spent two or three nights a week dropping bleu cheese olives into dirty martinis and messing up steak orders. I was living off my savings during this time and determined to work only a few shifts a week for passive income. I didn't want to compromise the habits I had now been refining for years. This night owl had since moved away from the dark side and had become an early bird.

After two years, however, my bartending skills had become a bit rusty. I wasn't as quick or sharp and speedy as I once was. I quickly realized that the "in the weeds" feeling of dinner rushes undermined most of what I had been practicing, in reference to prayer, meditation, and mindfulness—all the strategies that had allowed me to achieve some level of safety within my own body.

But I needed a paycheck, so I clocked in, did my best, had a great attitude, and hoped to make some money. As time went on, however, working there only grew more challenging.

Seeing women in cocktail dresses dining in with their dates, watching the servers pop open bottles of champagne tableside left me discouraged and defeated. I hated myself for having been "out there," and now I was back where I started. Now, instead of seafood towers and bubbly, I was wiping down the liquor bottles and mopping the bar floors at closing time. How far I had fallen.

It was around this time I began seeing a therapist. I desperately needed someone to help me navigate this world that I had yet to figure out. I also think I just missed talking and spending time in intimate settings with men.

I sat down on Chase's worn navy sofa and began talking about my least favorite subject: me. For nearly three years of my life, I was a professional girlfriend, and now, here I sat seeking advice on how to date. I needed to better understand what was and was not appropriate when functioning in normal society.

For instance, Logan needed continued reassurance that I was not seeing anyone else. Oftentimes, he would accuse me of it without reason, and I wasn't entirely sure if this was normal.

"Well, the fact of the matter is that he does not want you to know he is hanging out with other women," Chase said.

I just couldn't accept that. It was his initial honesty that led me to like him. He told me he was not seeing anyone else, and I said the same. Doesn't that mean we are dating? I wasn't sure how any of this worked.

I reconnected with Marcy, who was taking on a new business venture. We had met to discuss the vision she had of building a retreat center on her ranch in town. She showed me the blueprints and renderings and the next steps she was taking in the project. I wasn't sure how I could help, but if I could, I wanted to.

Logan and I had plans to grab dinner sometime after that. He asked me to meet him in the parking garage instead of at the front of the building to get in his car. It didn't seem like a big deal at the time, so I was happy to accommodate.

At the restaurant, I brought up Marcy's project, the vision, and the steps she had already taken to get it underway.

"That sounds doomed to fail," he said, taking another gulp from his wine glass before flagging the server over to order another.

"Have you ever written a business plan? Has Darcy ever built anything?" The way he asked the question made it seem like he wasn't looking for an answer.

"Her name is Marcy, and yes, she has actually built a very successful company," I answered.

"And you? What have you built?"

I grew quiet. I wasn't proud of the thing I had built.

"Let's just not talk business anymore," he said with food in his mouth. I hadn't felt paralyzed inside my body in so long. It was now growing familiar again. I shut down.

"I will always challenge you, Kelsey." His voice was demeaning, only a bit softer now. The tone of an apology without ever actually giving one.

"You're not eating? My ex used to do the same thing for attention. I'm not buying it."

I couldn't believe this was the same person I had spent weekends with at his lake house—the man I had shut down my business operations for. I was silent and just stared at my plate.

He later paid the bill and asked me if I was ready to go.

"I think I am just going to Uber home," I said quietly.

Scoffing, he responded, "Un-fuc*ing believable," before pushing out his chair and walking out the door.

It had been three months since I had closed shop, and I had never felt less desired. Logan barely texted me anymore, and when I did see him, it was when he would knock on my door past 10 p.m., in search of conversation and the white wine I always kept stocked in my refrigerator. I sat at my kitchen counter in black dress pants, feeling unremarkable, unaccomplished, and average. I perused pictures of me from former photoshoots and felt like I was mourning an ex as I counted down the minutes until I needed to leave for my bar shift.

Then I cracked. I made my website public again, opened my email, and sifted through them for the next couple of days, returning responses here and there. I threw myself into one task or another to delay the heavy onset of conviction I already felt ruminating inside of me, as though I had taken the lid off the cookie jar without actually having reached inside and pulled one out.

Then, it happened. A test? A sign? A sick joke? I received an email from a man named Ethan who had expressed interest in my *Monthly Exclusivity* package. The same package I had deterred Mr. San Fran from purchasing. One that was still priced at a healthy rate of $60,000.

You've got to be joking. Someone finally bites at this package while I am doing everything in my power to maintain some sort of moral and spiritual integrity.

I recognized Ethan's full name and picture, which was odd. I had met him at a film festival the previous fall, where I had been "working" as a filmmaker's plus-one. I was curious if the filmmaker had passed along my business card or if this was just by chance.

Certainly, this was a blessing from God. He is omnipotent, and in knowing I would eventually backslide again, maybe this was his way of making it worth my while.

Or maybe this is a test of my faith. To dangle an absurdly and obnoxiously large carrot in front of my face to see if I buckle.

I was suddenly Westley and Vizzini from *The Princess Bride*, going back and forth between poisoned wine goblets in the Battle of the Wits.

I decided it would be irrational not to at least entertain the offer. After all, he seemed nice when I met him. I emailed Ethan back and shortly thereafter received the deposit for a three-hour date next week to discuss my *Monthly Exclusivity* package.

It was the day before my scheduled date with Ethan, and I was a hot mess. I made up an excuse that I was sick or needed to travel at the last minute, and I returned his deposit without any discussion of rescheduling.

It was a different sort of self-harm I was practicing this go-around, like just rubbing a little cocaine on your gums so you don't snort a whole line.

I started going out with my co-workers from the steakhouse after our shift and winding up at underground cocktail bars until two in the morning. I filled that space of secrecy that "the job" once held for me, with drugs, alcohol, binge eating and bulimia, all in attempts to feel something physical to counteract my own despair.

Ethan continued to inquire, and I eventually did respond back. I informed him that since we had met at the film festival I had retired. That I was stepping away from the industry to pursue other career opportunities. Failing to mention, of course, that I was still waiting for *said* opportunities.

He was understanding and continued to be a gentleman. His heart came through in his words and not in a sappy or meek sort of way. Quite the opposite. There was strength and confidence but also an evident humility behind his written words. That being said, I could tell he was the type of man who typically gets what he wants.

He asked if meeting for lunch, and only lunch, was an option.

I agreed to give our date a second try. And then for a second time I ended up canceling and sending back his deposit. A week or so later I came around again. We rescheduled for a third time, and for a third time I canceled and sent back the deposit. I was not opening this door again that I had so aggressively fought to slam shut. Also, I needed to stop emailing him back mid-martini.

Chapter 33

2022

After a year and a half of attending church and three months of not working, I finally felt clean enough to be baptized. The late summer winds tousled the tops of the Black Oak trees that lined the new church property, and the sky was the perfect replica of watermelon as I was lowered into the waters of a small standalone pool. Connie, Marcy, and Alison were in attendance and standing close, taking photos and videos, and wrapped me in a towel once I stepped out. This was it. I officially felt clean.

I was still bartending and during the day getting together with Marcy to try and workshop and network for the retreat center. My church was hosting a mission trip to Costa Rica, and while my bank account was not encouraging me to go and *Eat, Pray, Love* off to Central America, I felt somewhat led to go.

I arrived with no expectations but with the sole goal of serving and saying "yes" to what was asked of me. The trip itself was a challenge for me on many

245

levels. I spent most of my days alone, and now I was in a group setting and bunking with three other women for the next week. I would skip lunch to wander down to the beach alone to recuperate. I felt the safest in silence and solitude, and it meant I didn't have to rise to anyone's occasion but my own.

We spent the week working with the local kids at the mission's head-quarters and delivering meals for families with an exceptional need in the community. We walked into homes made of mud floors and slab roofs whose owners greeted us with the most joyous and sincerest of smiles, expressing their gratitude for us blessing them with a visit and care package.

We visited the home of a woman suffering from ALS, who had not left her bed in three years. I held her hands in prayer as she looked deep into my eyes, as if no one had touched her with such intention in the longest of times. Muffled sounds escaped her barely moving lips as she attempted to speak. We left, and I broke down crying. I had spent thirty years outrunning my mind and dissociating from my body, and here this woman was stuck and imprisoned with a competent mind inside a body that failed her and left her in chronic pain.

We visited another woman who had left an abusive husband in Nicara-gua and fled to Costa Rica with her two young children. Her husband had beaten her while she was pregnant, and as a result, she lost the baby that she had been carrying for seven months. She told us she felt responsible for the loss and unworthy of love and forgiveness, that she felt cursed.

Appearing almost eclipsed under the shade of the carport, her eyes showed a lingering tiredness that I recognized too well.

The next morning, we met for worship, and I was overwhelmed with shame. I felt like a shell of a person and ended up confessing that day in that upper room to a group of twelve or so of my peers, ranging in ages from mid-twenties to late-sixties, that I was a fraud, an escort, and that I loved

Jesus so much. He had changed my life; He had revealed to me the truth and given me everything I didn't know I needed: friends, family, and community, and a heart. Each one of them met me with love and compassion. It should have been beautiful and fulfilling, but I just felt pathetic and exposed.

I didn't know what to do afterward or where to go. All I could think to do was run away. So I laced up my sneakers and went for a run on the beach. Down to the strip of sand that acted as the meeting point where the firm wet sand converged with the incoming tide. I sprinted as long and as far as I could until only one or two people were within sight, before collapsing into the sand with two throbbing Achilles as my mind marinated in regret for what I had just done.

"I don't know what I'm doing!" I cried out to God. All I wanted to do was drink and escape my past and the snapshots of men and moments that I didn't know how to forget. I envisioned the tide washing up further up onto the banks of the Nicoya Peninsula and simply sweeping me out to sea.

I returned home to Austin to the comfort of my own space and privacy, Torchy's Tacos on my doorstep, and a frozen bank account. An unusual amount of cash deposits had raised alarm bells. I hadn't talked to Logan much while I was away, but he knew when I was coming back, so he reached out, and I invited him over to my apartment for martinis. His martini wasn't dirty enough the first time around, so I got up to stir in more olive juice.

He took a judgmental sip. I waited to sit down until I received his approval.

"Better," he said.

I told him about my mission trip and my baptism a couple of weeks prior to which he responded with, "Good for you." And "I had that done when I was a baby." I couldn't seem to win with this guy.

I had played this moment between him and I repeatedly in my head. The myriad of mental movies depicted best and worst case scenarios and everything that could be found in between.

Logan worked in finance, so I decided to cater to his business side and gave him a brief overview of how my bank had essentially broken up with me.

"Kelsey, did you do something illegal?"

For a second, I genuinely entertained saying "yes" just on the grounds that it might impress him, even though the answer was "no." I was hired for my time and companionship. At no point in time was sex or any sort of physical intimacy contracted for. On the occasion when physical intimacy had taken place, it was always a decision made between two consenting adults—but that's not what I told him.

I was aware that I was not the only girl in his arsenal. It was a small town and an even smaller apartment community, and I made sure to keep everyone as an ally. As such, I was given the insider information more often than not, that there were reasons I was no longer invited to the lake house, and why he would ask me to meet him in the garage. So, I was just going to throw the pot of pasta up against the wall and see if our relationship was anywhere near al dente.

"Remember how I told you I had quite a few bad experiences growing up?" I asked. We had each shared with one another painful experiences from our past, so I tried to convey how false beliefs had shaped my bitterness toward men, that I wasn't proud of how those beliefs had escalated but that it did make for a lucrative income that was hard to walk away from; that it had stopped being part of my life once him and I started spending time together. I hoped that the last part might award me even the most miniscule form of compassion, and I told him I had made a living as an escort for the past couple of years.

The first words out of his mouth were "Like a prostitute?" His face was riddled with disgust in me.

The next words were, "Did you ever for one second consider how this would affect my health?"

It was, by all accounts, the worst case scenario I prepared myself for. My heart sank down into the pit of my stomach, through the floorboards, and down into the roots of the mountains that rested in the unexplored depths of the ocean. Silence. Stillness. Specks of dust and fibers from my wool carpet held my immediate focus, magnified by the light that pierced through the glass door of my patio, highlighting them against the black walnut wood floor.

The next handful of lines came non-stop.

"I have never slept with a prostitute! Now I have to get tested! You sold your soul to make a few bucks! What is wrong with your generation? Always wanting to get rich quick without putting in any effort! You're a liar and a cheat. If I had known you were a prostitute, I never would have gone near you!"

He stood up to leave but not before tossing back the rest of his martini.

I stayed seated as he let himself out and closed the door behind him. Not loud enough to cause a scene, but loud enough to leave an impression and to send his closing argument out with a bang.

I walked into my room, pulled back the covers, and crawled under them, laying on my side as I watched the lines of people press up against the overlook on the Congress Avenue bridge waiting for the bats to fly out into the evening sky. I wondered what it might be like to be one of them, to be normal and to perceive the bats as a unique sight to behold and not as a cauldron of hunters seeking to feed and constantly out for blood.

I ripped back my sheets and shot up out of bed. I had spent enough years of my life in depression over the words and actions of men, over my codependency toward them and the weight I placed in gaining their approval. I opened my computer and began to write. Everything.

Later, I found myself on Chase's navy blue couch as I eyed a dead plant on his desk.

"You know, Chase, that is quite depressing," I mentioned, noting the plant without leaves was mainly just a dead branch. With the amount he charged, you would think he could spare 99 cents for a mini succulent to take its place. He smirked, eyeing the plant almost endearingly.

"I am going to bring it back to life," he said with confidence.

I had little faith. It was that day in Chase's office, wearing my backwards cap and athleisure wear, that I woke up a bit more. Chase had unlocked and unshackled something inside of me when he said, "Just remember, his actions are not a reflection of your worth."

"What?" I needed him to repeat it. The sentence didn't make sense.

"His actions toward you are not a reflection of your value."

What a wild thing for him to say.

Chapter 34

HURT PUPPY

2022

I fought the temptation to go back to companionship, even with Logan out of the picture. In the days following *the night of the final martini*, Logan had asserted via text that "When the money runs out, you will go right back to it."

Back at the steakhouse, I could not have asked for a better restaurant to work at, better management, better coworkers or clientele. I just hated the person I became in the restaurant industry. Instead of making three thousand a night, I had since lost a zero on that figure. Instead of feeling confident in my dress and overall appearance, my long hair was held back, and I wore a buttoned up black vest that, even after bringing it to my tailor, still sort of made me look boxy. That was when I decided to reach back out to Ethan.

I figured there was no harm in meeting Ethan for lunch. Just lunch.

251

When I entered *my companion* mindset, life was instantly better. I missed this version of myself. I loved this version of myself. I texted Ethan upon my arrival,

Hot brunette in a navy dress.

We were seated at a table in the corner of the dining room, and I asked him if he had been to the restaurant before. It took him a few seconds too long to answer.

"I'm sorry," he said. "I think I had forgotten how beautiful you are!"

I chose to believe it was sincere. I felt it was.

Our three-hour lunch somehow turned into five, with two bottles of wine being both decanted and consumed. At one point, I turned to the wall behind me, admiring the large oversized mirror. Ethan suggested that I inquire if they would consider selling it to me. Instead, I turned to him and stated, "I'd rather have you buy it for me."

"Sure!" he said, through a caught-off-guard sort of laugh.

"Great! I'll send you the link tomorrow."

This version of me was strong and bold. I could ask this man I had barely met to purchase me a three thousand-dollar mirror, but I was never able to ask Logan to take his shoes off at my front door.

After that date, I raced home to my apartment and pulled on my black dress pants and top to match as I searched my phone for the closest scooter. Then I remembered I was hammered and was in no condition to operate a milk frother, let alone a scooter. So I called an Uber.

That night at work, I could not function. I sent out a flaming 32-ounce Tomahawk ribeye to a couple that asked for a simple 16-ounce New York Strip to share.

Back at my apartment, I thought about my afternoon with Ethan. I liked him. I would have loved to see him again, but I couldn't go back to that life.

If I went back for sixty grand, I would have gone back forever. There was no dollar amount that could satisfy me. There would never be enough.

But we did meet a second time at a dive bar to play pool and drink the worst old fashions known to man. They were so bad, somehow it made the experience that much more awesome.

"I see you were stretching the truth about your pool game!" Ethan said.

It's true, I had. I loved shooting pool. I just never really had anyone to shoot it with.

I couldn't get a good read on Ethan. On our first meeting, he barely gave me as much as a hug goodbye, and now we were shooting pool and talking. We were on the outskirts of downtown, and I thought of all the four-plus star hotels within a ten mile radius of that pool hall, figuring he would suggest extending our time together and opt to take a drive over to one of them. Except, he never did. We closed out our date with a casual hug by the dart boards and called it a day.

A few days later, he asked me if I wanted to grab lunch. He suggested a classic Austin staple located on South Congress. A place that just so happened to be located across the street from the South Congress Hotel and a block away from Hotel San Jose. I knew his play here. Overall, I did admire his intellect, and at times, I felt I had met my match when it came to playful badinage. Ethan had a way of accepting the things around him at any given time just how they were, while also always seeking ways to improve everything, to make something more efficient, more profitable, and to spark revolution.

We spent time just talking about life and sharing stories while also discussing the business operations of every place we stepped into—ways to increase revenue, drive business, and what have you.

The second round of margaritas came, and I awaited the idea and suggestion of heading over to a hotel. Still nothing. Again, he gave me a polite, almost neighborly hug goodbye. Not so much as alluding to wanting to be physical with me or biting even the tiniest of fashions to my ever-so suggestive remarks.

A week or so later, we met at a local coffee shop where we had planned to discuss the details surrounding my *Monthly Exclusivity Package*. Over tacos, the figure of $1.3 million was tossed around as a yearly sum. Retirement could wait another year.

The coffee shop he had recommended was next to a Marriott, so I figured today was the day he would pop the, quite literally, the million-dollar question. I was seated at a high-top table with Ethan when told me that I had failed to ask him an important question in all our time together.

"You're married," I said. I was already nodding my head in acceptance. I was the dumbest girl alive again.

He was right. It was the one question that I failed to ask. Mainly, in all my searches, I could not find an answer to that question. Then again, I stopped diligently searching after he had asked me if I would be comfortable joining him at public events, galas, etc. I had assumed, based on the questions, that he was not involved. Then again, in this industry, that is something you don't ask. It is an industry based on and off assumptions, and assumptions are not rooted in truth. Assumptions are what was keeping me shackled to this life.

Had I not yet learned my lesson to always ask the hard questions and to stop making assumptions? Rule number three: never make assumptions!

I had heard it all. Every instance or excuse. The men whose wives left them for their brother, best friend, or another woman. The widower, the divorcee, the man divorced two or three times over. The open marriages, the don't-ask-don't-tell policies within marriage. Just when I thought he was unique. Just when I had begun to let my guard down—this. I reacted poorly to the news. I felt more like a chump than deceived. I stood up from the table.

"Well, it was lovely meeting you, and I wish you the best. Also, don't you have something for me?"

He handed me an envelope out of his back pocket, and I walked out that coffee shop door. It was later evening I realized I had broken the number one rule. I had compromised the safe space I prided myself on creating, over wanting to maintain an aura of righteousness. I had judged him and condemned him for revealing the truth. I had put him down as a way to lift myself up. To justify me being there in the first place.

I texted Ethan and apologized for just that. He accepted my apology, and we wished each other the best.

It took about a month from the time Logan stormed out of my apartment to when he reached out with an olive branch, asking to talk. I invited him over where, ironically enough, I had just purchased an olive tree and was repotting it with a bag of soil on my kitchen island. I can't make this stuff up.

I was still unsure if I actually did anything wrong and was unsure as to why I was apologizing when he had told me I was disgusting in my own home. Nonetheless, I mindlessly lost myself in potting that plant, scooping soil and pressing it down securely as I rambled on about Jesus, some state trooper, my bitterness toward men, how my beliefs around not only sex work, but everything, had changed. I retreated to the bathroom to wash the dirt out from under my fingernails and collect myself.

I returned to the kitchen, and Logan made his way around the kitchen island and wrapped me in a tight hug.

"I didn't know you were hurting," he said. This was unexpected. He was once again the sensitive, caring, strong man that I spent the summer months with.

He went on to ask me about how I was going to afford to continue living in my lavish apartment, and soon after, I was again being scolded for lying and for "selling my soul for a few bucks."

I tried to convey that I was unaware and had a lot of misunderstandings as a result of unresolved trauma, all in hopes that he would hear me out.

That's when he yelled, "Your trauma is not my problem!"

I had no words, but my eyes did grow glossy even though my posture remained straight. He left before I could even ask him to go. My trauma was not his problem.

A few weeks later, I ran into him around the building. The conversation was cordial at first, friendly even. Then came the prying questions of what I planned to do for work, how I was going to afford to live there, and then finally the condescension.

"When your spigot runs dry—and it will—you will revert back to what you know!"

That's when I turned to leave, and he spat, "You're just a hurt puppy!"

I froze for a moment, my jaw clenched, before I continued to walk away.

"You're just a whore!" He yelled, in a twisting of the knife type of way. That's when I turned back and took a few steps closer to him. I looked directly into his eyes that had once entranced me.

"Fuc* you."

It wasn't one of my finer moments.

Chapter 35

WELCOME TO THE JUNGLE

2022

I had an established client of two years reach out during this time to suggest meeting up for "lunch" and only lunch, since he knew I was retired. I figured I had been able to do it with Ethan and others, so why not? Maybe I could be a companion who specializes exclusively in social outings void of physical intimacy.

Sam and I met at tour usual spot, and after a few margaritas, the agreement we had made about "just lunch" was soon disregarded. After a couple of drinks, under the guise of my alias, and in an environment that would slowly lead me astray from the boundary I had put into place. I ended up acting in accordance with exactly how all my last ten or so "dates" with Sam had.

Back at my apartment, I realized I had just undone four months of "sobriety" from escorting. New rule: no social dates.

Back on Chase's navy couch, we unpacked memories that I never much felt held any significance. The topic of holidays came up, and I told him I usually spend them alone, and then my birthday, which I had never celebrated.

"It's just an unlucky day," I told Chase. Eyeing the still, lifeless desk plant. "I don't understand how people expect everyone to drop what they are doing and celebrate someone."

Chase wanted to explore that thought.

"Let's see ... finding out my college boyfriend was cheating on me, catching my other boyfriend in the act of cheating, standing in a courtroom being sentenced to community service over an assault and battery charge I didn't even commit. Unable to drink a beer to celebrate twenty-first because I had practice the next day, and —."

I was reminded of those cherry red Beats headphones, the sound of that ripping duct tape, and Anthony. I had already cracked my neck two or three times that session. I had become so well-acquainted with the pain and discomfort in my neck over the years I had forgotten when or how it even began. It was only then that I was reminded as to why I could not fully turn my neck to check my blind spot on the right side of my Jeep.

I said it all with a straight face, like I was reading a recipe or giving someone directions. I had never spoken any part of that out loud, let alone the entire thing, and accepted that all of it had actually taken place.

I was mostly curious about Chase's reaction and whether I would be met with sympathy or pity. Instead, to dodge whatever bullet might come, I asked him if he knew the score of the Yankees game.

"I'm sorry that happened to you," he said.

That day made it more real than it ever had been. I always figured that being a woman just meant you were raped sometimes. And since I was a slut and a professional whore, I couldn't be mad when it happened occasionally. I thought of Brianna and the cat-calling in Morocco; my sister and those other brave women who not only stood up for themselves, but stood up on behalf of all women to let the world know we are not objects and we, as women, are not for the taking.

I had aligned myself with a false identity in college, over coming, alongside my sister, during maybe her most painful time. I turned and cowardly ran away. I chose artificial harmony, and to hide behind the more palatable masquerade that was identifying as an athlete, over seeing and hearing her when she needed to be seen and heard. I had unconsciously done to my sister what I felt my parents had done to me.

That's when Chase told me that I do not need to normalize my trauma. He was starting to make a little more sense each time.

I had quit the bar around this time. It was taking more of a toll on my mental health than anything else. I put an advertisement back up online to get back into escorting while I continued to apply to jobs around town. Hotels, administrative and clerical work—anything outside of the restaurant industry that might overlap with my background.

I had a three-hour booking scheduled for the next night, so after a morning walk, I spent most of my day inside my apartment, lethargic and depressed. At one point, I took a shot and cried out, "God, I don't want to do this! Why am I so messed up?"

I prayed from my heart at that moment, puffing up the eyes that had just been de-puffed by an ice roller. I asked God to, once more, deliver me from this sin I planned on carrying out.

I pulled up my email to check to see if my date for the evening had reached out to re-confirm. He had, going on to explain how he had overdone it at brunch while in town visiting friends and that he hoped I would forgive the inconvenience. Before I could finish reading the email, my phone went off, alerting me of a payment received.

I will be sending you the balance shortly, and I hope you will consider seeing me again in the future.

Around that time, I attended a church function where the pastor performed the humbling act of washing one of the leader's feet. While the pastor took a cloth to the man's feet, I was hit with a motion-sickness-like feeling. I had always thought this was a beautiful part in the Bible where Jesus washes the disciples' feet, yet I was feeling sick in a panicky sort of way.

It was back at my apartment that it hit me why I had been so disturbed. I was reminded of Anthony from back in college and his foot fetish. I didn't understand how that man still had such a strong hold over me after nearly a decade.

I went off the rails around that time and booked a trip to Boston where I was scheduled to collect $13,000 during my quick three-day visit. Except, I left after one day with half of that. I had forgotten how miserable I was when I "toured" and centered my days around my greatest source of shame. I felt death all around me as I grieved the Holy Spirit.

Clients I hadn't spoken to in years came out of the woodwork around this time. Many to rekindle or confess, others for closure. One client, a ridiculously handsome cardiologist, wrote me a love letter that would have given Nicholas Sparks a run for his money. The line, "If I held on any longer, I would have never let go," gave me confirmation that the feelings had not been one-sided. The temptation to run back into the arms of these men, many whom I knew genuinely cared for me and were willing to pay me to do so, was off the charts.

It had been two years since Nathan—a tall, dark, and handsome man a small handful of years older than me—had fled my apartment forgetting his socks, while I was in the middle of shaking a margarita. I had not seen him since my rate was $500 an hour, and I was still operating out of my old apartment.

Back then, Nathan was the only client I actually looked forward to seeing. He was the type of man I could picture myself dating. We would go golfing, to basketball or soccer games, or fill our Yeti's with spicy margaritas and spend the afternoon at Barton Springs. Time with Nathan back then gave me a dose of normalcy.

"It's so great to see you," he said. I could tell he meant it.

"I missed this," he said. "This is rare, do you get that?"

I did, and I do. It was why Logan used to wander down to my apartment at night when we were still on good terms. He would say the same thing. We give the love we want to receive, and I had always wanted to be seen and heard. It was why I was so good at my job.

"I'm sorry I gave you the wrong impression back then," Nathan said. "I was separated when we met."

It didn't matter much to me what he was when we met. It mattered more now as to *why* we were rekindling. Seeing him after two years felt like going back to your high school after graduation or reheating up takeout french fries.

Nathan was an entrepreneur but referenced the non-profit he had worked for the majority of his life. He spoke of *The Company* vaguely. I never asked questions that would hit too close to the mark, but after we grew comfortable with one another, he revealed to me that his non-profit was actually a cult he was born into.

That day at lunch he dropped the line, "I'm pretty sure you have a file."

"I'm sorry, a file?" I asked, concerned.

"They were tailing me for a bit while we were seeing each other and then apparently individually for a bit after. Don't worry, it's not a big deal." he said as he took a bite into his sandwich.

"Not a big deal?" I asked, smoothing out the top of my dress.

"What are you doing?" he laughed.

"Looking for a red dot on my chest, what does it look like I'm doing?"

"Listen," Nathan began, "I made my peace with them and honored my commitments. It's been two years. I've missed you. For a while, I considered dating you, and I was trying to figure out how I was going to change my life to make that happen," he said.

"Then what happened?" I asked.

"*The Company* called me and said they were watching us from across the street from your place, so I left without my socks."

Chapter 36

YOU LIKE MY HANDWRITING

2023

Each New Year's Eve, I write myself a letter to read the following New Year's Eve. That year I opened the previous year's letter and was disgusted by what was written. I wrote about how God would deliver me from *this job* in His timing, and that a job would come my way sooner or later. I reminded myself to give myself grace.

More self-deception. I didn't need to give myself grace. I needed a plan. I needed to keep my eyes fixed forward. I wasn't going to let another year of my life go by riddled with indecision, backslides, fear, and still being involved in sex work.

But I still returned to the steakhouse and asked if they would be open to having me work a couple of shifts a week. The answer was yes, and I was so grateful.

The following week I was back in that black vest, stirring Manhattans and trying to remember the steak menu.

Bobbie was one of the steakhouse's regulars. She had jet black hair, light blue-gray eyes, and a sense of humor that alluded to how smart she was. Bobbie wore bright red lipstick that matched the Old World red wine we poured for her from a Coravin.

"I hadn't seen you in a while! I was asking the boys about you!" she said.

I was the only female bartender, so I told Bobbie that they kept me around just long enough to put a woman's touch on the place and give it a deep clean. I told her I was navigating a career, but these guys always welcome me back through my trial and error.

That's when Bobbie said, "Well, honey, I'm going to tell you right now: this is not a permanent place for you. If you are not happy where you are right now, just know that it's temporary. You have greatness written all over you, and I noticed it the first time you were behind this bar. You are destined for great things, and to tell you the truth, I was excited when I did not see you back here for a few months because I knew that most likely meant you were probably pursuing your purpose because it had finally come that time. You have a big mark on your life, and I'm just happy to have met you when I did. Keep your eyes up."

I was speechless. I was trying not to cry behind the bar. Another occasional angel. Bobbie had spoken every word that I so desperately needed to hear. I knew myself so well by then, what was good and bad for me and places I shouldn't be. Why was I here? Because it was familiar, and toxic familiarity is so much more comfortable to survive in than to risk failure within the uncharted and unknown. God had spoken a different plan and purpose over my life, and I was still pursuing false and dated dreams from before I met Jesus. The door had been flung open, but I was still choosing to hang around inside that yellow house on the corner, the one with the old oak out front.

I walked up to the manager on duty at the end of the night and said that unless they truly needed me, there was no need to put me on next week's schedule. This would be my first and final shift. And just like Elisha taking fire to his yoke of oxen, I would not leave room for a back slide this time around. I would finally burn this plow.

The following Sunday, I drove out to Dripping Springs for church. I was restless and unfocused the entire service, which was not like me. After the service, I grew increasingly agitated and went up for prayer for the first time in a very long time. Marcy and Tara, the pastor's wife, prayed heavily and with authority over me. When I opened my eyes afterwards, the colors of everything around me were brighter. The outdoor air felt cooler and more alive against my skin. Even the sun felt warmer, and I felt lighter, less dense.

I went straight home after church that day, opting out of brunch and throwing on my workout clothes to go for a walk around Town Lake. That walk somehow felt different from any and all walks I had taken before. Just moving seemed like less of a challenge, and there was a greater sense of connectivity to everything around me. Is this how normal people feel?

My self-destructive habits were gone. I did not look out onto my balcony and think, I should jump off it. I didn't seek out opportunities to drink or be reckless or self-sabotage in any way. The constant need and desire to escort stopped, and my compulsive need to drink and overeat stopped too, and with that so did my bulimic habits. I would have a drink every now and again, but mainly my interest in it dissipated. When temptation did present itself, it seemed like more of a choice to be made than an urge I needed to satisfy or a task I needed to conquer. No longer was I enslaved to my sins.

A few months later, while listening to our pastor speak one afternoon at the main campus chapel, Connie just put her arm around me, and Alison lovingly placed her hand on my knee before Marcy flashed me a big smile. I didn't know why at that moment I almost just started to cry. I tried to remember how long it had been since someone just touched me. I hadn't the faintest clue how starved I was for human touch and connection, how all those years in every facet of the sex industry I had been overcompensating for it. I had never felt safer in my own body or around others.

I prayed silently and in my heart for my family that day in the chapel, that they one day would come to know Jesus and, as a result, would finally have interest in getting to know me. It was then I realized I couldn't blame my parents for not knowing how to express or show love to me. You cannot share with others what you do not have. The only reason I now knew how to love was because these three women had shown that love is, in fact, a verb. It is an action and a state of being. In that "space" Viktor Frankl talks about, we can consciously choose to love or not love each day. And in choosing to love and to do it often, we make love a habit. It was Aristotle that said we are what we repeatedly do. Even though he was referencing success and excellence, in essence, we are the sum of our thoughts and our character is the entirety of our actions.

After the service, Alison pulled me in for a big hug. After a few seconds, she pulled away, and a large smile extended across her face.

"Adopted!" she said. "I just heard the word adopted!"

Regardless of how my parents might react to my past decisions, I let go of that fear that day. No longer would I continue to worry about additional rejection or a continued estrangement. God had given me a family though this church, and He now called me a child of his own.

I was still searching for jobs one day when I received a text from a familiar, though unsaved number, on my Bat phone, what I called my burner phone.

It was Ethan. And given that the phone had been shut off and locked away, I now realized that the text was sent a week prior. He had sent me a link to a magazine article referencing his company cleaning house and that he had been let go in the process.

#FunEmployed? Too soon? I texted back.

We decided to meet for coffee the following week to catch up and flip the script.

"You can call me, Kelsey," I said. We met at that same coffee shop where we had last seen each other six months earlier.

I told him that if he was coming to me for a job that I was, unfortunately, on a hiring-freeze. I then asked him why he had waited so long to reach out. I had been sarcastic in my delivery and was not looking for a legitimate answer, but that's when he told me he was battling cancer. That in the short time we had known each other, it had progressed and had now spread to other parts of his body.

This was new for me. I had seen clients with various chronic illnesses and disabilities but never a man who was told his days were numbered. There had been so many men who had sought out my companionship for nothing more than social interaction. Then there was the exact opposite, as the years I worked mainly took place during the Covid pandemic. I had undergraduates at the University of Texas inquiring about booking with me in hopes I would consider taking their virginity. Given the uncertainty of the times or any promise of a future, many saw it as their only option if they wanted to experience what it was like to "be a man" before the world ended.

Those were the emails I always replied back with an intentional response, conveying the importance of hanging on to something so meaningful, along with a polite decline.

Yet, here Ethan was spending his time drinking bad old fashions and shooting pool with me, without wanting much more from me than to exist fully in the present moment, void of judgment, pity, or conversation surrounding his cancer. He wanted to get to know me, and still, it was so hard for me to believe or accept.

Ethan asked me what I was doing for work and said he wanted to help. That's when I told him I had heard that one before. I did say that when he landed his new gig, I expected to be his first hire. *In the event he could afford me.*

"And will that be competing with your former salary or current salary?" he asked.

"Well played." Yup. I still liked him.

A month or so later I received another link to my non-Bat phone, announcing Ethan as the new CEO of some tech company. I had suggested he hire me as his executive assistant, and we got together the next week to discuss it. He had asked me to bring my resumé, but when he asked for it, I handed him a separate paper that read *37 Reasons Why You Should Hire Me.* I reminded him that I preferred to work remotely, only on Wednesdays, and that if he played his card's right, there could be a part II to that list in the near future.

"I think number seventeen is my favorite," I said.

"Can fly a single-engine in a pinch?" he questioned.

"Oh snap, I meant eighteen," I responded.

"Good to quite good at bartering for goods in various languages," he read as he continued down the list.

"Can drive a manual transmission in platform heels while eating a breakfast burrito."

"Yes." I responded. "And twenty-six is also a skill that sets me apart from the competition."

"You like my handwriting," he read and smiled. "I do like your hand-writing."

That was when he told me that the position I had inquired about had already been filled. My heart sank.

"You told me I was a shoo-in!" I said. Disheartened, but not surprised, I moved the orange rind around my old fashion glass as a means of distraction.

"You are a shoo-in! I have something else in mind," he said, with con-tentment.

He went on to describe a job that seemed both pretty self-explanatory and entirely too official. I responded to the suggestion with: "I can't do that! I have never done that before! I have no experience!"

"Don't worry. You will be great. I think your skillset would fit great in this position."

I had so many jokes, but I tried to maintain a straight face. It wasn't working.

"You know what I meant." he responded.

I was at a point where I believed in myself, while also fairly confident that between YouTube and repeated failure, I could pretty much learn anything.

"Let's back track," I suggested. "Is the monthly 60k still on the table?"

"Ha! This will be great for you! I think this is the perfect job for you!" Ethan exclaimed.

It was all too far-fetched. I had men offer me jobs before, but the job always dried out once their interest in me did. I wasn't sure what the catch was here, only that if I wanted to whore myself out, I would be doing it for a lot more, and I wouldn't need to enter the corporate world at thirty-one to do it. I would believe he was being sincere when I received the offer letter.

I didn't like this waiting game and how Ethan had once been the one seeking me out, and now I was the one waiting for a call back. My rent alone was running me $4,200 a month, and I was quickly sinking. I planned to move out of my apartment when my lease was up in July, only, I had nowhere to go. With no income, I would not be able to show three months of bank statements with income to rent anywhere! Two years prior, I was bidding on million-dollar condominiums, but now my grocery list consisted of canned tuna, popcorn, and avocados to cut costs. It was good that my bulimic habits had halted because even that seemed like a luxury I could no longer afford.

God showed up and provided for me in these months, though. One month, a settlement check for $1,500 came in the mail, a payment from a class action lawsuit brought against one of my former employers I was only then just finding out about. I had not spoken to John in over a year and had never asked him for money. But I called him up out of the blue and asked if he would give me $1,000 to cover my rent. He answered with a "yes" with no questions asked. I told him I might have a job, but I was unsure how it would pan out.

"Just remember Kelsey, He doesn't call the qualified, He qualifies the called." An envelope was "anonymously" dropped at my concierge later that morning.

A few weeks later, I received a payment from Wayne for $2,500. I had not spoken to him in over a year, or seen him since that day in his truck on my run, but attached to the payment was an apology for the "light-stalking" after I had cut ties.

I met with Ethan several weeks later to discuss the job and what could be expected in incredibly vague terms. I didn't understand why he wasn't seeking favors from me yet or how I was once a sex symbol that had since been reduced to a charity case. On two occasions, I made an advance and a move on Ethan only for him to completely deny me.

"Kelsey, I will not be a cliché!" he said firmly.

I'm worthless. I'm ugly. I'm dumb, I'm fat. I'm pathetic, I'm trash. The thoughts I thought I had overcome resurfaced as a result of the refusal, which I perceived as rejection.

"I am trying to help you with your career. Just give me time," he stressed.

I was again a sitting duck. One that didn't understand why my codependency was spilling out of me like a busted can of biscuits. I didn't want a job in corporate America. I did not want to be a person who hated their life, and I didn't know life without prostituting myself in one way or another. I had never been able to survive in the light, and again I was stuck in my own body and stranded as me.

Chapter 37

A MAGNITUDE OF SUDDENLIES

2023

"Looks like your pickleball game is better than your pool game!" Ethan shouted from cross-court. We traded in our paddles for a couple of dark beers and some bean bags before making our way over to the cornhole boards. We clinked our beer glasses together, and the taste of roasted dark chocolate and malt once again proved to be the perfect pairing for a chilly late-spring afternoon.

I looked around at the small handfuls of people that corralled themselves outside of the brewery. Couples and friend groups that had brought their dogs.

"Is this what normal people do?" I asked Ethan as I tossed a beanbag.

"What do you mean?" He asked.

All these years, I just thought I was wired as an introvert, but maybe I was just a hurt puppy. Even just playing cornhole on a weekday afternoon was so alien to me.

"Never mind," I said.

I had already interviewed with three of his company's executives, and I asked Ethan if there were any updates.

"It is definitely raising some red flags," He responded.

"She has no experience!" "What is her work history again?" "She has never worked in the industry?" "How do you know her again?" He said that no one could rationalize hiring me. That's when he reminded me that the funny thing about being the boss is that you call shots.

My eyes locked onto the point in the sandpit that met the crabgrass. My last days of freedom seemed to be upon me, and my worst fear was crouching at my door. Mediocrity.

During this time, I prayed, read my Bible, fasted, prayed some more, meditated on His word, and read my Bible some more. I clung to the verse "Your word is a lamp to guide my feet and a light for my path," (Psalms 119:105) during this season.

I had exactly three months left on my lease on my current apartment. After assessing my finances, I shouted out to God again.

"God! Please find me a place to live for $1,000 a month! It's the only way I can crawl out of this hole!"

Two weeks later, an offer letter arrived in my inbox. I had a job. I started in two weeks. The next day, a woman from my church sent me a text message. She heard I was looking for a place to live in Dripping Springs and asked if I would be interested in renting the guest house on their property.

I replied within two seconds and asked what the rent would be.

"$1,000." She replied.

He did it again.

April rolled around and, with that, of course, came Tax Day, the same day Connie had asked that I give a short-hand version of my testimony at our church's women's event. I told her that I was a little stressed because I owed the government a boatload of money on that same day ... but sure! I'll put my entire reputation on the line for the sake of serving as Court Jester.

You're the best! she texted back.

I never saw my life as abnormal or unique. I have two parents that are still married, that live in Connecticut, and own a Goldendoodle. Yet, as I gripped the microphone that day, noticeably quaking with uncontrollable anxiety, all I could think was that many in the room would react the way Logan had to my truth. I feared I would be seen as the destroyer of marriages, the poster child for their own hurtful experiences with divorce or infidelity. That everything I would try to convey would be overshadowed by the word "slut."

The Trinity were the only women at the church who knew my backstory at that time, and I figured that many in the crowd would hear my story and never speak to me again. On that stage, I spoke to the spiritual darkness I had walked through and normalized most of my life. How I had been so blind to my own toxic thought patterns and self-sabotaging behaviors. That it wasn't until I began reading the Bible in search of truth and in discovery of God that everything began to change. Jesus led me to the truth. Jesus brought me to that church in Dripping Springs.

After I finished speaking, my prediction was proved false. Many of the women had similar stories or experiences and could relate to my message in some way. Some told me that certain parts of my speech had set them free from strongholds they were dealing with. I met with so many women from my church after that day who shared with me their own stories and struggles of whatever they felt I might be able to relate to or empathize with. For over two years, I feared that my church community, upon discovering my biggest source of shame, would hate me. But just like that spot in the cornhole pit where the sand met the crabgrass, my shame was met with a shift in my perspective. I discovered how my mess went on to prove there is nothing too messy for Him to redeem.

I gave that speech on a Saturday, and that following Monday was my first day of my first corporate job. I was thirty-one years old. I awoke at five that morning, read, prayed, meditated, journaled, got in a workout, and blew out my hair—all before sitting down at my desk at nine. I was born for this corporate world! Ethan called me to give me a quick Teams tutorial, as I had no idea what anything was.

"And this is how you screen share," he said.

"Oohhhh" I watched the screen intently, probably sounding and looking like one of those Minions from *Despicable Me*.

By the time the company-wide call started, I was afraid to touch my computer, paranoid that I would accidentally turn on my camera or somehow remotely delete company files. I was hired in a mid-level management role but was placed in an entry-level role at first, where I was trained in and learned basic tasks. After a few weeks, I had the hang of it, but I was told by my supervisor that I was to remain in that position for a full six months.

I watched as others later hired for my same role were placed on a completely different path. Most weeks, I was given busy work to complete and had little to no interaction with anyone. I sought training and opportunities to shadow or observe others in my role and was denied. My reporting supervisor passed me off to someone in another department and checked in with me once a month, while I watched as others in my position received training and direction. Once again, I was discarded when I was not of immediate benefit. Never in my life had I felt more rejected, more incompetent and directionless. More worthless. I had gone from getting paid to drink martinis at cocktail bars, to this.

After three months, I didn't even try to hide it from Ethan.

A Magnitude of Suddenlies

I would rather hurl myself off my balcony or go back to screwing strangers than to work at this company!

I texted in fury, waiting for the clock to strike five, signaling the end of the business day so I could take a walk around the lake. I was laying on my sectional in my living room and reminded of the client who had purchased it for me. At least when I was enslaved to my sin, I had a fat bank account and clients that sent me furniture from CB2.

"You don't see it because you're in it. I am working behind the scenes," he said. "I see the bigger picture. Things will get better for you very soon."

He asked me to be patient. I asked him to just fire me.

I could live with a drastic pay cut, but I was really living my worst nightmare. I was living a mediocre life enslaved to a desk and subject to traditional business hours.

The rumors at work had only grown worse with time. The cliché ones that made their way back to me stating that I must be sleeping with the boss, how a woman with no experience and a poor excuse for a resumé doesn't just "land" a mid-level corporate job without dishing out sexual favors to get there.

I did my best to remind myself that none of it was personal, that none of this was permanent. I believed the promises God had spoken over my life and that there were lessons to be learned at this stage to work toward them. I brought myself back to the bee that was trapped on the wrong side of the glass and tried to see past my immediate circumstances.

At the same time, the thoughts of suicide slowly crept back into my mind. I was back in college. I was a self-conscious, anxious, nervous wreck. Then, one morning, I received a phone call. My friend from back in Connecticut had decided to take his own life. I grieved differently than I ever had before. A gnawing pain clawed away inside of me as I recalled the feeling of utter hopelessness all too well. The drying out of your soul that takes place within you and leaves you questioning whether the unknown of what death might hold could be any worse than the valley of death that is you.

I spent hours crying and crying out to God in the pitch-blackness of my walk-in closet. By the end of the second day following my friend's death, I decided to rummage through my safe and plug in my Bat phone that had been shut off for three months now. It would boost my spirits. It would bring me comfort. Amidst this corporate rejection, I would read love letters from my fans and see the invitations that awaited me.

My latest email was from a client that I had not seen in three years. He expressed interest in flying me out to Scottsdale in the event I was still in the biz. Getting out of Austin for a couple of days seemed like just what the doctor had ordered. So, I booked a flight out to Arizona—in economy.

Bob had booked me for my minimum of three hours, even though I typically didn't travel for less than five. Different times. In the room, I tried to remember if Bob had always been this old. Like, *much* older than I remember.

My mind was putting up a fight and refused to shut off or allow me to "tap in" to my other personality, to compartmentalize. I excused myself to the bathroom to try and get a better grip on the situation, attributing the knots in my stomach to the acidity from the wine to better help me cope. I was a professional. I had done this hundreds of times before. I would stay the course and close the deal.

I looked deeply and intensely into my eyes in the ring-lit mirror. I had come to like the woman that looked back at me, even if she didn't have a place in the world just yet. The clarity and clear conscience that came with not living this life anymore was valuable. *What am I doing here?*

"God," I prayed, my hands resting against the marble countertop. "I don't want to do this. If it is in your will, will you once again get me out of this? And if it's not in your will, can you please consider doing it anyway?"

I returned to Bob who, in my absence, had taken the liberty of removing his tie and loosening the top few buttons on his shirt. I picked up the bottle to fill our glasses a bit. I didn't really care if he felt I was stalling. We had two hours left and I was going to drag this out for as long as humanly possible. Here, I controlled the timeline. I held the power. Before I could pick up our glasses, however, he reached for me and began kissing me all over. This wasn't helping my nausea. After only a few seconds I pulled away.

"Woah! Slow down there, cowboy!" I said.

I picked up our glasses to raise another toast before setting my glass down on the coffee table on the other side of the room. When I turned around, Bob pulled me in again before he spun me around and pushed me onto the bed, where he began kissing and feeling me all over.

"I missed you so much!" His mouth traveled across my face, the breathy words heard over the faint clanking sound of a belt buckle.

I found myself again in that in-between space, the one where I could let go of whatever kept me tethered to the present moment and surrender to it. Or I could take back control of the timeline. Whatever it was, I needed to decide now. It was only a few seconds until my mind would just collapse into my body, before the patterned and trained version of myself would take over.

"I need a minute," I said, pushing myself further up the bed to escape him. He lifted off me briefly, enough for me to momentarily collect myself before he collapsed back on me. That's when I realized he only lifted off me to kick off his pants, and now he was reaching up my dress to pull down my underwear.

All to say, the entire scenario ended with me kicking him square in the face, shouting "Get off of me!" with some very non-Christian verbiage placed somewhere within the mix. I grabbed my handbag and locked myself in the bathroom, fairly certain I had just broken Bob's nose.

I heard his cursing through the door, and I prayed for him to leave. Then, I felt his anger reduce to desperation. "Baby! I'm sorry! I thought you were into it! I thought we were just playing around!"

I wasn't sorry that I gave Bob a bloody nose, or that I honored my "No Refunds" policy. It wasn't pretty, but God certainly offered me an out. This part of me was officially dead and gone. It was the last job I ever took.

Back at church in Dripping Springs, I felt worthy of being there again. Each day further from my old lifestyle gave me clearer vision and a better understanding of who I could possibly be. I prayed individually and collectively with the members of *the Trinity* for Ethan's recovery, for the cancer to be completely removed from his body.

I often cried when I prayed for him. I didn't understand why he was fighting for me, why he believed in me when I didn't believe in myself, or why he would risk jeopardizing his career and professional reputation over a girl he barely knew. It didn't make sense why my life or career should matter when his entire life hinged upon his health, which was in jeopardy.

Ethan had invited me to his home in Austin for a family-and-friend's barbecue. I wasn't entirely sure why he invited me, and what didn't make sense back then was typically terrifying.

At the party, I listened to the live band from the lawn while admiring the school of neighboring terra cotta roofs scattered in the valley, sprinkled among canopies of Live Oak and Texas pecan trees that stretched as far as the eye could see. Next to me sat a beautiful and spunky blonde by the name of Kate. Her husband was a guitarist in the band, and she was a corporate flight attendant.

While I was still at the steakhouse, I had taken up flying lessons to act as a "stand-in" for all of the reckless behaviors that had left large chunks in my daily routine. I was working toward my private pilot's license, but between my corporate working hours and lack of income to support the endeavor, that hobby had been put on hold.

"You have to come to this event in Austin!" Kate exclaimed. She described an aviation networking event that would be taking place in two weeks. I had never been to a networking event, and the idea of attending one gave me anxiety just thinking about it. I figured for that reason alone, I should probably attend.

Chapter 38

WHEAT FROM CHAFF

2023

The morning of the networking event, I texted Kate confirming our original plan to meet up ahead of time. Her flight back to Austin had been pushed back, and she was now not expected to return to Austin until ten or so that evening. I had been on the fence about attending anyways, so I made the executive decision not to go without her. Then, I thought a room full of people I did not know, and whose opinion of me I couldn't care less about, was probably the perfect place for me to practice being myself. So I got dressed and hopped in my Uber to head to its host location—a brewery on the East Side.

The ratio of men to women at the event was about 7:1, so I already felt incredibly confident reading the room and figuring out who I should make my target. It wasn't until I realized that everyone introduced themselves by first and last name that I realized I'd never used my full name to introduce myself. I listened in on my own delivery to see how my full name sounded pressed together.

In the middle of the event, I turned around to have my attention captured and held for just a few seconds too long by a man in a navy sports jacket. The man introduced himself to me as Ben. I introduced myself to him as Kelsey.

Ben was a lion among sheep but also a sigma among betas and wannabe alphas. It was evident he was smart and calculated, and I saw how those around him defaulted to him for answers and approval. He was more than handsome, but his demeanor is what attracted me to him the most. Past all that was a man who masked his intelligence and one whom I had never enjoyed talking to more. A group of us left the brewery and made our way to a bar across the way. Murals and graffiti art tattooed all four sides of the cement and stone building, and ivy gathered and scaled its walls.

The bar was near full capacity, which made me nervous. Ben must have sensed that, and he reached over and took my hand in his as a supernatural peace descended upon me like a dove. He led us through the crowds to what should have been a non-existent, open bar seat.

We talked for upwards of an hour ordering rounds of Naked and Famous cocktails before a very intoxicated woman physically pulled Ben away from me for her own entertainment. That small window allowed me enough time to realize it was late and I needed to go. I didn't like being out this late. I called my Uber and, in two minutes, gave quick goodbyes to all the men I had met that night and a large Irish goodbye to Ben. I exited the bar and stepped into the Uber, conveniently parked up against the curb. I closed the door and reached for my seatbelt to see a man in a navy sports jacket running out the side door in a frenzy.

Seeing me in the Uber, I raised my hand and waved goodbye to Ben through the backseat window.

Ben lived in Dallas but reached out to see if I wanted to get dinner the next time he was in Austin. I did, and so we did. His visit also just so happened to fall on a day that Ethan was having another party at his house. A few executives from our company were in attendance, and Ben and I dined with one of them and his wife afterwards downtown.

All was and went fine until Ben and I ended up in an argument after dinner. At this time, I was hyper-sensitive to anything that might even resemble disrespect. I had gone from getting paid to go on dates with men who treated me like a queen, and I was prepared to walk away from anyone who exhibited behavior similar to Logan's.

Ben and I parted ways that night and did not speak until nearly a month later at a similar networking event like the one in Austin, only this time it took place in San Antonio. After the event, a few of us flocked to a spacious hotel lounge that at first glance resembled, although quite modern, a Medieval ale house. Dark wooden lounge tables held drippy ivory pillared candles, and exotic bouquets. The lounge itself smelled like a mélange of leather and chai. At the room's center was an oversized wrought iron chandelier, and under it, in walked Ben—with another woman.

The two of them joined our group, but by the end of the night, the woman had departed, and Ben and I had since warmed up to one another. We decided to go on a hunt for some late-night food as Ben and I trailed behind the two others in route to a food truck park a few blocks away. When we arrived, one of the men in the group pulled me aside.

"You know Ben's married, right?"

Never had I been more unprepared to get the wind knocked out of me. Strike three. I fled the scene and walked until my feet hurt from my heels before I called an Uber and headed back to my hotel. I was still the dumbest girl in the world.

In a text, Ben had said there were probably a lot of things we had not got around to talking about. And that was that.

Soon after, it was my last downtown sunset watching the bats from my balcony. The guest house in Dripping Springs was an absolute blessing. I was in over my head at my apartment downtown. Plus, I felt some distance from it would be good for me.

When I arrived in Dripping Springs, my movers began hauling boxes and furniture from the moving van into the humble abode that was my new home. The owners had left a piano that I had asked the movers to place against the far wall. Upon lifting it up, a handful of dead beetles and scorpions lay underneath it.

"Nope! Nope! Everything back on the truck. We are going back downtown!" I shouted.

"You're out in the country now!" one of the moving guys said as I rifled through one of my boxes for my handheld vacuum.

That night, I turned on my bedside lamp and opened my Bible to read a few pages when, in the corner of my eye, I noticed a large black beetle slowly inching its way toward me across my white duvet. I screamed bloody murder. Grabbing a tissue to rid my bed of it, I took a flashlight to the rest of my bed and noticed a couple of other tiny black bugs hanging out at the base of my comforter. I lost it. I was hysterically crying as I texted the family who owned the home and stripped my bed to start laundry with extra hot water.

Terry, one of the owners, rushed over with some pest spray and a flashlight.

"I swear we never would have rented to you if we had known there was a bug issue!" she said.

"I'm sorry. I'm just a hot mess. No one at thirty-one really dreams of being single and living in someone's guest house!"

I realized how terrible it sounded after the words had left me. "Not that I'm not grateful!"

I slept on the couch with a light on and a flashlight in hand and got up every few hours to rewash my bedding. That night, I was reminded of all the people I never fell asleep next to and all the other times where I woke up to things being done to me. It made the bugs seem less threatening. Although still equally disturbing.

In every possible way, I made the Lord my refuge in that season.

Chapter 39

LIKE REAL PEOPLE DO

2023

I met up with Ethan for coffee and breakfast tacos a couple of months after the move. I had now been at the job for six or so months. He asked how Ben was. I told him he was married. His eyes genuinely hurt for me.

"That's okay, it's not like it was Freshman Idol or anything," I said.

"And what is Freshman Idol?" Ethan asked.

It was our team's version of controlled hazing. Every freshman on the team had to take the mic and sing karaoke in front of the entire team and coaching staff en route to away games. For someone like me, it was mortifying.

He asked how work was going, but I just kept silent.

"Stick with it," Ethan said. "I'm making changes."

He was, and he had. Ethan had heard the rumors and was aware of some of the mistreatment. He had already assigned me a new supervisor and had made a lot of drastic changes within the company for the better. I trusted him when he said he was looking out for me.

I figured if anyone at the company was thinking rationally, maybe they would have drawn the conclusion that if I *was* sleeping with the boss, I would have negotiated five times the salary I was receiving, a *Porsche 911*, and free access to his personal jet. Not a mid-level position where I stared at a screen all day. In any right, this season was teaching me how to control my emotions and was refining every aspect of my character.

"How's the new place?" he asked.

"How's the cancer?" I replied. He smirked. He gave me the updates, and I made a mental reminder to send in a prayer request to my church that afternoon. I sent one every couple of weeks to have the church pray for his healing.

I dunked my breakfast taco into some green salsa, "Of all the hookers you could have made your charity case, I'm still semi-certain I am grateful it was me," I said before biting into the taco. I loved my friendship with Ethan.

"I hired you for your talent and ability to grow into something much bigger than you, yourself, probably anticipate," he remarked.

I was reminded of the story of Ruth and sitting in that smoothie shop window with Lena years before. I was the foreigner here. I had done nothing to deserve the kindness this man was showing me. Like Ruth, I knew God was strengthening and shaping me through the trials. All I could do was strive to be diligent, hardworking, and in possession of unwavering loyalty to God. In turn, I would forever show unwavering loyalty to Ethan for taking a chance on me.

It had now been a month since the event in San Antonio and my last communication with Ben.

Even with the possibility of something romantic with Ben now ruled out, I was still interested in the sales job at his company he had mentioned wanting to hire me for. I used it as the excuse to strike back up a conversation and to resolve our differences. I didn't like burning bridges. Not anymore at least. We planned a call for a few days later.

As expected, it was a bit awkward—until I realized I didn't care. He talked about his company, the role, the timeline, and business in general for about half an hour. Then he mentioned how small his industry was, in addition to how I handled myself in both environments and events. I knew where he was going with this.

"Well—someone made a comment, and it made me start to think," Ben began. "Here is this girl that shows up to these events with some hours of flight time, not really knowing anyone."

He was connecting all the dots. Seeing me engaging one-on-one with the men there. Showing up alone.

"I don't know where I'm going with this," Ben said.

I think we both knew exactly where he was going with this. I told him to speak his mind, and if he had a question, he should ask it.

"Well, at one point I wondered if you might be a pro."

I had a strong feeling he wouldn't react like Logan. But, if he did, I would know for certain I was not interested in working for him. So I told him the truth: "Yes. I used to be an escort, but that was a long time ago."

Also, that I was not there to solicit anyone, I just really loved flight school and was looking to network and find ways to continue to pursue my private pilot's license without quitting my full-time job.

I then asked him, point blank, if he was married. That was when he told me he was separated and had been living alone for two years. I quickly lost all interest in the sales job.

I flew to Dallas to spend the weekend with Ben, who picked me up outside baggage claim. I had never had a man pick me up from the airport before, and as silly as it sounds for all the flights I took in all those years, it was something I always wished would happen one day.

I let go of my suitcase, allowing it to slightly roll away as I jumped on Ben in a huge embrace as he walked toward me. I loved him then, but I knew I loved him that first night we met and he grabbed hold of my hand. We spent the weekend in one long never-ending conversation. He had planned for us to meet another couple who were close friends, and I had to remind myself that that was something people normally do. A normal thing that I had no experience with.

Thank goodness his friends were amazing because I was fairly quiet and didn't know how to be myself just yet. Unsure how to express that I didn't like my job but that it was by the grace of God that I even had one. I didn't know how to convey my dreams and ambitions because I wasn't yet sure what those were. During dinner, I realized that this was the first double date I had ever been on. I leaned over to tell Ben, and that's when he started laughing. Then he corrected me and said that by that logic, my first double date was with him and my company executive and his wife back in Austin. That made this one my second.

We finished up at dinner, and someone suggested we try a new club across town. When we arrived, our hands were stamped, and we entered a dark tunnel where spot and multi-colored strobe lights came into view as we drew nearer. The bass of the music sent shockwaves that my gums, still sensitive from whitening them that morning, seemed to now be extra sensitive to as a result.

We parted and walked through a beaded curtain that opened up to the club. Red, blue, and green laser beams shot around us sporadically, highlighting hordes of people in the crowd and drawing attention to the cages that dangled from the ceiling. Inside of them were women dancing as fog machines continued to cloud the room. This was too much. An onset of vertigo came over me, which collided with the smell of weed, a scent and a drug I could never get behind.

"Was this normal?" I asked myself. *"Is everything fine?"*

That's when Ben grabbed my hand. I felt safe again. I ignored the voices in my head that attempted to remind me I was a hurt puppy. I reassured myself I could be a team player, that I could fall in love with this moment. That's when a confetti gun loudly popped off and streamers of every color fell from the ceiling, and I jumped out of my skin. A parade of young women passed by dressed, although barely, in royal blue lingerie. They carried sparklers in each hand, which they had hoisted in the air and were waving them back and forth.

Was this normal? Outfits I had worn in the privacy of hotel rooms were now club uniforms? Am I that outdated? I didn't understand how any of this was normal, and everything around me felt oppressive and like a nightmare I had already woken up from.

I needed to leave, and my chest was collapsing as if at any moment the roof might cave in, or someone would grab me and rape me in the bathroom. Fragments of men and moments came flooding back. Snippets of low-lit hotel rooms. The men. The outfits. The money. That maroon-patterned bedspread, the smell of duct tape, the way the air conditioning felt before and after on my skin.

Thankfully, it wasn't Ben or his friend's scene either. We soon left.

Chapter 40

KISHI KAISEI

Japanese Proverb,

"Wake from death and return to life"

2023

Back in Dripping Springs, I set my bags down inside the doorway of my winsome casita in the country, flicking on the kitchen lights to evade the black mass of nightfall that fell far outside and away from city or street lights. I couldn't deny that God had provided this home for me when I needed it the most or that it was starting to grow on me. I couldn't deny that I had just spent the most amazing weekend with Ben, being myself for what seemed like the first time. I also could not deny that, in the corner of my eye, there was a second black mass on the floor in front of the refrigerator. I could not deny that I had come home to a tarantula in my kitchen.

A few months later, I flew to an aviation conference with Ben in none other than Sin City. The irony. As a result of the two networking events, I had connected with a handful of people in the industry. One man by the name of Chris encouraged me to go pitch myself to the CEO of his company.

They were hiring for a sales position, and Chris suggested I be proactive in approaching the CEO in order to set myself apart from the competition.

The idea of the job did sound enticing, but from where I was sitting in my current role, most things did. Also, I had no intention of "pitching" or selling myself because what did I actually have to boast about? Outside of the way in which Jesus had radically saved me, I had nothing to share that would place me ahead of any competition. I was aware that on paper I was completely unremarkable. The only way I believed I could set myself apart would be to have a one-on-one conversation that was not in passing, but deliberate and intentional. The skill that the entirety of my past had shown me I was an expert in.

On the final day of the conference, I grabbed lunch with Chris and the CEO when the CEO asked me, "So, what did you think of the conference?"

The truth was I barely attended the conference. I was working my nine-to-five most of the time. But could I say that? Would it make me sound unprofessional? Like I wasn't a go-getter or interested in the industry?

The three of us had been talking casually and cracking jokes, and then there was a shift in all of it. I realized this was an interview. It mattered, and I had to be me. I started trying to prove myself in the next sentence, just like in the past with the next play, the next practice, or the next opportunity. I felt compelled to validate that I belonged there, that I was worthy of investment.

At that moment, the CEO to my left and Chris on my right were the sum of every man who had not paid me, had told me I charged too much, who had hurt or abandoned me. They were the crux of every man who told me I was unqualified and replaceable. The entirety of my life, everything I had learned up to that point had led up to this singular and defining moment. Except I had no idea how to be myself and still did not understand how to thrive in a world that I had never felt accepted in.

Kishi Kaisei

I wasn't sure if I was supposed to demonstrate assertiveness and executive decision-making or if I should be docile, quiet, and polite. I ended up just coming across as rude and making absolutely no sense. I left the lunch thinking that I was not only a poor excuse for a Christian but an overall human being.

I walked the casino floor and sat down at a bar top tucked away by a row of slot machines. I people watched those on the casino floor and wondered about the conversations running through their minds. Were they trying to outrun themselves or their current realities? Who was gambling for a rush of meaning, a fleeting window of success, or felt that this might be the only place they belong?

I was witnessing my former belief system in action before my eyes. I had always lived for the next ca-ching and had placed the things of value—my identity, my self-worth, my safety, and future—on the various betting tables of this world.

Then, a reverie of the past took hold of my thoughts, and I was back in that preschool yard as the leaves danced across the lawn. For a moment, the smell of wet grass and the morning dew overpowered the smell of cigars from the men who puffed their smoke to my left. And it hit me: I cared what that CEO thought about me. I cared what both those executives thought about me. The character flaw that I couldn't seem to outshine, outrun, or exfoliate off my person. The secrecy of my past that continued to haunt me and leave me treading water in a sea of residual shame. I still had not dismantled my first core belief. I still sought the approval of others as I searched for belonging.

I spoke to Chris later that afternoon who told me that the CEO had said I was "incredibly unimpressive."

Somehow, it was everything I needed to hear. I laughed in his face.

"He's wrong!" I said almost joyfully.

I was so certain that man could not possibly be right. I thought of the many Egypts that God had led me out of and looked at where I stood that day. The things I used to believe, my former state of mind, and frigidness of my heart. I didn't care if that man thought I was unimpressive because I finally believed I am everything God's word tells me I am.

I am a new creation in Christ (2 Cor. 5:17), a child of God (John 1:12), and a branch of the true vine (John 15:5). I am chosen (Eph. 1:4), adopted (Eph. 1:5), redeemed and forgiven (Eph. 1:7). I am no longer a slave, and I am set free (Gal. 5:1). I am a Masterpiece (Eph. 2:10). I am all these things, so that CEO is just plain wrong.

My job in tech got better after I decided to get out of my own way. After I realized fear had no place in my future and that my identity was not subject to or would be influenced by the opinions of others. That the only audience I needed to play to was one. I humbled myself before the Lord, and opportunities arrived, and blessings followed.

2021

On a separate day in Hope Chapel I stood in the back, listening to the band play while praying that God would see me, that He might forgive me even though I didn't know how to change. In my shame and through tears, a woman with dark hair, cat-eyed glasses and a flawless tan came into view. Alison took my hand in hers and told me that God wanted her to share something with me. That's when Alison said, "He said you are redeemed. You are restored. You are clean."

Alison didn't know me back then, nor did she know what I did for a living at that time or what those words meant to me at that exact moment. Three words that, even through my sin and shame, I have thought of every day since that worship night at Hope Chapel nestled in the valley on Marcy's ranch.

Redeemed. Restored. Clean.

PRESENT DAY

Seated on a patio in Manhattan, Ben and I enjoyed our individual omelets. A plate of French toast covered in berry compote and powdered sugar was placed in the center for us to share. His irises, the color of caramel, seemed to melt before my eyes.

There was a resurgence of peace and of safety that swept over me when we were together and while he was close. It took me a while to believe Ben meant it when he said, "I am not dating you for your past but for who you are right now."

It was as if I was meeting a little bit more of myself at the same time Ben was. Each morning felt like the first day of something new.

We held hands and walked through Central Park, and I was grateful for the moment, as well as every prayer God did not answer that had led me to that place, at that time, with Ben. A patient love. A love I would not have been ready to fully give to another, let alone fully receive, before that moment. A love I would never place above or prioritize over God.

With Ben, the time of day never mattered unless we were en route to a reservation or factoring in driving time to the next airport. The only currency exchanged is time, which is generously given and weighted heavier than silver or gold.

Dale Carnegie said, "A person's name is to that person, the sweetest, most important sound in any language."

And when Ben spoke mine, it felt light, homey, and perfect; the whipped creamed atop a Belgian waffle.

One of the following weekends, Ben and I took a road trip from Austin to San Antonio to visit Renée and Steve, the gentleman she had been seeing for the past six months or so. I had never seen my friend more authentically happy, more naturally her true self. Steve was empathetic to a great deal of the struggles Renée faced. He himself had lost a child to addiction, a similar addiction Renée's son was still battling. Steve wasn't thrilled about her work, but it didn't affect his love for her, and over time she adjusted her practices and slowly began to transition her business.

The following morning, Ben and I searched the kitchen cabinets for coffee mugs. Steve and Renée were already awake and enjoying their morning cups out on the patio. We filled our mugs with morning Joe and made our way outside to join them.

"I love that about you," Ben said, as he pulled open the sliding glass door.

"What's that?" I asked.

"I didn't want to say anything because I didn't want you to stop. But while you were fixing the coffee, you were humming."

EPILOGUE

I never could hit *flow* in my basketball game. I didn't play loose or relaxed and always tried to control the game instead of letting the game come to me. Lacrosse was the sport I started playing because I hated softball. As such, I was never stressed about my performance. I lived in a state of *flow* on the lacrosse field for so long. I had game sense, skill, and field vision. That was, until it mattered. Until it became my idol and the thing that defined me, gave my life purpose, and was the sole reason I was getting out of bed in the morning.

While I was escorting and when it didn't matter who I was, I learned how to become myself. Through escapism and under the guise of an alias, I discovered a part of myself that, while confident, driven, and compassionate, led me to confront all the falsities of my immediate reality. It is not God's desire for us to live in a state of fight-or-flight. We are meant to exist in a state of *flow*. Our identity is meant to be found in Him and through Him.

During this writing process, I asked Lena if I could use her real name to tell bits of her story and how it more than intertwined with mine. Her response began with "Absolutely," and it ended with "I am not ashamed of my past. The depth of my messiness, the deception I was in, and the shame I held only points more powerfully to His glory. My worst moments are highlights of His glorious resurrecting power at work within me. I've seen the truth about my past, and it has opened so many doors for the gospel."

She then referred to her past as a "trophy" and not a curse. Today, Lena still resides in Zanzibar, and while dozens of women have left sex work for good, she has shared the gospel with hundreds of people. Her ministry has since expanded, and the gospel is being preached to sex workers, addicts, and those incarcerated. Her ministry is growing every day.

I once asked Lena for evidence of God's existence, and she reminded me why it is called *having faith*. God went ahead and answered my request anyway. My narrative is one long chronological list of all the times He intervened, saved, or delivered me with and without my awareness. He never stopped chasing after me, and finally, there came a point where I could no longer deny His love for me. He wore me down with love and kindness and never stopped fighting for me. In loving God, I learned how to love myself.

I am reminded of a quote from *Tuesdays with Morrie*, by Mitch Albom, "Love wins. Love always wins."

In the book of Ruth, Ruth, a Moabite living in Bethlehem, goes out to the fields to harvest grain. That field is owned by a man named Boaz, who allows her to harvest grain in his fields with his other workers. Boaz looks favorably upon Ruth, even though she is an outsider and a foreigner. He allows her to eat at his table and looks over her as she gathers grain during the harvest. It is a story of God's protection and blessing, and in more ways than one, Ethan was a Boaz to me.

Epilogue

The last time I spoke with Ethan, his doctors couldn't find his cancer anywhere—the same cancer that nearly a year before had spread across his body. In time, those prayer requests soon transformed into a praise report.

Later in the book of Ruth, Ruth lies at Boaz's feet at the threshing floor, a place where women were not allowed to be. Ruth pulls the corner of Boaz's garment over herself and asks him, "Spread the corner of your covering over me, for you are my family redeemer" (Ruth 3:8-13).

I have found that intimacy is both the issue and the solution. We cannot go through life without experiencing intimacy, and we cannot experience it if we refuse to confront ourselves. Entering into a relationship with Jesus is asking Him to show you who you truly are in the eyes of our Creator and Father. In all seasons and every instance, He covered me.

Hosea 2:14 is one of my favorite verses: "But then I will win her back once again. I will lead her into the desert and speak tenderly to her there. I will return her vineyards to her and transform the Valley of Trouble into a gateway of hope."

It was in that guesthouse in Dripping Springs that God enveloped me with peace and calmed me with assurances. It was there, a place that I would have never chosen to go, where He whispered tenderly to me and gifted me this book. God will meet you wherever you are. In your pain, hurt, abandonment, or dejection. You are not beyond redemption or past forgiveness. With him, there will be no Swiss Cheese!

Transitioning out of my self-sabotaging habits to throwing myself at the feet of Jesus took discipline and time to develop that endurance. Now, His comfort is all around me. I have been called out of the grave and redeemed, and I can attest that Lena was right that day in Boulder: A moment in the Lord's presence is greater than any drunk or high [or amount of money] I could ever receive.

In a world that continues to build upon the rock of fleeting pleasures, choose to invest in the eternal and unfailing intimacy that is found in Christ. Choose a life filled with unconditional love because everything without it is mediocre. For I have seen firsthand that wisdom is better than folly, just as light is better than darkness (Ecclesiastes 2.13-14).

I encourage you to ask the hard questions, to ask yourself why you find yourself in a pattern of undesirable places, to get to the root of why you allow words spoken over you to assign you an identity. In the search for truth, He will expose the lies and shine light in dark places. He has a plan and purpose for your life, and it is beyond wordly comprehension.

And remember:

"Wisdom and money can get you almost anything, but only wisdom can save your life," (Ecclesiastes 7:12). And that is what Jesus, the ultimate grapefruit spoon, did for me.

ACKNOWLEDGEMENTS

The only reason this book was made possible was because so many individuals shaped and influenced my journey.

To all the occasional angels mentioned throughout this book whose names I do not know: the man who scooped me up out of a totaled car, the man who changed my tire on the side of the Jersey Turnpike and the conductor on the Amtrak line all those years ago. To "Bobbie" from "the steakhouse" for being the tipping point I needed to propel forward, push past my comfort zone, and dream bigger. A giant thank you to you all.

To "John," the man who gave me my first Bible and who pointed me in the direction of the church that instilled in me a new belief system, I am forever grateful. Thank you for believing in me and seeing my potential before I could do either of those things for myself.

To "Ethan," the man who took an interest in my career and took a chance on me, thank you for challenging me and offering hope and guidance.

To Jeff Racho for your support throughout this entire process & your supernatural brilliance surrounding legal ethos.

A sincere thank you to Miles McGriff and Dr. Carol Lingbarger. Each of you had a profound influence on how I view health and wellness. Your guidance and support shaped my habits for the better, helping me adopt a healthier lifestyle and make positive choices each day.

To Pastor Brock and Stephanie Stamps, for being the leaders in the Dripping Springs community that you are, and for building and shepherding the church that led me closer to Jesus.

I would like to additionally thank Marcy and Dr. Antonio Jimenez for your encouragement in writing this book, your inspiring faith, and the endorsement you provided.

To Ash Abraham for the monumental role you played in the editing process, and to each individual at the Fedd Agency who made this book come to life.

Also, a large thank you to the following people: Jenn Rousseau, Toni-Ann Bucknor, Emily Walsh, Lena Wadsworth, Rebecca Collins, Dr. Caitlin Swallow, Connie Hagen, Alison Keber, Joan Daniels, Jordan Kruise, Connie & Frank Grygier, Pastor George & Montie Oakes, Pastor Skip Preston & Gaby Navarro-Preston, Pastor Derek & Jill Welborn, John Gamble, Erich Sanchack, and The Pierson Family.

Additionally, a profound thank you to Paul Martinez for your unwavering support and contributions; your vision, drive, heart, and encouragement.

And a supreme thank you to Nina Chodniewicz. Thank you for believing in the story I wanted to tell.